TYLER COWEN (Ph.D.) holds the Holbert L. Harris chair in economics at George Mason University. He is the author of a number of textbooks and other thought-provoking works and writes the most-read economics blog worldwide, marginalrevolution.com. He has written regularly for *The New York Times*, writes a regular column for *Bloomberg View*, and contributes to a wide number of newspapers and periodicals.

D0122011

Additional Praise for *The Complacent Class*

"*The Complacent Class* is refreshingly nonideological, filled with observations that will resonate with conservatives, liberals, and libertarians. . . . A useful corrective to the conventional wisdom that American ingenuity, sooner or later, will revive a low-growth economy."
　　　　　　　　　　　　　　　　　　　　　　　—*The Wall Street Journal*

"[*The Complacent Class*] provides an open invitation for the reader to think deeply."　　　　　　　　　　　—Derek Thompson, *The Atlantic*

"Cowen does a marvelous job of turning his Tocquevillian eye to today's America."　　　　　　　　　　　　　　—*Financial Times*

"Timely and well-written."　　　　　　　　　　　—*Foreign Affairs*

"[Cowen] is a skilled stylist and polished debater. . . . [*The Complacent Class*] will undoubtedly stir discussion."　　　　—*Kirkus Reviews*

"Cowen's predictions take on a different coloring with the results of the 2016 presidential election, and it will be fascinating to see whether and how they come true."　　　　　　　　　—*Publishers Weekly*

THE
COMPLACENT
CLASS

THE COMPLACENT CLASS

The Self-Defeating Quest for the American Dream

TYLER COWEN

PICADOR   ST. MARTIN'S PRESS   NEW YORK

picadorusa.com • picadorbookroom.tumblr.com
twitter.com/picadorusa • facebook.com/picadorusa

Picador® is a U.S. registered trademark and is used by Macmillan Publishing Group, LLC, under license from Pan Books Limited.

For book club information, please visit facebook.com/picadorbookclub or email marketing@picadorusa.com.

Designed by Steven Seighman

The Library of Congress has cataloged the St. Martin's Press edition as follows:

Names: Cowen, Tyler, author.
Title: The complacent class : the self-defeating quest for the American dream / Tyler Cowen.
Description: New York : St. Martin's Press, [2017] | Includes bibliographical references and index.
Identifiers: LCCN 2016049031 | ISBN 9781250108692 (hardcover) | ISBN 9781250108708 (ebook)
Subjects: LCSH: Social mobility—United States. | Social classes—United States. | United States—Social conditions—1980- | United States—Economic conditions—2009-
Classification: LCC HN90.S65 C69 2017 | DDC 305.5'130973—dc23
LC record available at https://lccn.loc.gov/2016049031

Picador Paperback ISBN 978-1-250-15377-7

Our books may be purchased in bulk for promotional, educational, or business use. Please contact your local bookseller or the Macmillan Corporate and Premium Sales Department at 1-800-221-7945, extension 5442, or by email at MacmillanSpecialMarkets@macmillan.com.

First published by St. Martin's Press

First Picador Edition: March 2018

10 9 8 7 6 5 4 3 2 1

To the rebel in each of us

CONTENTS

ACKNOWLEDGMENTS

For useful comments, edits, and discussion, the author would like to thank most of all Tim Bartlett and Michael Rosenwald and Teresa Hartnett, but also Bryan Caplan, Yana Chernyak, Carrie Conko, Natasha Cowen, Michelle Dawson, Veronique de Rugy, Jason Fichtner, David Gordon, Kevin and Robin Grier, Robin Hanson, Garett Jones, Daniel Klein, Randall Kroszner, Edward Luce, Megan McArdle, Stephen Morrow, John Nye, Jim Olds, Hollis Robbins, Daniel Rothschild, Reihan Salam, Alex Tabarrok, Peter Thiel, and surely some number of others whom I have neglected or forgotten unjustly.

THE
COMPLACENT
CLASS

THE COMPLACENT CLASS AND ITS DANGERS

Disruption has been the buzzword of the decade. And it's true that there have been some significant changes afoot, from the wiring of the whole world to the coming of unprecedented levels of multiculturalism and tolerance. But as important and yet neglected is a story that's happening alongside and to some degree in reaction to all of that change. It involves people making decisions that are at first glance in their best interests—that is, they are economically and indeed socially rational decisions. But the effects of these decisions at the societal level are significant, unintended, and not always good. They have made us more risk averse and more set in our ways, more segregated, and they have sapped us of the pioneer spirit that made America the world's most productive and innovative economy. Furthermore, all this has happened at a time when we may need American dynamism more than ever before.

Americans are in fact working much harder than before to postpone change, or to avoid it altogether, and that is true whether we're talking about corporate competition, changing residences or jobs, or building things. In an age when it is easier than ever before to dig in, the psychological resistance to change has become progressively stronger. On top of that, information technology, for all the disruption it has wrought, allows us to organize more effectively to confront things that are new or different, in a manageable and comfortable way, and sometimes to keep them at bay altogether.

Given the growing success of the forces for stasis, I see *complacency*—a general sense of satisfaction with the status quo—as an increasingly prominent phenomenon in American life. And I've coined the phrase *the complacent class* to describe the growing number of people in our society who accept, welcome, or even enforce a resistance to things new, different, or challenging. These people might in the abstract like some things to change, they might even consider themselves progressive or even radical politically, but in fact they have lost the capacity to imagine or embrace a world where things *do* change rapidly for most if not all people.

This movement and this Zeitgeist have now become so pervasive that we could even speak of *the complacent classes*, but when I stick with the singular form, it will be to emphasize the underlying unities behind differing situations. Consider, for instance, three tiers of the complacent class, differing in terms of income and education and opportunity.

I. The Privileged Class.

Members of the privileged class are usually well educated, often influential, and typically stand among the country's higher earners, though not always in the top 1 percent (which starts at around $400,000 a year). They correctly believe their lives are very good, and they want things to stay that way awhile, of course wishing to elevate as many others as possible. These individuals tend to be tolerant, liberal in the broad sense of that word, and often quite munificent and generous. They fit the standard description of cosmopolitan and usually take an interest in the cultures of other countries, though, ironically, many of them have become sufficiently insulated from hardship and painful change that they are provincial in their own way and have become somewhat of a political target (from both Donald Trump and Bernie Sanders in the recent campaigns). Because they are intelligent, articulate, and often socially graceful, they usually seem like very nice people, and often they are. Think of a financier or lawyer who vacations in France or Italy, has wonderful kids, and donates generously to his or her alma mater. I think of these people as the wealthiest and best educated 3 to 5 percent of the American population.

2. Those Who Dig In.

The individuals who dig in are more likely to be of middling station when it comes to income and education. They are not at the top of their professions for the most part, and they may have professional jobs, such as being dentists, or nonprofessional jobs, such as owning small businesses. Still, by either global or historical standards their lives are nonetheless remarkably good, and full of "first-world problems." Many of them are doing better than what we think of as a typical middle-class existence. But because they hold a lot of their wealth in the form of their homes, and in some cases have legitimate worries about their long-term employment, they do not have the luxury of not worrying about money. Further, pressures from the costs of housing, health care, and education intensify the money issue for them, and they do have to worry about financing retirement. They hope to hang on to what is a pretty decent life, whatever its stresses and imperfections may be. Think of a mid-level teacher or health care worker who is trying to keep the neighborhood in good shape, get the kids into a better college, and save something for a still-uncertain future, all contemporary methods of trying to dig in.

3. Those Who Get Stuck.

Those who get stuck are the individuals who, among other combinations of possibilities, may have grown up in highly segregated neighborhoods, received a subpar education, were exposed to significant environmental toxins like lead paint, have parents who drank in excess or abused opiates, were abused as children, became alcoholics or drug abusers themselves, or perhaps ended up in jail. Their pasts, presents, and futures are pretty bad, and they are not happy about their situations. A lot of these people never really had a fair chance. Think of a single mom with a poorly paid retail job and no college degree, or the ex-con who has dropped out of the labor force because he can't find a decent job and is now trying to get on disability.

Despite the divergences in their situations, what these groups have in common is a certain level of social and emotional and indeed ideological acceptance—a presupposition—of slower change. More and more, America consists of people who belong to one of these three groups and are more or less OK with this division of the spoils.

You might think the group at the bottom cannot possibly be complacent about their situation, but by standards of recent history, indeed they have been when it comes to their actual behavior. As we'll see later, the numbers show this pretty clearly. They have been committing much less crime, engaging in much less social unrest, and embracing extreme ideologies such as communism to a smaller degree; if anything, they have been more disillusioned than politically engaged. I'll consider later in the book whether the Ferguson riots and the election of Donald Trump and other unusual current events might be signaling an end to this trend, but the point is that we have been building toward stasis for about the last forty years. Whether or not you think the break point has come just now, to understand why the stasis eventually must fall apart, first we must see how and why it has evolved.

The good news is that more and more Americans are entering the upper tier than ever before—it's nice to have something to be complacent about. Recent income data indicates that a core of about 15 to 20 percent of the American population is doing extraordinarily well, in terms of both income and also social indicators, such as happiness and health outcomes. There is an ongoing collapse of the middle class, as is often reported in the media, but the underreported upside is that some of the middle class is graduating into the upper class. The bad news, however, is that the accompanying structures are not ultimately sustainable for the broader majority of the population. As overall social and economic dynamism declines and various forms of lock-in increase, it becomes harder to finance and maintain the superstructure that keeps stability and all of its comforts in place. The most talented of the middle rise to the top, while a lot of other forms of mobility slow down and congeal, thereby heralding the loss of dynamism and, eventually, control. And so the complacent class is but a phase in American life, rather than Francis Fukuyama's much-heralded "End of History." Still, for whatever cracks may be showing in the edifice, the complacent class defines our current day, even though we are starting to see parts of it crumble before our eyes.

One of the great ironies of the situation is that those most likely to complain about the complacent class are themselves the prime and often most influential members of that class themselves, namely what I call the privileged class. When we hear Progressives criticizing high income inequality or conservatives bemoaning America's fall in global stature, you might wonder, *If they are complaining, what makes them so complacent?*

The defining feature of these groups of people is, most of all, the lack of a sense of urgency. Our current decade can be understood by comparing it to the 1960s and early 1970s. The Watts riots of 1965 put 4,000 people in jail and led to thirty-four killed and hundreds injured; during an eighteen-month period in 1971–1972, there were more than 2,500 domestic bombings reported, averaging out to more than five a day. I'm not *advocating* these tactics, of course. My point is that, today, there is an entirely different mentality, a far more complacent one, and one that finds it hard to grasp that change might proceed on such a basis. Yet in the 1960s and 1970s, not only did riots and bombings happen, but large numbers of influential intellectuals endorsed them, defended them, and maybe led them to some degree. Back then the privileged class was not always so complacent because a large number of those individuals were far more willing to disrupt the social order. Today the critique is penned, and the enemies of reason and progress are condemned, but then the page is turned and the complacent class turns its attention back to the very appealing comforts of everyday life.[1]

HOW DID SO MANY PEOPLE BECOME SO COMPLACENT?

The forces behind the rise of the complacent class are quite general. For better or worse, the truth is that peace and high incomes tend to drain the restlessness out of people. For all the revolutionary changes in information technology as of late, big parts of our lives are staying the same. These days Americans are less likely to switch jobs, less likely to move around the country, and, on a given day, less likely to go outside the house at all. For instance, the interstate migration rate has fallen 51 percent below its 1948 to 1971 average and has been falling steadily since the mid-1980s. There has been a decline in the number of start-ups, as a percentage of business activity, since the 1990s. There are also fewer unicorn miracle growth firms, there is less corporate churn and turnover of new firms replacing older firms, and there is a higher market concentration in the sectors where we can measure it. The average American is older than ever before, and so is the average U.S. business.

There is also much more pairing of like with like, whether it has to do with marriage, the associations we belong to, or the income levels of the neighborhoods in which we live. In our biggest and most influential cities, segregation by income has become so glaringly obvious that few people think it can be reversed. And many of America's trendiest cities, including cities with quality universities, are among the most extreme for segregation by socioeconomic class. I'll be giving specific numbers throughout the book, but those are some key external metrics by which we can see and measure the growing complacency in American life.

The clearest physical manifestation of these ongoing processes of segregation is NIMBY—Not In My Backyard. Building new construction gets harder and harder in many of our most important cities, and the ratio of rents to median income in those locales has been rising steadily. American life is more segregated by income than ever before, and the new innovations we are creating are cementing rather than overturning this trend, which is backed most of all by city and county laws but also by our own desires for suitably nice living quarters and experiences.

But NIMBY is just one specific physical manifestation of a broader mentality of stasis. There is also:

NIMEY—Not In My Election Year
NIMTOO—Not In My Term Of Office
LULU—Locally Undesirable Land Use
NOPE—Not On Planet Earth
CAVE—Citizens Against Virtually Everything
BANANA—Build Absolutely Nothing Anywhere Near Anything

One upshot of this current Zeitgeist of community-enforced social stasis is that our physical infrastructure won't get much better anytime soon. Every time a community turns down a new apartment complex or retail development, it limits America's economic dynamism by thwarting opportunities for those lower on the socioeconomic ladder. The relative absence of physical construction also makes it harder to put people back to work when bad times roll around, and, at a deep psychological level, it gets people used to the idea of a world that more or less always looks the same, albeit with an ongoing proliferation of trendy restaurants, boutiques, and people walking around with earbuds, texting and staring at their smartphones. I don't mean that as snark; those are nice neighborhoods enjoyed by many Americans, including myself. Still, what has been lost is the ability to imagine an entirely different world and physical setting altogether, and the broader opportunities for social and economic advancement that would entail.

Indeed, in this new world the performance of income and social mobility is rather disappointing. In spite of the people who are doing great, the data indicate that the upward mobility of Americans, in terms of income and education, which increased through about 1980, has since held steady. Partly this is because the economy is more ossified, more controlled, and growing at lower rates. It's also because it is much more expensive to move into a dynamic city, an option that gave many a way of making economic progress in times past. Two researchers, Chang-Tai Hsieh and Enrico Moretti, estimate that if it were cheaper to move into America's higher-productivity cities, the U.S. gross domestic product (GDP) would be 9.5 percent higher due to the gains from better jobs. Yet no one thinks that the building restrictions of, say, San Francisco or New York will be relaxed much anytime soon. Most of the complacent class just doesn't see building restrictions as an urgent issue, and even if they understand the problem intellectually, as many of them do, the selfish incentive to make changing restrictions a priority just isn't there.[2]

We've gone in relatively short order from a time when the physical world and its infrastructure were vital, ever-changing, and all we had, to one in which, at least for younger people, they increasingly play second fiddle. The visions of earlier science fiction were about how different things would look and how much more rapidly we would get around, for instance using the now universally cited flying car. In past generations, people moved through the physical world at ever faster speeds, whereas today traffic gets worse each year and plane travel is, if anything, slower than before. The passenger train network is not growing, and bus lines are being shut down, both reflections of America's decreasing interest in mastering travel and mobility across physical space.

The big practical questions for the postwar generation were about what we might place in the physical world and how that would exert its effects on us, because the physical world was viewed as a major source of inspiration. Would it be cities reaching into the heavens, underwater platforms, or colonies in outer space? All of these possibilities were embedded with futuristic architectures and also utopian ideologies, such as space travel bringing humankind together in cosmopolitan dreams of peace. Those options seemed like logical next steps for a world that had recently been transformed by railroads, automobiles, urbanization, and many other highly visible shifts in what was built, how we got around, and how things looked. But over the last few decades, the interest in those kinds of transportation-based, landscape-transforming projects largely has faded away. Elon Musk's hyperloop plans will remain on the drawing board for the foreseeable future, and the settlement of

Mars is yet farther away. Urban progress is less transformational and more a matter of making more neighborhoods look and act like the nicer neighborhoods—namely gentrification. When it comes to transportation, mostly we are hoping to avoid greater suffering, such as worse traffic, cuts in bus service, or the rather dramatic declines in service quality experienced in the Washington, DC, Metro system.

I argue that the physical world matters no less today, but we are in denial about its power and relevance. We seek to control it, to hold it steady, and to marginalize it ideologically by worshipping Silicon Valley and elevating the value and power of information. We're much more comfortable with the world of information, which is more static, can be controlled at our fingertips, and can be set to our own speed. That's very good for some people—most of all the privileged class, which is very much at home in this world—and very bad for others.

The final form of stasis has to do with how and where we place our individual bodies. Most of all, it seems we like to stay home and remove ourselves altogether from the possible changes of the external physical world. Amazon, of course, can provide nearly everything now. Prepared meal services such as Hello Fresh will send you all the ingredients you need to make a meal. Wash.io will come pick up and do your laundry. Need an oil change? Press a button on an app and your oil change arrives a few hours later. Want to watch your kid play little league baseball? You can do that on Apple TV. Americans can literally have almost every possible need cared for without leaving their homes. This is a new form of American passivity, where a significant percentage of the population is happy to sit around and wait for contentment to be delivered.

The other side of this staying-home coin is the demise of a cherished American tradition: car culture. Buying one's first car was once an American rite of passage, and car culture was glorified in rock and roll from Chuck Berry through Bruce Springsteen and beyond. Driving in a car meant a rhythm, a freedom, and an individualism in which you alone steered the wheel and chose a location and, within limits, a speed for getting there. Car culture was an individualistic culture and of course not always in responsible ways, as the death toll from driving indicates. But today, only about half of the Millennial Generation bothers to get a driver's license by age eighteen; in 1983, the share of *seventeen-year-olds* with a license was 69 percent. Today, social media and the smartphone are more important both practically and symbolically. Mark Liszewski, executive director of the Antique Automobile Club of America Museum (Hershey, Pennsylvania), remarked: "Instead of Ford versus Chevy, it's Apple versus Android. And instead of customizing their ride, today's teens customize their phones with covers and apps. You express yourself through your phone, whereas lately, cars have become more like appliances, with 100,000-mile warranties."[3]

Apart from this shift in mentality, cars are harder to afford for a lot of young people due to sluggish wages and rising college tuition. Furthermore, there has been a migration of Millennials into larger cities, where Uber, bike lanes, and car-sharing services make owning one's own vehicle less important. Cruising, or taking the proverbial joy ride, just isn't that big a deal anymore, and each year the Americans who do have cars are driving fewer miles with them.

America's future is likely to bring a much greater use of driverless cars, which will be a major gain in terms of safety and convenience. But just think of the reorientation in terms of cultural and emotional significance: It will be the cars controlling us rather than vice versa. The driver of the American car used to drive an entire economy, but now the driver will be passive, and what will the culture become?

This new orientation would have seemed deeply strange to our ancestors, but we are trying to talk ourselves into seeing this obsession with digitalized information as normal. Anthropologist David Graeber expressed the point nicely when referring to his attempt to watch one of the *Star Wars* installments:

> *Recalling all those clumsy effects typical of fifties sci-fi films, the tin spaceships being pulled along by almost-invisible strings, I kept thinking about how impressed a 1950s audience would have been if they'd known what we could do by now—only to immediately*

realize, "actually, no. They wouldn't be impressed at all, would they? They thought that we'd actually be doing *this kind of thing by now. Not just figuring out more sophisticated ways to simulate it."*[4]

THE ROOTS OF THE COMPLACENT CLASS

These more complacent dynamics in American life started, in their most general terms, in the early to mid-1980s, although in each chapter I offer more exact detail on the timing of specific mechanisms, some of which required the spread of the internet to come to fruition. In terms of attitudes, the 1980s were important because America was coming off the social and political turmoil of the 1960s, the youth movement, the Vietnam War, rock and roll and drugs, and the economic troubles of the 1970s. The Reagan recovery seemed especially dramatic to those who had lived through the earlier periods, because all of a sudden, everything seemed to be coming together again. Economic recovery resumed, American power again seemed to dominate the world, it was "morning again in America," traditional patriotism returned to fashion, and global communism was to fall shortly thereafter. Collectively, as a nation, we used this newfound wealth and prestige to dig in, to protect ourselves against risk, and to build and cement a much safer and more static culture. So many features of the country became nicer, safer, and more peaceful, but as an unintended side effect, a lot of the barriers to advancement and innovation were raised. Ultimately America decided it didn't want a redo of all the turmoil of the 1960s and 1970s, and it did what was needed to stop that from happening.

This added social stasis came roughly at the same time as a slowdown in the rate of technological progress, starting in the 1970s, as I outlined in my earlier book, *The Great Stagnation.* In 1973, the oil price shock and then some bad policy decisions hurt the American economy a great deal. The American government eventually repaired most of the policy mistakes, such as excess inflation, but since that time innovation and productivity growth have been relatively slow, and only the tech sector has been truly dynamic. America has been trying to run a new industrial revolution with a limited number of engines while checking potential losses for the well-off and upper middle class. You can think of this book as detailing the social roots for the resulting slow growth outcome and explaining why that economic and technological stagnation has lasted so long and why, for the most part, it has failed to reverse itself.

Sadly, the villain is us. Most Americans don't like change very much, unless it is on terms that they manage and control, and they now have the resources and the technology to manage their lives on this basis more and more, to the country's long-run collective detriment. America declines in the sense that it is losing the ability to regenerate itself in the ways it did previously, as during the postwar era or the Reagan revolution or even the good times of much of the Clinton administration. But Americans, at least the American "haves," are pretty happy within that decline. Overall, as a nation, Americans are sufficiently happy that they don't even notice their starring role in the stultification of what has been and still remains the world's greatest nation.

The slowdown and stasis in American life is not just about building and how we manipulate physical space. It's not exactly breaking news to point out that our political system has creaked to a standstill. Polarization is part of that story, but it's also true that an ever-increasing percentage of the federal budget is on autopilot, with only about 20 percent available to be freely allocated, and that number is slated to fall to 10 percent by 2022. In 1962, about two-thirds of the federal budget had not been locked in and could be allocated freely. Today, however, it is harder to have a meaningful debate about how the money should be spent because most of the money is already spoken for, and that is a big reason why problems of polarization—which have always been present—have become harder to solve.[5]

This change in the nature of the federal budget, and this quest for ever more guarantees, is one of many ways in which America's pioneer spirit has been replaced by a kind of passivity. In the meantime, politics becomes shrill and symbolic rather than about solving problems or making decisions. If politicians can't offer voters solutions, they can at least come up with rhetoric and symbols to motivate their supporters to fight for them. Yet the harsh exchanges across different points of view mask an underlying rigidity and complacency: For the most part, American politics does not change and most voters have to be content—or not—with the delivery of symbolic goods rather than actual useful outcomes.

One thing most Americans agree on in politics—for all the complaining about the bank bailouts—is that there should be more guaranteed and very safe assets. The Federal Reserve Bank of Richmond has estimated that 61 percent of all private-sector financial liabilities are guaranteed by the federal government, either explicitly or implicitly. As recently as 1999, this figure was below 50 percent. We're also more and more willing to hold government-supplied, risk-free assets, even if they offer very small or zero yields—negative yields in the case of many foreign securities, such as those from Japan or Switzerland. Plenty of commentators suggest that something about this isn't right, but again the push to fix it is extraordinarily weak, especially since that would mean someone somewhere would have to take significant financial losses.[6]

There is a Zeitgeist and a cultural shift well under way, so far under way in fact that it probably needs to play itself out before we can be cured of it. The American economy is less productive and dynamic, Americans challenge fundamental ideas less, we move around less and change our lives less, and we are all the more determined to hold on to what we have, dig in, and hope (in vain) that, in this growing stagnation, nothing possibly can disturb our sense of calm.

THE NEW CULTURE OF MATCHING

Even when we do get a big breakthrough, its impact is not in every way revolutionary. Paradoxically, Americans can use innovative, ever more efficient information technology to *slow down* the change in many parts of life and to become more rather than less settled. Not long ago someone tweeted at me: "Hope you write more on angle that Internet w/ its ready, free amusements takes edge off human ambition."

Without conscious intent or explicit planning of anyone in particular, rapidly evolving technology has turned us into a nation of matchers. Today it is easier than ever before to be on a quest for people like ourselves, for an indistinguishable mate, for the ideal hobby, for the perfect meal and the perfect app to photograph our pets. We match on our own, or, more and more, algorithms guide us. Match.com matches us in love. Spotify and Pandora match our taste in music. Software matches college roommates. LinkedIn matches executives and employees. Facebook helps us reconnect to our past—our old neighbors, our old boyfriends—and more generally even brings us to just the right news and advertisements, or at least what we think is just right.

The bright side is that these processes also lead us into a lot more exciting foreign travel, or perhaps to encounters with people who truly have different outlooks than we do and who can communicate that to us online or later maybe even in a personal meeting. Still, even with these most positive and diverse of cases, there has been a fundamental shift of societal energy away from building a new and freer world and toward rearranging the pieces in the world we already have. There was something to be said for less-compatible, more challenge-laden accidental pairings with all their conflicts and messy resolutions. At the end of the day, you weren't quite satisfied with your pairings, and so you felt you had to go away and do or build something great, because you had no notion of just waiting for the next social network–based encounter to come along. The great adventures of life, the surprise of strangers, of strangeness, of the electric and eclectic moments of happenstance, and also of extreme ambition, are slowly being removed by code as a path to a new contentment. We are using the acceleration of information transmission to *decelerate* changes in our physical world.

From an economic perspective, a lot of the matching of the contemporary world is great. Buyers are less likely to be disappointed with their purchases—they get what they want, and that means consumers are doing better than GDP statistics indicate. A more intense matching of top intellects, made possible by email, social networks, better job recruiting, and easier travel and collaboration, leads to higher peaks of cooperative achievement and excellence—these days the very best collaborators are more likely to work together in our most productive firms.

Or consider better matching in the context of marriage. One study from 1932 found that over a third of the people in one part of Philadelphia married someone who lived within five blocks. A more recent study showed that of the couples who married between 2005 and 2012, more than one-third of them met online; for same-sex couples, that figure is almost 70 percent. Even if love doesn't always work out, most Americans embrace this freedom of choice because it expands our horizons, helps us feel in control, and most importantly gives us what we really want, or at least what we think we want.[7]

But again, this matching brings a very real collateral downside, no matter how comfortable life may feel in the short run. America's prowess at matching means more segregation by income and educational status and indirectly more segregation by race in many parts of the country, even as racial tolerance has never been higher. It is price and rental rates that are driving different groups apart, not outright prejudice, so that good matching technologies can separate us more rapidly and more effectively than ever before. There is also more assortative mating of high earners and high achievers—the investment banker will marry another investment banker rather than a next-door neighbor or high school sweetheart or secretary. That's great for wealthy and accomplished couples, but it is harder for many others to break into these very exclusive pairings.

CALM AND SAFETY ABOVE ALL

Physical disruptions, in the form of riots or violent protests, are these days harder to accomplish, and most Americans seem less interested in them than during the 1960s and 1970s. Americans value civil disobedience less and obsess over safety more. Even the prison riot—which always was doomed to failure—is mostly a thing of the past. There is today nothing comparable to the 1971 Attica prison riots, with about forty hostages taken, the arrival of hundreds of state troopers, and, by the end, forty-three people dead, including ten who worked for the prison.[8]

When it comes to the streets or political events, the police use managerial science and information technology and surveillance to control potential "troublemakers," and most Americans approve or maybe even demand more such control. Rather than busting heads, the wiser police departments confer with consultants and public relations experts on how to defuse potential troubles. Ferguson and related demonstrations may well be the start of a new and countervailing trend, as I discuss in later chapters. Still, until very recently, the overall thrust of the last forty years has been toward more peaceful public gatherings and far less confrontation. Toward this end, although the American legal system has allowed police to place quite severe restrictions on rights of public assembly, the demand for peace and calm and safety is so high that this is barely a public issue at all, and this development is another form of the NIMBY mentality.

Current philosophies and aesthetics mirror this shift toward the calm. The metaphysics of the big political debates of the 1960s now strike us as absurd. In the 1970s, intellectual, angst-ridden American teenagers noodled over Nietzsche, the meaning of the counterculture, and the classic Russian novels of ideas. Woody Allen satirized these books in his movie *Love and Death*, and it was assumed that enough of the viewers would catch the references. These days Jane Austen is the canonical classic novelist, with the *Wall Street Journal* even referring to "the Jane Austen industry." And a lot of her stories are about . . . matching. For better or worse, these stories are less concerned with the titanic struggle of good versus evil—can you imagine Mr. Darcy shouting, as would a Dostoyevsky character, "If there is no God, then everything is permitted!"? Instead people are afraid of having their calm disturbed, so the frontier issue in many colleges and universities is whether to put "trigger warnings" on school curricula, out of fear that somebody will be offended or traumatized by what we used to welcome as radical and revisionist texts. I don't actually mind trigger warnings and in fact I use them myself for some of my classes. What I find strange is that they have become such a well-known and controversial social issue. That is a far step away from the 1960s, when the battle was over the right to denounce authority, sometimes sliding into outright advocacy of violence, as with the Black Panthers and the Weather Underground.[9]

In the 1970s, American gay culture was a source of innovation, restlessness, and outright rejection of traditional bourgeois values. Over the last decade, we've seen the mainstreaming of many LGBT communities and their incorporation into a very stable and legalistic status quo. As a result, there is certainly more happiness, more equality, and more justice, all good things. Yet gay culture as a driver of radical change—rather than as satisfied contentment—probably peaked in the 1970s and early 1980s, with the evolution of sexual mores and the evolution of disco, house, and other musical forms out of "outsider" gay communities, as well as the Pop Art of Andy Warhol and Keith Haring.

The 1960s was also an era that called for greater freedom with drug experimentation. But of all the drugs that might have been legalized, American citizens chose the one—marijuana—that makes users spacey, calm, and sleepy. LSD attracted great interest in the 1960s for its ability—for better or worse—to help users see and experience an entirely different world, often with different physical laws. That is now out of fashion. Crack cocaine, a major drug of the 1980s, can rile people up, but for a few decades now it's been losing ground to heroin and other opioids, which relieve pain and induce a dreamlike stupor and passivity.

The other drugs that have boomed are the antidepressant medications, including Prozac, Zoloft, Wellbutrin, and the like. In the 1990s, there was a great deal of angst, and several best-selling books, about how Prozac was calming users down but perhaps stealing their personalities or removing their authentic selves. These worries are mainly gone, as the quest for greater calm is now seen as being of overriding importance. Katherine Sharp, who wrote one of the seminal studies of antidepressants, notes that we're just not that into personal authenticity anymore, and furthermore social media have busted our notion of having a "true self" for the medications to ruin. The necessity for ever greater calm creeps along, and the next frontier is that it is becoming common to give drugs for schizophrenic and bipolar individuals to disruptive children under five years of age. In 2014, in fact, 20,000 such prescriptions were written for children under the age of two. The debate over the propriety of antidepressants seems to be largely over, and tens of millions of Americans are continuing to enjoy their medicated sense of calm.[10]

Medication became the accepted answer to attention-deficit/hyperactivity disorder (ADHD), or supposed ADHD, some time ago. (Reading through the current debates does not exactly inspire confidence that we've got the matter figured out.) Somehow kids are supposed to match the levels of calm and composure we might find in mature forty-seven-year-olds. Estimates vary, but according to some, almost 20 percent of American boys and 10 percent of American girls, ages fourteen to seventeen, have been diagnosed with ADHD, yet that concept, with the attention deficit disorder label, wasn't even formally introduced into the *Diagnostic and Statistical Manual of Mental Disorders* until 1980, although there were earlier and far more marginal notions of hyperactive and hyperkinetic children. According to another related estimate, 10 percent of American teenagers currently have had medication prescribed for ADHD; whatever the exact numbers, it is commonly agreed that there is a kind of epidemic of diagnosis and medication. Maybe these medications help some of these children, but again the net social pressure is to force everyone to focus, and not always for the better. To make sure no one is too disruptive, we have elevated the power of our institutions to restore or ensure tranquility, most of all our schools, the government, and the medical establishment.[11]

Medication is not the only reason why American kids have become calmer and more tranquil. In 1965, the most common leisure activity for American kids was outdoor play. Recent surveys suggest that the average American nine-year-old child spends fifty hours a week—by direct comparison, nearly seven hours a day—or more looking at electronic screens, which include televisions, computers, and cell phones. For the average American teenager, there are estimates ranging as high as seventy hours a week in front of those screens. I don't find that so easy to believe, but it's obvious we're less physically mobile, and we're picking up these screen-staring habits at ever younger ages.[12]

In the 1970s, a game called dodgeball—one variation of which was known as bombardment—was popular in American schools. The premise was to throw a hard, inflated ball at the players on the other side with as much force as possible, to see if they could catch it without dropping it. The face and the belly were two popular targets for each hurl, and of course the most fearful and intimidated players had the most tosses sent their way. At least in my elementary school, it wasn't unusual for a kid to get whacked in the face and leave the playing field crying. I recall my gym coach barking out, "Suck it up, kid!"

Flash forward to 2015, when a school district in Washington State bans the game of tag on the grounds of its excessive violence. From now on, those schoolchildren are supposed to keep their hands to themselves during recess. There is a Facebook group called "Supporting tag at recess," but so far it has yet to triumph. The restrictions, however, go far beyond tagging or touching other people. In late 2015, I read of a seventh grader who was told his *Star Wars* shirt was not allowed in school because it portrayed a weapon, namely, a lightsaber. There is also plenty of talk these days about banning football, for fear that many concussions can lead to permanent brain damage. Several decades ago, these questions didn't even come up for consideration.[13]

These days schools are occupying students with the safest possible activities, most of all homework, and also classifying them more thoroughly through more testing. According to one estimate, a typical student will take 112 mandated standardized tests from prekindergarten through the twelfth grade.[14] Parents have begun to revolt, but most of these tests are probably here to stay, as school bureaucracies change only slowly and the longer-term trend is indeed toward more tests.

Given all that, it should not come as a total surprise that Millennials are not such an entrepreneurial class. The share of Americans under thirty who own a business has fallen by about 65 percent since the 1980s. It can be debated how much this is the spirit of the times, high levels of college debt, or maybe just a sluggish economic environment, but in any case, the safe upbringing of the Millennials matches the worlds they build for themselves later on. John Lettieri, who was a cofounder of the Economic Innovation Group, has argued that "Millennials are on track to be the least entrepreneurial generation in recent history."[15]

Even in our vocabulary and usage of words, these moves toward greater safety are evident. The very word "disrupt" once applied to an angry kid in class, or maybe a broader political struggle; now it is more likely citing the overturning of a long-successful business model by a digital interloper, a purely peaceful activity. And we're not even aware that by most measures, in spite of a few highly visible examples, such as Uber and AirBnb, disruption in the world of business is down too. Contrary to common impressions, America is creating start-ups at lower rates each decade, and a smaller percentage of those start-ups is rising to prominence, as we see in more detail in chapter 4. We're not even managing peaceful disruptions, much less violent ones, at our earlier rates.

The big losers from a lot of these trends are the unskilled men, including those with the less peaceful or more violent inclinations. The contemporary world, for all of its virtues—indeed *because* of those virtues—is not very well built for some chunk of males. Current service jobs, coddled class time and homework-intensive schooling, a "feminized" culture allergic to many forms of conflict, postfeminist gender relations, and egalitarian semicosmopolitanism just don't sit well with many men, most of all those who have no real chance of joining the privileged class. Whether or not it is politically correct to admit it, I believe a lot of men have tendencies toward the brutish, but in today's America, those tendencies are suppressed. Again, this is largely a positive development, but still we need to face up to the fact that many people don't like it when the world becomes nicer. They do less well with nice. And eventually they will respond by behaving badly, whether it is at a Donald Trump rally or through internet harassment.

Just look at the numbers. Female median wages have been rising pretty consistently, along with female education, but the male median wage, at least as it is measured and adjusted for inflation, was higher back in 1969 than it is today.[16] (Admittedly the measurement is not tracking actual living standards very well, but that such a measure is even possible speaks volumes.) A lot of men did better psychologically and maybe also economically in a world where America had a greater number of tough manufacturing jobs. These men thrived under brutish conditions, including a military draft to crack some of their heads into line. Those problems of permitting and also constraining masculinity are too-often forgotten, and our neglect of those issues will help ensure that today's *complacency cannot last.*

For all of our interest in controlling and often thwarting change, this stagnation cannot and will not last forever. In all systems, pressures build for change, and the more we shunt aside or postpone those pressures, whether through segregation, poor mobility, political dysfunctionality, sluggish productivity and debt-financed economic growth, or a general disengagement and miasma of spirit, the stronger they become. Eventually, we will see the latent tensions building and begin to understand that changes can be postponed but not avoided. Ultimately that means that our current dilemmas will continue until they reach their breaking points. Sadly, there isn't any "fix" above and beyond waiting for some parts of our current institutions to crumble away and eventually be replaced.

I argue that in the longer term, social change will boil over once again, in uncontrollable ways, or, to borrow a phrase from urban economist Richard Florida, America is headed for a "Great Reset." A Great Reset is what happens when you postpone change for too long, and it is like opening up a valve on an overheating engine; there is a sudden rush of outward force, and not always in a pleasant or orderly manner. In medieval times, for instance, the Catholic Church sought to shut down a lot of theological dissent. For a while this worked, but eventually the result was a far-reaching and fundamental process known as the Reformation, which had major political, economic, and religious ramifications for centuries.

As for the present day, unpacking the ongoing trends suggests that many of them cannot continue or will not always converge in a peaceful fashion; rather they will explode into some major revolutions farther down the road. The first very visible indication of the Great Reset was the financial crisis of 2007–2008, which punctured old myths about the efficacy of the American financial system and revealed that the country is on a fundamentally lower path of economic growth. Many individuals cannot expect to find a good job at all.

The further playing out of this Great Reset will, as I explain in more detail in the last chapter of this book, involve a major fiscal and budgetary crisis; the inability of our government to adjust to the next global emergency that comes along; impossibly expensive apartment rentals in the most attractive cities; the legacy of inadequate mobility and residential segregation; a rebellion of many less-skilled men; a resurgence of crime; and a decline in economic dynamism, among other social and economic problems. Eventually stasis will prove insufficient and big changes will have to come, whether we like it or not.

And this is another reason why our current, relatively happy, change-avoiding world is not an entirely comfortable proposition. We may not welcome all of the fairly radical changes that are to come sooner or later, but we're postponing having to deal with them in favor of short-term comforts.

We have created the complacent class. We own the concept and indeed we *are* the concept. It is in fact our greatest but also our most dangerous innovation. Someday we may break it too.

2.

WHY HAVE AMERICANS STOPPED MOVING, OR IS YOUR HOMETOWN REALLY SO SPECIAL?

You decide to move. Not just to a bigger place in the same town because you had another kid, but far away, to another town, where you don't know anyone. Maybe you're leaving a high-stress job in a big city to a basic nine-to-five in Colorado, where you plan to take up skiing and legal marijuana. Or maybe you're leaving the West Coast for a biomedical start-up in Boston, a fracking job in Oklahoma, or to follow your spouse, who will be running a small factory in Athens, Ohio.

The decision to move reflects something very fundamental about one's life. It is the physical embodiment of the desire to change many things. Some moves are forced by external circumstances, but more often than not a move across states stems from a personal vision and a desire for proactive change. People move for better jobs, for marriages, for a different climate, for new and different social networks, or sometimes just to shake things up. People have moved to enjoy the sexual freedoms of San Francisco, to imbibe the fast-paced life of New York City, to cash a check from the automobile factories of Detroit or Tennessee, or to retire in the sunshine of Florida or Arizona. Picking up and moving is, to most people, daunting, to say the least. It can require selling a house, finding a new one, borrowing money for the transition, finding a whole new set of friends, learning a new area, new directions, new favorite restaurants, getting used to new sports teams, saying "pop" rather than "soda," not to mention helping family members adjust to all of these new things. Even in this age when it's easier than ever to stay connected with old places and learn about new ones, the physical dimension of our existence means a move of house will bring a lot of irrevocable change.

You don't move unless either you have to or you are serious about living through a lot of personal change. As James M. Jasper put it in his book *Restless Nation*: "The purpose of moving is self-transformation."[1]

Economists see migration as a kind of investment. You give up something in the short run, namely the home, job, friends, and conveniences, in the hope of achieving something different and better somewhere else. In the beginning, the move isn't supposed to be easy, but it's a sign of hope, faith in the future, and a belief that a new start can lead to something grander and more glorious.

Americans traditionally have thought of themselves as the great movers, and indeed that was true in the nineteenth century and even through most of the twentieth. In history, Frederick Jackson Turner's 1893 *Significance of the Frontier in American History* described the American West as an outlet for our national energies. The classic American novel—Mark Twain's *Huckleberry Finn*—is about a restless journey, a move, and an escape from a previous life, for both Huck and Jim. Herman Melville's *Moby-Dick* was an epic novel of adventure, global travel, and a risky quest to confront God by hunting a vicious white whale. Jack Kerouac entitled his 1957 manifesto *On the Road* to reflect an ethos of travel, discovery, and rootlessness, a vision also reflected in the 1969 road movie *Easy Rider*. But starting in the late 1980s, things changed, including in American literature. Today's top novels are more frequently about well-educated, dysfunctional people who live in Brooklyn or the suburbs and who are not entirely happy with their rather well-heeled lives. There are more likely mentions of espresso than the settling of the frontier or of moving to another state to shake up the unhappy routine of one's daily life.

IS YOUR HOMETOWN REALLY SO SPECIAL? • 25

In the old TV show *I Love Lucy*, the Ricardo family leaves New York for a new life in California, for twenty-seven full episodes, and then later in the series they settle in a Connecticut suburb for a better life. For the Seinfeld characters in the 1990s, the journey to the West Coast ends up as little more than a fun vacation, and it is hard to imagine the main characters detached from Manhattan for very long.

Much earlier, the French visitor and commentator Alexis de Tocqueville was struck by the degree of geographic mobility in America, most of all in the westward direction. In the mid-nineteenth century, he wrote: "Millions of men are marching at once toward the same horizon; their language, their religion, their manners differ; their object is the same. Fortune has been promised to them somewhere in the west, and to the west they go to find it." He didn't just mean the far West; he also noted how rapidly the state of Ohio was transformed from being empty to full of capital and settlers, and after that many of the residents of Ohio moved on to Illinois. This earlier America also saw plenty of migration to the farther West, even in light of great hardship along the trail, unpredictable weather, difficult-to-navigate river and mountain crossings, and the risk of violent attack.[2]

In the latter half of the nineteenth century, the residents of the United States were more geographically mobile than even those of Great Britain, which at the time was considered a very mobile society due to its political unification and relatively free labor markets. Cross-country moves were made by almost two-thirds of American men older than thirty years, whereas only a quarter of British men did the same. In the United States, over a third of the moves were of more than one hundred miles, whereas in Great Britain, only 6 percent of the moves were of more than one hundred miles; the fact that the United States is a larger country, and thus its inhabitants naturally more prone to long moves, does not countermand how this mobility shaped the American national character. Just about everyone in the world thought of America as a highly mobile and indeed adventurous nation. The fact that most American families had not been settled in the same area for centuries, with ties to local cuisines and dialects and traditions, as was often the case in Europe, helped with this mobility. Furthermore, there was a frontier to be settled, first in the Midwest and then in the West. During some of America's worst times, such as the Great Depression, this extreme geographic mobility kept the unemployment rate from rising even higher than it did.[3]

If California ended up as the place where "the future happens first," this was in part because the state was settled by restless migrants who wanted yet more migration on top of their earlier decision, or the earlier decisions of their ancestors, to move to the United States. This mininion of migrants within a nation of migrants birthed Hollywood, a lot of the best of American popular music, the environmental movement, the social revolutions of the 1960s, and of course Silicon Valley and the personal computer, not to mention the revolutionary contemporary view that nerdiness is fundamentally cool. If you have a new idea and want to work and realize it, California probably is still the very best place in the world, a fact that shows the long-standing American connection between geographic mobility and innovation. All that moving around gave America an active, dynamic ethos.

The mobility of Americans wasn't limited to those with enough resources to pull off a comfortable geographic transition; it also shows up in the histories of our poor, downtrodden, and oppressed. Millions of African Americans, fleeing Jim Crow and also seeking better jobs, moved to the North, Midwest, and West, mostly from the American South, over the course of the early to mid-twentieth century. At the peak of this migration, about 30 percent of African Americans in the South moved northward, from 1920 through the 1960s, and more than 4 million southern-born African Americans ended up living elsewhere by 1980. Even if, as data suggest, the migrants on average did not end up with better jobs or higher wages than those who stayed behind, they were at least able to escape the oppressive cultures from which they came. The natural response to disquietude was to look for changes in one's natural and physical environment.[4]

Even for people who didn't move permanently during these earlier eras, there was significantly more mobility back and forth between regions. Nicholas Lemann, in his classic study of African American migration, wrote: "For a time, in the late 1950s and early 1960s, it seemed as if the whole black society of Clarksdale and the Mississippi Delta had transferred itself to Chicago. Everybody was either living in Chicago, or back and forth from Chicago, or occasionally visiting Chicago."[5] This was a way to earn more money and see more of the world, but without cutting ties altogether with one's home community. Muddy Waters is one significant creator who made the move from the Delta up to Chicago, and it is from that geographic transition that electric blues, and eventually rock and roll, was born. The story of African American popular music in the twentieth century is above all a story of migration and creative adaptation to new environments. It was in the large, noisier nightclubs of Chicago that Muddy Waters plugged in his guitar and made it electric, so that his music could be heard above the drinking, arguing, and overall hubbub of the audience.

Later, Great Society programs from the mid-1960s helped drive African American mobility at a time when some of America's manufacturing jobs were starting to disappear. By 1981, the legacy of the Great Society had generated 2 million additional government jobs, mostly funded by new federal programs in health, education, and other aspects of the welfare state. Blacks ended up in these jobs at disproportionate rates, and as of 1970, 57 percent of black male college graduates worked for the government, as did 72 percent of black female college graduates. Most of these jobs were funded by federal money, but they were run through state and local governments, and getting one very often required moving. If the state of New Jersey was your new employer, you probably couldn't live near Memphis.[6]

Currently there is a trend for African Americans to move back to the South, or sometimes to the West, but overall that is a modest development. In total, only 4 percent of African American families are moving along the lines of that trend, so this is nothing like the great migrations of times past.[7]

As late as the 1980s, when I was living in Germany, I recall bragging to my German friends that about a fifth of American households picked up and moved in a given year. At that time, America was living through an economic boom that saw high GDP growth and rapid job creation, while much of Europe was mired in persistent double-digit unemployment. Although my German friends already had the sense of America as a highly mobile country, they nonetheless found that statistic almost impossible to believe. For so many of them, their aspiration was to buy a house, or inherit one, in the city or region where they grew up and where their parents were still living. That offered the comfort of a familiar dialect, foodstuffs from childhood, old friends, and of course parents who would someday help with babysitting. Often they would move once, to attend university on a temporary basis, and then return to their hometown or home region.

Back then, America really was special when it came to geographic mobility. But since the 1980s, the United States has become a lot more like Europe with regard to moving house. Americans don't all go back to their hometowns the way many Germans do, but they do, more and more, find a favorite area, invest in the transition costs, and then stick with it. Americans have become much less restless in movements across the country, and more people are looking to simply settle down and entrench themselves.

Here is this change in a single number: The interstate migration rate has fallen 51 percent below its 1948–1971 average, and that number has been falling steadily since the mid-1980s. Or, if we look at the rate of moving between counties within a state, it fell 31 percent. The rate of moving within a county fell 38 percent. Those are pretty steep drops for a country that has not changed its fundamental economic or political systems. You might think that information technology (IT) would make it easier to find a job on the other side of the country, and maybe it has, but that has not been the dominant effect. If anything, Americans have used the dynamism of IT to help ourselves stay put, not to move around.[8]

For the most part, this decline in mobility is not fundamentally about changing demographics. Long-distance moves have declined considerably for all age groups, for homeowners and renters, and also for dual-income couples, so neither aging nor the difficulty of relocating a two-earner couple explain America's recent lack of motion, even if those factors are driving the behavior of some specific individuals. Aging does seem to explain why Americans move around less within their counties, as it is harder to pick up and move when you are old, but it doesn't explain the big decline in residential mobility across longer distances such as states for, say, purposes of retirement.[9]

If anything, changes in demographic variables make the American mobility decline all the more striking. Education, in particular, is one major driver of mobility; data from the 1940 to 2000 U.S. censuses indicate that the long-distance migration rates of college graduates are about double those of high school graduates. (Interestingly, it is the high school graduates who are more likely to move *within* their county.) And an additional year of schooling implies a 3 percentage point increase in the chance a man lives outside of the state he was born in. That makes intuitive sense, because an individual with an advanced degree is more likely to receive a high-wage offer that might make moving profitable. College also makes individuals aware of job opportunities—often distant ones—they otherwise would not have known of, and it gives them a network of geographically diverse peers. Furthermore, the very act of going away to college primes individuals for future mobility, prying them away from their local social networks for a few years and getting them used to the idea of being far from home. But here's the catch: Americans are better educated than ever before, and that makes it all the more striking that residential mobility is down.[10]

African Americans today have become especially immobile, and to an unprecedented degree. If we look at data on the last generation, 76 percent of African American mothers gave birth in the same state that their mothers did, whereas for white women that same figure was 65 percent, circa 2010. Using the Panel Study of Income Dynamics, the best database of its kind, it is possible to trace a subset of 4,800 African American families from a cohort born between 1952 and 1982. If we consider the progression from youth to adulthood, 69 percent of that cohort remained in the same county, 82 percent remained in the same state, and 90 percent remained in the same region of the country. A generation earlier, the comparable numbers were 50, 65, and 74 percent, all lower. Adjusting for income, homeownership, and other demographic characteristics does not fundamentally eliminate this mobility gap. African Americans have gone from being an especially mobile group to an especially rooted one.[11]

WHY ARE AMERICANS STAYING PUT?

If it's not mainly demographics, what lies behind the greater interest in staying put?

One big reason for the decline in residential moving stems from a decline in job switching. If people are less likely to change jobs, they are also, for obvious reasons, less likely to move. And if we look at job reallocation rates—a rough measure of turnover in the labor market—they have fallen more than a quarter since 1990.[12]

Among the most written-about job phenomena these days is that of the flexible gig economy, as reflected in individuals who work as Uber drivers, for example. That is indeed a significant change in transportation for many of us, but it is not the major trend in the labor market as a whole. Nor has globalization turned all jobs into temporary or transient posts. The data show that job transitions are down and individuals are more likely to spend a long time with a single employer than ever before. And upon reflection, this shouldn't come as a surprise. Some evidence suggests that longer job tenure is driven by the aging of the workforce, as older people are more likely to be settled in their careers. Furthermore, employers like finding quality workers and investing in them and building them into durable and valuable cooperative teams. That process has become more important as specialization in the workplace has gone up, because individuals have to work together all the more. Finally, in a world with less-rapid job turnover and a lower rate of entry for new businesses, it isn't as easy to switch jobs as it used to be. Many people are simply stuck rather than enjoying a wonderful deal.

According to the data, the hiring rate has declined more than the firing rate, a fact that induces workers to stay put when they have tolerable but perhaps not ideal jobs.[13]

To give this some concrete numbers, in 1998, 44 percent of workers had five or more years on the job, but as of 2014, this number had increased to 51 percent. The percentage of workers with less than one year on the job had fallen from 28 to 21 percent.[14]

Another factor in the decline of American geographic mobility is the decline in American geographic *diversity*. That is, different parts of the country are no longer so dissimilar from each other in economic terms, compared to the earlier world, where most automobiles were made in Michigan, most heavy industry jobs were in the Northeast, and most movies were made in Hollywood. Since the golden age of manufacturing in the postwar era, American regions have lost much of their distinct economic flavor, blurring into a mélange of more or less indistinguishable service sector offerings. Each region has its shopping malls, its hospitals, and its schools in what is now a nationally recognizable sameness. If you are a nurse, or a medical technology assistant, or a teacher or yoga instructor, you can consider working in any reasonably populated part of the country. Those jobs are virtually everywhere. The dentist job outside of Cincinnati just isn't that different from the dentist job outside of Denver, and so in this regard Cincinnati and Denver have fairly similar economic profiles, at least compared to the United States of fifty years ago. A dentist doesn't have that much reason to move from Cincinnati to Denver or vice versa; instead he or she will pick a preferred city and stick with it. And while these jobs pay more in the big cities, that premium is to some extent offset by higher rents and other costs, such as more crowded living conditions. Historically, jobs and higher earnings have been a major reason why Americans have moved, but that reason is declining in importance.

When jobs are based in manufacturing, or in resource extraction, the economic motive for moving is pretty clear. You move to a factory job in Detroit or, as of late, a fracking job in North Dakota. After the price of oil falls, you might move back to a service sector job in Durham,

North Carolina. But manufacturing jobs typically pay higher wages, all other things being equal, and thus they pull in labor when the jobs are there. In the United States, for workers without a college education, manufacturing jobs still yield a premium of $1.78 an hour, or over 10 percent. In some states, the manufacturing premium for these jobs is over 24 percent. Those wage premiums attract the ambitious, but today manufacturing jobs are only about 8 percent of national employment, and that rate is projected to decline further.[15]

Economists sometimes refer to an "index of regional specialization," which is a numerical measure of the economic differences across regions. In economic terms, Detroit is very different from Houston if automobile production is a big part of the Detroit economy and oil production and refining are nil, while the opposite is true for Houston. Similarly, if oranges are grown in Orange County and potatoes are grown in Idaho, those two regions are again economically different. Of course, many regions have pretty similar economic profiles. If you go to the suburbs of both Atlanta, Georgia, and Columbus, Ohio, you will find more or less the same blend of retail and services.

As we have homogenized our physical spaces for some time, so too has American regional specialization been declining. If we split the country up into the nine regions of the Census Bureau—New England, Middle Atlantic, South Atlantic, Mountain, Pacific, and so on—the regional specialization for manufacturing in the U.S. economy reached its maximum point in 1914. Most of the significant declines have come since the late 1940s, and those declines have been steady. In other words, the motive to move for manufacturing jobs has been falling for well over sixty years. Circa 2015, it is unusual that a manufacturing job unique to one region of the country is a major reason for a cross-state change of residence.

There is one category for which regional specialization is steadily rising, and that is agriculture, where specialization has mostly *increased* since the beginning of the available data series in the 1870s. It's easy to see why agriculture should be different in this regard. Due to reasons of weather and water, some parts of the country are intrinsically more efficient than others for food production. It makes sense to grow wheat in Nebraska, produce milk in Wisconsin and Vermont, and harvest potatoes in Idaho. Quick transport and refrigeration allow these supplies to reach the entire country, whereas in most of the nineteenth century, separate food supply networks were clustered around each city. That said, the number of jobs in agriculture has been decreasing steadily, so this increase in agricultural regional specialization hasn't driven a lot of internal U.S. migration. It has meant, however, that Mexican and other Latino field workers have spread out to many different parts of the United States, such as the agricultural parts of the Midwest and the Pacific Northwest. In that sense, regional specialization still does drive a lot of migration, but not usually for native-born U.S. citizens; we'll see soon that native-born Americans have outsourced much of their geographic mobility to immigrants, especially Latinos.

Another factor behind the mobility decline is that American regional economic convergence stopped some time ago. It used to be the case that the poorer regions of the country were catching up to the wealthier regions in terms of income. That meant people had some reason to move to the poorer states. They were creating lots of new opportunities at a faster pace than the more established states, and furthermore, real estate prices there often had not caught up with their burgeoning success. A high-paying job combined with a cheap house presented a significant incentive to move, and so for a long time, the states of Arizona, California, Florida, and Nevada were growing more quickly than average and also pulling in a lot of population. But the 1880 to 1980 phenomenon of regional catch-up has been gone for a few decades. The relative rank order of differing regions has become more static, and these days no one expects to find northern Louisiana gaining ground on Brookline, Massachusetts, much less Silicon Valley. That lock-in in turn has diminished the incentive to move house to another region, because the people from the poorer regions can't afford the higher rents of the wealthier regions, nor do they have the skills to get the jobs there. This logic is self-reinforcing: Since fewer people are moving, it is harder for poorer regions to catch up because they can't pull in the new talent.[16]

Another part of the economic story behind our moving less has to do with the much-discussed issue of rising inequality. Typically talk of inequality focuses on wages, but it is also true that rates of return on capital have grown less equal for American companies. That is, some companies, such as Facebook and Google, are extremely profitable, whereas many others aren't doing well at all. This is more the case than it was during, say, the 1960s. Economists would say that returns on capital have become more dispersed over time and show higher variance. There is also evidence that most of the rise in inequality has been *across* firms rather than *within* firms. A given firm is more likely to be either a "winner firm" or a mediocre one compared to before, as I discuss in more detail in chapter 4.

So how does all that tie into job mobility? Well, the American economy is evolving into a tiered system of high-pay, high-productivity companies on one hand and lower pay, lower-productivity companies on the other. This tends to reduce aggregate job turnover. People with good jobs in the high-pay, high-productivity companies don't want to leave them. If you are a secretary or administrative assistant at McKinsey, you probably are paid more than if you were doing similar work at the local animal shelter. At the same time, McKinsey wants to hire people with experience in the high-pay productivity sector. So moving in or out of these two tiers can be difficult, which means that workers have lower incentives to change jobs and in turn lower incentives to move across state lines.

Note also that, on average, larger firms are replacing smaller firms, especially in American retail. Larger firms have lower rates of job destruction and also lower rates of job creation, and again that slows down job market turnover and also moving.[17]

Some of the decline in labor mobility may stem from the law itself, specifically the growth of occupational licensure. In the 1950s, only about 5 percent of workers required a government-issued license to do their jobs, but by 2008, that figure had risen to about 29 percent. Partly that increase stems from the ongoing shift away from manufacturing jobs to service jobs in the American economy. But an insidious process has been going on at the same time: a slow but steady accretion of professions that have sought and received government protection against outside entrants. While once only doctors and medical professionals required licenses to practice, now it is barbers, interior decorators, electricians, and yoga trainers. More and more of these licensing restrictions are added on, but few are ever taken away, in part because the already-licensed established professionals lobby for the continuation of the restrictions. In such a world, it is harder to move into a new state and, without preparation and a good deal of investment, set up a new business in a licensed area. The data show that individuals in tightly licensed occupations demonstrate lower levels of cross-state mobility. For instance, men in heavily licensed occupations are less likely to move across state lines than men in less heavily licensed occupations, even after adjusting for demographic variables that might cause the two groups to differ. Those same men, reluctant to cross state lines and lose licensure rights, are not less reluctant to move around within their states, where they keep their licenses.[18]

It's also harder to fire workers than it was several decades ago, in part because of fear of lawsuits over discrimination, as American society has steadily become more litigious. This means that some employers will be less likely to hire in the first place, in order to minimize their lawsuit risks. They look more for the kind of workers they will not need to fire or not need to replace anytime soon, which also slows down the pace of job turnover.

Counterintuitively, some of the increase in job stability probably has come through globalization, even though global trade is a much-maligned force when it comes to job stability. In the short run, globalization does export some jobs from the United States, but it leaves the country with a more stable set of jobs overall. In essence, Americans have kept a lot of the stable jobs at home and exported a lot of the less-stable jobs abroad, such as to maquiladoras in Mexico or factories in China. These are production-sharing relationships, and much of the burden of adjustment is put on countries where people are less used to stability and comfort than are American workers. In this regard, that giant sucking sound of job loss to places abroad has not been so bad for American workers in every way, at least once they get past the immediate costs of the initial transition. America has kept a lot of the more stable service sector jobs and sent some of the country's previous labor market volatility overseas.[19]

There is another kind of outsourcing that I mentioned briefly, but it has attracted relatively little notice: Americans are outsourcing their mobility and capacity for economic adjustment. When there is mobility in the American labor market, it comes disproportionately from Mexicans and Mexican Americans. When a negative economic shock hits some city or region in the United States, the natural response is for some labor to leave that region and move elsewhere. Of course, not everyone needs to abandon the area, but some people should want to move on. Yet, if most Americans are less mobile than before, who is going to pick up and leave? More and more we see that mobility coming from Mexicans living in America, especially those who are relatively recent arrivals. Mexican-born Mexicans are less likely to have strong regional roots in America, and furthermore a nationwide network of Mexicans—often from the same state or region of Mexico—can help with relocation. A Mexican moving from Houston to Chicago, for instance, will have a relatively easy time finding compatriots from back home with whom to share an apartment. Upon arrival, there will be familiar foods, familiar faces, and a support network, all based on a set of connections from back home in Mexico or perhaps other parts of Latin America.

The net result is this: Cities that have a high number of Mexican-born Mexicans have relatively flexible responses to labor market trouble, and cities without those Mexicans have less flexible responses. Just as Americans hire Mexican immigrants to cook meals in restaurants, or to help build homes, among many other jobs, so are Americans using Mexicans to relocate for them. No, I don't mean the manning and packing of the moving truck (though that too); I mean the actual moving itself.[20]

Another possibility, consistent with the data but hard to prove, is that American geographic mobility has declined because workers are better matched with their jobs. Workers either develop what is called "firm-specific productivity," such as when a boss gets to know a specific set of employees very well, or they carve out firm-specific perks, such as capturing the office with the best window view or working with the best support staff in the company; often those gains cannot be replicated elsewhere without a lot of time and investment. That ability to settle in comfortably decreases the incentive to switch jobs, companies, or economic sectors. It is possible that these better matches are more common than in earlier decades and thus job mobility is lower, and then geographic mobility is lower too. This is again speculation, but job-specific productivity may be higher when work has more to do with learning and coordination with a team of coworkers and less to do with brute physical force.[21]

Another less-positive possibility is that workers receive less surplus gain from jobs. That is, you try to take the job you think is best for you, but once you get there, the net gains just aren't that great. The boss demands more from you, the value of your health insurance benefits declines over time, your coworkers turn out to be disappointments, and so on. And let's say that kind of benefits erosion will happen for most jobs you take. Well, in that case, it wouldn't so often be worth the costs of picking up house and moving to a new job. Even a job that seemed better wouldn't stay that much better over time, if it was even better at all. And so people will stay put to a greater degree. It is hard to demonstrate this hypothesis, but it is consistent with broader evidence we are seeing from labor markets at a time when economic growth and productivity growth are slower than in previous decades. Middle-class wages are stagnant, bosses monitor worker performance through surveillance more and more, and the value of pensions and benefits is eroding, so perhaps the upside of moving to new jobs just isn't that high anymore, relative to staying put.[22]

By the way, the two groups whose job mobility has dropped the most are the young workers and the less-educated workers, and thus those groups are more vulnerable and more exposed to the likelihood of a protracted spell of unemployment. Men have lost more job mobility than women have, and that too has hurt their labor market performance, especially in response to the Great Recession. Switching jobs is often one of the best ways to get a promotion or a wage boost, and if people are less likely to switch jobs, it will be that much harder for them to get ahead. Lower geographic mobility and lower or stagnant income mobility are two sides of the same broader problem, namely, excess stasis in general, at a fundamental cultural level.[23]

And here is a striking way to think about some of the underlying cultural shifts, given that mobility is often down the most for the less-skilled workers. In such a setting, poverty and low incomes have flipped from being reasons to move to reasons *not* to move, a fundamental change from earlier American attitudes. The older notion of moving to a city, by train or bus, and staying in a flophouse, or with relatives, until one finds a decent job is harder to pull off these days.

HOW HARMFUL IS THE MOBILITY DECLINE?

This decline in geographic mobility shapes American lives. The settled are likely to know their surrounding area better, so they will know the best restaurants, the most effective and cheapest plumber, and how to drive from one place to another. Residents will function more effectively in their environments and have longer-standing social contacts, if for instance they need someone to pick up the kids from school or help out with running a bake sale.

At the same time, there is inarguably a loss of dynamism. A new city or state forces people to rethink their assumptions about the best ways to do things and about what their lives really should consist of. A move forces individuals to start working with a whole new set of people and business practices; even if this change is not always for the better, the resulting creative ferment will breed change and progress. A dynamic, moving society may be less comfortable personally, but it is likely to be more innovative. Just contemplating the prospect of a move can force people to start reexamining how they are spending their time, their future job plans, and who the friends they really can count on are.

Lower mobility even may be a factor behind some of the outrageous real estate prices in some of America's biggest and most attractive cities. Let's say, for instance, you know you are less likely to want to move in the future, for whatever reason (this may be especially true for two-income professional families). You will wish to make sure the place you choose to live will help you climb career ladders or change jobs, even if you don't change cities or move house. You might also think you should choose somewhere to live that will give you the latitude to change hobbies, lifestyles, circles of friends, and so on. If you really think you are not going to move, that initial choice faces a lot of pressure to be the right one. So what will people do? A lot of people will wish to settle in or near very large cities with lots of jobs, lots of economic sectors, and lots of amenities. Cities that have enough size and diversity to fit the interests of both people in a couple. That means New York City, Boston, Los Angeles, Chicago, and San Francisco. And so the rents and home prices in those locales become exorbitantly high, in part because only large and well-developed places offer nonmovers the flexibility they may turn out to need.[24]

The mobility decline also makes American labor markets more sluggish, because moving to another part of the country traditionally has been a good way of finding a new job. But these days, in response to an economic crisis of a given magnitude, American workers move around less than they used to. They are less likely to move across states and more likely to accept unemployment or perhaps to leave the labor force altogether. That is their choice, but still it is bad for the American economy as a whole, because the unemployed are producing less, they are probably suffering psychologically, and they may be a burden on taxpayers. Lower geographic mobility is one reason why the rate of unemployment stayed high for so long after the onset of the financial crisis, compared to, say, the Reagan recovery of the 1980s.[25]

Most troubling, the numbers also show that those who most need to move are, on average, the least likely to do it. Individuals who have been willing to move geographically have maintained their previous levels of income mobility, whereas the expected incomes of nonmovers have fallen steadily since the 1980s. The "income mobility gap" between movers and nonmovers thus has been rising steadily since that time. It is hard to tell whether geographical immobility is causing income immobility in this context, or vice versa, but most likely a bit of both is going on here.[26]

One recent "experiment" in forced mobility, the relocations that followed the catastrophe of Hurricane Katrina, reveals the potential of mobility to elevate the movers. The hurricane rendered many lower-income parts of New Orleans unlivable, and reconstruction was slow, if it happened at all. Homes remained waterlogged or destroyed, and basic infrastructure went unrepaired for a long time. For many people, returning home simply wasn't an option, so they resettled around the country, with the region surrounding Houston, Texas, picking up the largest share.

So what happened? Well, sociologist Corina Graif wanted to know. Toward this end she traced 711 of the displaced households, and her results reveal much about the transformative power of moving, particularly for poor and less-advantaged communities. A great majority were African American, and many were Hispanic. And what happened? The average incomes of their new neighborhoods were about $4,400 higher than those in their old neighborhoods; the average poverty rates of the new neighborhoods were lower (from 26 to 22 percent), and the new neighborhoods were typically less racially segregated. Although it remains to be seen how all this will translate into subsequent upward mobility, there is at least a plausible case that the new neighborhoods are much better at the very least for the younger children in these families.[27]

Another piece of evidence for benefits of mobility comes from the Moving to Opportunity study, based on a 1990s program designed to see whether moving to less-poor neighborhoods would help poor people escape poverty. Thousands of very poor families were offered "moving vouchers," financial incentives to move to nonpoor neighborhoods. The new neighborhoods had to have a poverty rate of 10 percent or less, and the vouchers were arranged so that the difference in rents would be picked up by the government. The families were then tracked, and the goal was to ascertain how much an improvement in neighborhood quality would in turn improve social indicators.

Economists Raj Chetty, Nathaniel Hendren, and Lawrence Katz examined the data on the effects of the Moving to Opportunity program and found that the children who switched neighborhoods when they were young enjoyed much greater economic success later on. In particular, if they moved before their teen years, their incomes were 31 percent higher when they became adults, a significant effect. They also were more likely to attend college—5.5 percentage points more likely, or a 32 percent increase relative to the control group. To put that all in numerical terms, if a child moved into the new and better neighborhood at age eight, it would translate into a gain of gross income of about $302,000, or if discounted at 3 percent (it doesn't all come at once), a present value of $99,000 in additional earnings over a lifetime. Positive gains were measured across all five sites, and for whites, blacks, and Hispanics, if measured as separate groups, and also for boys and girls.[28]

One striking outcome of the experiment was that more families— 52 percent of them—turned down this opportunity than accepted it. This finding is further evidence that excess inertia and status quo biases are limiting the prospects for the improvement of America.[29]

Furthermore, a closer look at the Moving to Opportunity study indicates that it probably *underestimates* the positive impact of moving on poor Americans. In other words, the study showed real gains from even very small changes in neighborhood quality, which suggests that bigger changes in neighborhood quality might be better yet. For one thing, the black and Latino families, even if they switch neighborhoods, do not leave the broader social status hierarchies that are to some extent still holding them back. Furthermore, many of the movers ended up moving back to the old neighborhood or somewhere similar in terms of socioeconomic indicators; the neighborhood switch was perhaps never regarded as permanent. For the children, the new schools were, in terms of test scores and teacher/student ratios, not very different from the old schools. In Chicago, for instance, a lot of the program recipients simply moved from a very bad South Side Chicago neighborhood to another slightly less bad South Side Chicago neighborhood. In New York City, many of the program participants were living in the Martin Luther King Towers, a housing development in Harlem. Many of the movers switched to an area called Wakefield in the North Bronx, near the border with Westchester County, only about ten miles to the north of their original neighborhood. Some of the other families moved to an area called Soundview in the Central Bronx, only six miles to the north of their original neighborhood.[30]

Finally, there is other evidence for neighborhood and integration effects. An older study, of Chicago's Gautreaux mobility program, for instance, found that children who moved out of public housing to the city suburbs were more than twice as likely to attend college, compared to those who stayed behind. Fifteen years later, these youth ended up living in better neighborhoods, although the data are incomplete on their more detailed outcomes. Although the Gautreaux study lacked some rigor, a very recent and also state-of-the-art study, of housing demolitions in Chicago, also shows the upside of residential mobility. The children who were forcibly displaced by housing demolitions were, as adults, 9 percent more likely to be employed, and they earned 16 percent more than those who were not so displaced.[31]

This lack of geographic mobility also is probably holding back our income mobility. It is much harder for Americans to migrate successfully to some of the most economically dynamic American cities. In the "good old days," you could pick up your bags and move into New York, San Francisco, or Los Angeles, among other places, and find a middle-class job, almost certainly one with a pay hike over what you might have been earning in rural America. Perhaps more important, the chances for further advancement were greater too, much greater, once you moved to the big city.

But today, high rents, resulting both from talent clusters as we might find in Manhattan or the Bay area and from restrictive building codes, make it harder to move into major cities as a path for upward mobility. Obviously, it's no longer that easy to pick up your bags and move into an affordable place in Greenwich Village or, for that matter, Harlem, but even as you work your way out—to Jersey City, or easy-commute towns like Maplewood, New Jersey—you see the cost of renting or buying skyrocketing. For a low-skilled worker, the higher wages in those cities do not always make up for the much higher rental costs. And the reason is that those cities are so, so expensive, at least in the parts where most productive workers are willing to live.[32]

Compare today to the 1950s. At that time, a typical apartment in New York City rented for about $60 a month, or, adjusting for inflation, about $530 a month. Today you can't find a broom closet in the East Village for that amount. Even in the South Bronx there is gentrification, and some new apartments are going up for a projected $3,750 a month for a small-one bedroom abode. Many parking spaces in fact cost more than the going rate for a 1950s NYC apartment.[33] Or to put that 1950s rent in perspective, the U.S. median wage at that time was about $5,000 a year, so a typical New Yorker spent as little as 10 percent of salary on rent, or perhaps even less to the extent that New Yorkers were earning more than other typical Americans. Today this is but a wild dream as a typical New Yorker spends about 84 (!) percent of the national median salary on rent. As recently as the 1980s, the suburbs were more expensive, but today the central cities have the most exorbitant rents and home prices.[34]

It's not just that the rents were so cheap back then. In most American cities, if you rented a midlevel apartment, you could send your kids to a midlevel-quality school district. In New York City, that hasn't been the case for a long time, so a lot of middle-class families in the city have to think about sending their kids to private schools, which can run tens of thousands of dollars a year per kid.

If it were cheaper to move into major American cities, the country's economy would be stronger and many more Americans would have an easier path toward a higher salary and a brighter future. Two aforementioned researchers, Chang-Tai Hsieh and Enrico Moretti, set out to measure just how big a problem this has been. They noticed that within the United States, the dispersion of worker productivity across different cities has gone up. For instance, New York, San Francisco, and San Jose have become especially high-productivity cities, compared to, say, Brownsville, Texas; the size of these gaps has been growing over time. Those large gaps mean that the American economy could become much richer if more workers could be moved from the low-productivity cities to the high-productivity cities; that would increase income mobility too. The researchers estimate that "[l]owering regulatory constraints in these [high-productivity] cities to the level of the median city would expand their work force and increase U.S. GDP by 9.5%." In a $17 trillion economy, that is indeed a huge effect—you can think of it as an extra $1.7 trillion in upward income mobility.[35]

The culprit, however, is the NIMBY mentality and related anti-growth obstacles. Residents in Manhattan, San Francisco, and many other high-productivity locales just don't want all of those new people moving in, and so they have passed overly strict building and land use regulations or in some cases they have limited infrastructure so that adding more residents just isn't practical. Without good bus or subway connections, for instance, a lot of neighborhoods just don't work for people with jobs downtown.

And more cities are entertaining regulations on building. For instance, the growing cities in the American South may over time increase their land use regulations to maintain what is a new and growing exclusive status. Hsieh and Moretti estimate that increasing the toughness of land use regulations in the South to a level comparable with those of New York, San Francisco, and San Jose would cost the American economy about 3 percent of GDP. At the moment, the United States is divided into cities and states that are relatively static for new building, such as San Francisco, and those that are relatively dynamic for building, such as Atlanta and Texas. But the static areas evolved to that point for a reason: Current arrangements suit the interests of incumbent homeowners. Twenty or thirty years from now, there is a far greater chance that the dynamic parts will have turned static than vice versa. For that reason, future American residential mobility may be still more restricted than what we are observing today.

The growing geographic stasis of American life has another negative consequence, which I've already hinted at and will explore in greater detail in the next chapter. In many parts of the country, we are seeing segregation by race, income, education, and social status make a noticeable comeback. And we have good reason to believe that segregation brings significant negative consequences. Let's now take a closer look.

3.

THE REEMERGENCE OF SEGREGATION

I've noted that the stasis of our current age is not comfortable for everybody. For every member of the privileged class, there are more people who have been locked out of enjoying many of the fruits of economic and social progress. Your outcome depends a lot on where you live and who your peer groups are. And in these regards, America overall has been becoming less integrated and more segregated by a number of standards, even though relatively few people have deliberately chosen to make this country a more segregated one. There are, nonetheless, growing divides across many parts of American life, whether based on income, education, socioeconomic status, or race, and those divides are becoming increasingly sticky and difficult to unravel. Any story of change slowing down has to consider the reality that "digging in" isn't good for everybody, because in the longer run, it disrupts a natural flow of people across jobs, across geographic areas, and across socioeconomic peer groups.

Quite simply, a closer look at the phenomenon of segregation can help us understand why the complacent class shouldn't be so complacent after all. At any point in time, segregation can be a relatively or even very comfortable outcome for those in more advantageous positions—for instance, those parents who have enrolled their children in the most exclusive schools and who live in nice neighborhoods. But most forms of segregation ultimately corrode the basis of prosperity and innovation and eat into the trust and seed capital of society. That is the position America is in today. Rather than a fully consistent process of ongoing integration, this country has seen widespread cocooning and digging in, with the final collective result being tougher implicit barriers separating various socioeconomic groups.

These trends of increasing segregation show up in the aggregate numbers, but if you think about it, you probably can see it in some of the details of your own life, at least in many parts of this country. Circa 2016, you can see a black president on your television or internet screen, but that doesn't mean you're going to see more neighbors of a different race than you would have seen a few decades ago. Or if you do, you're much less likely to see such individuals outside of your income class, even if they are not of your race.

The Ferguson, Missouri, and Baltimore riots of 2015 took a lot of people by surprise, especially a lot of white people, and the proximate cause of these events was an accumulating pattern of police violence and misbehavior. But the deeper underlying roots of these and subsequent events were that the civil rights movement never really triumphed, and since then some economic forces have brought a lot of reversals when it comes to racial justice and fair treatment. After the legal and economic gains of the 1960s, a lot of people, both black and white, had a vision of ongoing racial amelioration. Maybe race relations would improve slowly, but they would improve nonetheless. After all, an integrated society is better than a segregated society for virtually everyone, so a taste of additional integration should lead to further advances. Over time, America was supposed to approach being, if not a racially blind nation, a much more integrated nation, and with that integration would come a greater degree of fairness and a lot more mixing of different kinds of people, including across the races. The election of President Obama was supposed to herald a new era of race relations.

This optimistic vision often seems to be true, especially if you inhabit the suburbs and spend a lot of time running after ethnic food and studying immigration, as I do. But in some key regards that progress never quite came to fruition, including for black-white relations and sometimes especially for black-white relations. When it comes to the residential and education worlds, America just hasn't gotten that much better at mixing socioeconomic groups, and that is yet another part of just how set in its ways the country has become.

In reality, the country is aging, and this matters for the degree of mixing. Think of yourself, or most of your friends. When you were in high school and college, you tried a lot of different things, tried out a lot of different styles and identities, and perhaps were not yet settled in to a definite career and set of friends. As you progress into your later years, you settle into a career, meet fewer new people, have less time to spend with them, and perhaps move into a permanent residence. You don't go to as many parties, and maybe you are married rather than dating and circulating with friends in the quest for a mate. By the time you hit fifty, you are more settled in your ways, in your connections—social, commercial, and otherwise—and you are probably not making too many additional close friends as the years pass, at least not compared to your earlier days. It could be said that you are mixing less, and the reasons for those changes are pretty intuitive and near universal. (On the bright side, I do know of some people who are exceptions.)

OK, so now consider the United States as a country. America is aging, and will get older yet. American businesses and cities are older and more established, and the frontier was settled long ago. The national identity is fairly mature, and it can be said that America is, as a country, not in high school anymore. Measured in terms of political continuity, it's actually a lot older than many European nations. So we should not be entirely surprised to learn that in some ways the country is mixing less effectively, especially internally, and this is showing up in less mixing by income, education, and social class, and across one of America's longest-standing fault lines, the black-white racial divide.

So when police misbehave, and taped recordings of that misbehavior comes to the attention of citizens, it does not happen in an atmosphere of harmony and slowly increasing progress under commonly lived public institutions. Many Americans know or at least instinctively feel that the ideal of equal treatment is in some ways receding along the horizon. It may not always or even usually be a matter of deliberate prejudice, but if you don't live in the right neighborhood or go to the right school, you can't count on getting fair treatment or even tolerably acceptable treatment. As we'll see, the system just hasn't evolved in those directions, and thus a persistent sense of injustice remains, and sometimes festers, thereby creating the potential for trouble.

I see these trends in my own life. I've lived in northern Virginia for a long time, and sometimes I think back to the 1990s, when I would shoot baskets in a neighboring town called Vienna, Virginia. Vienna was and still is an upper-middle-class small town in an upper-middle-class part of the country, well above average in terms of income and quality of life and quality of schools. And in those days, Vienna was mostly white, but this small neighborhood within Vienna, one of Virginia's historically black neighborhoods, was nearly all black. While it wasn't as affluent as those surrounding it, it was firmly middle class, with residents enjoying good schools and a high degree of public safety. And it wasn't the only such neighborhood in the area either; in the adjacent city of Fairfax, another upper-middle-class venue, there was a lively and well-maintained black neighborhood. Every morning I would see a rather antiquated convenience store on the corner and young black kids waiting for the school bus while I drove past to enter George Mason University. Again, this neighborhood was right next to well-off, mostly white enclaves.

Today all that has changed—these historically black neighborhoods within Vienna and Fairfax are gone. In the case of Fairfax, that old convenience store has been replaced by a shiny new mini-mall with a bright pizza restaurant, a Vietnamese pho restaurant, and a gourmet market and deli that sells fine wine, New York–style bagels, and extra-virgin artisanal olive oil imported in small batches from Greece. The first housing development you see when you turn into the neighborhood is called, distressingly, Royal Legacy. The townhomes are stout and large, fairly homogeneous, and have that oppressive upper-middle-class look. A quick online real estate search found some prices quoted at $744,999 for 2,300 square feet.

As rents and real estate prices went up, many of the former residents sold out or moved out. Today, if you visit either of these neighborhoods, you don't notice anything special about their ethnic or racial composition; they look just like the other parts of Vienna or Fairfax. They are no longer all-black or mostly black neighborhoods, and they also have many more Asian residents. You even could say that the *neighborhood* is more racially integrated than it used to be, at least according to the formal numbers, given the influx of Asians and Latinos. But the notion of mixing different socioeconomic groups has weakened or gone away, and those towns have been gentrified. In terms of income and class, both areas are now pretty homogenized in terms of social status. They no longer are districts where one part of America rubs shoulders with another, even though you will find many more well-to-do immigrants living next door to well-to-do Americans.

To be sure, these neighborhoods, and these black neighbors, were not *forced* out. No KKK member burned a cross on these lawns, and no discriminatory laws were passed. Having lived in northern Virginia since 1989, and also between 1980 and 1983, I have observed personally that it has become less discriminatory over time. In the last two presidential elections, it was a notable source of support for President Obama. Unlike in the early 1980s, Confederate flags are no longer seen and for the most part are no longer tolerated. But in lieu of that racism has come the complacent class, and so when it comes to black-white proximity, many parts of the region are more segregated than before, without overt or in many cases even conscious racism. We may feel good that the all-black neighborhoods are a thing of the past, but their dissolution is very much a mixed blessing because they were smack in the midst of some quite prosperous territory. Blacks have not been *pushed* out, but many of them have been *priced* out. This has been a core mechanism through which America has slowed down its residential mixing and done a more exact job of matching rich to rich and poor to poor. What we'll see in a moment is that this simple story about two Virginia neighborhoods reflects broader national trends.

WHAT KIND OF SEGREGATION IS GOING ON?

I'm going to consider a number of different and indeed contrasting forms of segregation and their measures. As you'll see, that will include segregation by income, by education, by social class, and of course also by race.

For all their differences, I think these varying metrics are pointing toward a broadly common picture: that significant parts of the United States are less mixed than before in terms of income, social class, race, and also overall feel. That is, since the 1990s, a lot of the trends have been negative rather than positive. The new segregation is superficially based on economics but more deeply rooted in a culture of matching—rich to rich and well educated to well educated—and a culture of stasis; namely, that economic change is not coming as quickly as it was during the 1950s or 1960s, or for that matter the 1990s. Most of this new segregation is not rooted in direct racial or social class animus, even though some of this animus persists. The new segregation is the result of the increasing ability of Americans of means to sort with people who are like themselves in terms of education and income and social class and then to be happy—or at least complacent—with the results of that sorting.

I'll start with segregation by income, which is the easiest to see of all the contemporary segregating developments. Furthermore, the inability of lower-income groups to afford a nicer neighborhood is a fundamental force behind some of the other segregations as well, because money, and what we can afford, drives so many other decisions in contemporary America.

Segregation by income grew dramatically over the period of 1970 to 2000, with some respite in the 1990s, but then faster yet during the period of 2000 to 2007. For instance, in 1970, only about 15 percent of families lived in neighborhoods that were unambiguously "affluent" or "poor." By 2007, 31 percent of American families were living in such neighborhoods. At the level of school districts, segregation increased as well between students eligible for free lunch and those who were not. In other words, those students who were eligible for free lunch were more likely to be grouped together than in times past. There is thus a thinning out of the middle and the creation of "rich" and "poor" sociological bubbles into which we are sorted. For where you live, income matters more than ever before, as can be shown by a simple perusal of the apartment ads for most of America's leading cities.[1]

Income segregation for black and Hispanic families grew especially sharply between 2000 and 2007, and that form of segregation is now considerably higher than it is for white families; that is, black and Hispanic American families are less likely to live in income-mixed neighborhoods. As we will see later, this fact has diminished their chances to enjoy some of the drivers of upward mobility, such as exposure to better schools and safer neighborhoods, just as they have been priced out of some very nice parts of Fairfax and Vienna, Virginia, as I explained earlier. In other words, income mixing is being denied to some of the groups who might benefit from it most, again mostly as a result of broader social structural forces—especially high rent due to gentrification—rather than due to explicit racism or prejudice.[2]

So where is income segregation happening at its most extreme? It's basically the Amtrak corridor at the most income-segregated end of the distribution—with Bridgeport–Stamford–Norwalk, Connecticut, coming in at the top, followed by New York City, Philadelphia, and Newark to round out the top four. The list then diversifies, with four main Texas cities (Austin, not El Paso) in the top fourteen for segregation by income. The Detroit metropolitan area is where segregation by income has gone up the most from 2000 to 2007, and that may have been driven by the exodus of middle-class residents from the city; perhaps this will be somewhat reversed by the modest revival of gentrification in that city. Still, overall, in these parts of the country, mixing by income is doing the worst.[3]

Notably, the list of the ten most segregated American cities, by income and education, includes four metropolitan areas in Texas. Since there has been a significant net movement of population into Texas, many Americans are opting for this segregation as part of their future, whether they know it or not. In many locales, the segregation model is passing a kind of market test as measured by the flow of Americans from one set of places to another. It might be more encouraging if the more-segregated areas were being rejected, but population flows show that is not the general trend. Again we see mechanisms by which some kinds of segregation increase, without anyone necessarily intending segregation per se.

SEGREGATION BY EDUCATION AND CULTURE

Moving beyond income, what about other metrics of segregation? What are some other ways in which individual decisions are limiting the physical mixing across different groups of people? The reality is that the breaking of America into different groups, while often driven by money, is in fact not about money alone. Education and social class are also very important as segregators and dividers.

The most heavily segregated cities, across a variety of metrics, including education, social class, and sometimes race, tend to be what urban researchers Richard Florida and Charlotta Melander label "high-tech, knowledge-based metros." That is again a sign of the complacent class at work. For instance, we can look at where the working class is least segregated from the non–working class as one metric for the mixing of social classes. That list of least class-segregated cities is Hartford, Providence, Buffalo, Virginia Beach, Orlando, Milwaukee, New Orleans, Rochester, Las Vegas, and Cincinnati, in that order. There is plenty of "Old America" on that list. To drive the point home, look at the large metropolitan areas where the working class is *most* segregated, and that list starts with Los Angeles, Austin, Dallas–Fort Worth, and Washington,

DC. If you have any doubts, the next five metropolitan areas for "working class most segregated" are Raleigh, San Francisco, San Jose, Houston, Charlotte, and Columbus. Hello, future: Those are the cities that receive breathless write-ups in airline magazines as the fun places to work and visit, and they are where a lot of people want to move, at least if they can afford to. Quite frankly, those are the parts of America where people feel very good about themselves.[4]

If we look at all metropolitan areas, rather than just the large ones, Durham–Chapel Hill, Bloomington, and Ann Arbor—all college towns—climb into the top five for segregation of the working class away from the non–working class. That is again the somewhat incestuous self-clustering of the complacent class rearing its head. Due to their major universities, those towns all have lots of knowledge workers, people proficient in IT or biotech, lots of skilled labor, lots of creativity, and people working hard to get ahead—all features that, it turns out, correlate with residential segregation by education and social class.[5]

Along related lines, Florida and Mellander also find that racial segregation is positively correlated with areas that have a lot of high-tech industry, with those that have a preponderance of people in the so-called creative class, who hold jobs requiring creative skills, and with those heavily populated by college graduates. Segregation also tends to be found in places with relatively high percentages of gay and foreign-born populations—think of San Francisco as having a fair share of both, but also a lot of neighborhoods with mostly white people. Median rent in San Francisco just passed $5,000 per month for a two-bedroom apartment, and so most people, even in the upper-middle classes, feel that residence in the city involves too much financial hardship. These days the poor in San Francisco are pushed into a smaller and smaller group of neighborhoods; the poor and middle-class residents of this region have responded with staged protests against the tech companies for bidding up the rents so high. Outside the city, in Silicon Valley, the region of East Palo Alto was considered a kind of ghetto as recently as the 1990s; it now has multimillion-dollar cottages and bungalows for sale.[6]

One way to put it is that segregation, when it comes to minorities and the less educated and the working class, tends to be correlated with those qualities of cities that we regard—along other dimensions at least—as trendy. At the end of the day, many residents of Park Slope, Brooklyn, or Ann Arbor, Michigan, for example, are morally opposed to segregation and would be horrified if you pointed it out in their neighborhoods, but still the process continues and indeed intensifies. Ending it simply isn't that much of a priority for anyone, or at least not a high-enough priority to induce people to live in less-desirable neighborhoods when they can afford something better, most of all for their children.

The metropolitan areas where the creative class is least segregated from the rest of society tend to be small areas, not large ones, and thus they don't shape the nation so much. The city with the lowest level of creative-class segregation turns out to be Mankato, Minnesota, with a population of just under 40,000 residents. Its largest employer is the Mayo Clinic, it is renowned for its high quality of life, and in 2004 it was rated as the funniest city in America by Hallmark Cards, all according to Wikipedia. And that is followed by Lewiston-Auburn, Maine; St. Cloud, Minnesota; Joplin, Missouri; and Rome, Georgia, none of which are major shapers of cultural or national trends because indeed a lot of the trends are toward greater segregation. I don't intend any slight to those places, but they do not seem to herald the future of America or its creativity. They are more like throwbacks to an earlier America, albeit with some successful service industries to keep them prosperous and to fund quality levels of local public services. In other words, the more mixed and socioeconomically integrated areas don't seem to be the ones that represent the future of America.[7]

Or consider the metric of segregation by educational achievement, which you can take as another rough measure of a kind of segregation by social class. The large metropolitan areas where those without a high school degree are *least* segregated are disproportionately a cross-section of Old America, namely towns that were once dependent on manufacturing and earlier modes of transportation, most commonly rivers, lakes, and canals. The top ten include Pittsburgh (#1), Louisville, Buffalo, St. Louis, New Orleans, and Cincinnati. Once again, while elsewhere the level of segregation is a larger problem, the broader trend is arguably a bigger worry, as we again see Old America serving as a bastion for some kinds of continuing but endangered integrated existence.[8]

Who is driving this segregation? The data show that the rich and well educated are keener to live together, in tight bunches and groups, than are the less well educated. Democrats cluster themselves more tightly than do Republicans, in part reflecting their stronger preference for urban areas, and that urbanization itself may tilt people toward the Democratic Party. And if we look at professions? Well, the so-called creative class is more clustered than the working class. Ironically, it's these groups—the wealthy, the well educated, and the creative class—who often complain about inequality and American segregation with the greatest fervor. The self-selection process is running its course, and how people are voting with their feet often differs from what is coming out of their mouths.[9]

One implication of these measures is that the affluent and well educated in America may be especially out of touch, no matter how ostensibly progressive their politics. A high-income family, for instance, is less likely to live in a mixed-income neighborhood than is a poor family. When it comes to understanding the circumstances of differing socioeconomic strata of America, high-income groups may not be so well informed when it comes to intuitively grasping America's real problems, or at least having a sense of what other Americans might feel those problems to be. Unfortunately, this form of residential segregation has characterized the data for about the last forty years. By now, however, this process is sufficiently extreme that we can have a political phenomenon, such as the election of Donald Trump, foreseen by hardly any of America's elite political commentators. In fact, those same commentators explained away some rather obvious poll-based evidence showing Trump's popularity within the Republican Party at the time.[10]

THE SEGREGATED COLLEGE TOWN

Most people think of college towns as politically progressive places guided by a pro-multicultural, antidiscrimination ethos. But in practice? It is striking how many of the most segregated smaller metropolitan areas are college towns. Some college towns with especially high levels of racial segregation, and educational segregation too, are Ann Arbor, Durham–Chapel Hill, Tucson, Gainesville, and College Station. These are the places where you need a high enough income to live in the good part of town (which gets bigger by the year), and there are also sharp divides in terms of education and social connections, and so these cities tend to be racially segregated to a high degree. A lot of lower-income people just aren't that interested in paying extra to live around college professors.

The colleges themselves, for all their embrace of affirmative action and the rhetoric of diversity, are typically highly segregated bastions of well-off, well-educated (by definition), and ambitious future high achievers, and they make the tone of the town all the more that way. Ironically, America's ethic of tolerance, as it has evolved, is a double-edged sword when it comes to integration. It has created a new set of entry barriers, as if only the right kind of "tolerant" people are supposed to be living in particular neighborhoods, or maybe only they can afford it or only they feel comfortable there by fitting in. The college culture sounds tolerant when you talk about it at a cocktail party, but on the ground, the reality is less rather than more mixing and again the cementing of America's social and also economic stasis.[11]

Richard Florida and Charlotta Mellander have ranked the most and least segregated areas in the United States, using metrics of income, education, and also occupation. By these measures, the most segregated area is Austin, Texas, where wealthy, college-educated professionals are least likely to live near their less-educated counterparts in the area. But if you know Austin a bit, this makes some sense. There is a yuppie downtown Austin, with America's biggest Whole Foods branch, tech start-ups, women wearing Loft clothes, and some of the most expensive real estate in Texas. Even the barbecue is highbrow there, made of expensive cuts of meat and carried by well-dressed servers.

Drive out by the airport, and you're more likely to see a taxidermist, shops selling burglar alarms and car parts, and strip joints. There is again barbecue, but in smaller and less glamorous settings, often trailers, and it makes the best of inferior cuts of meat. And the easiest way to see the transition between the different Austins is to head out of downtown, going east on Cesar Chavez Boulevard. Once you cross Route 35, the shops for women's creams are gone and suddenly you see outlets for "cash advance," immigration and criminal defense services, piñata party supply, a "flying trapeze" jumping area, and of course guns, Austin Gold and Guns being my favorite. People sit on their ramshackle porches rather than up in their riverview condominiums.

These different parts of Austin are not far apart in terms of miles, but the boundaries are clear. You're in either one or the other. Hipster coffee shops and used book stores are now starting to move east of Route 35, but the longer-run trend has been for yuppie Austin to push out lower-income, lower-education Austin.

The gentrification of Austin is affecting every facet of the city's life, including its heralded music scene. The official motto is "Live Music Capital of the World," but with a median home value of $272,250—and rising—it is harder for musicians to make ends meet. More Austin musicians are moving into the less-salubrious parts of town—about half of the city's musicians are eligible for publicly subsidized housing—or moving away altogether. Another problem for musicians is that no one wants them practicing and making so much noise in the newly gentrified neighborhoods, so they either have to move out or invest in expensive sound-proofing. When all is said and done, the gentrification of Austin may not have entirely positive effects on the city's creativity in the longer run.[12]

At the same time, the upside for Austin is obvious. In 1970, only 17 percent of the adults in Austin had a college education. By 2009–2013, this number had gone up to 45.6 percent.[13]

RACIAL SEGREGATION: UP, DOWN, OR SIDEWAYS?

The growing segregation by income can help us understand how racial integration has been evolving. The good news is that the nation as a whole has become modestly more racially integrated since 1993, after a deeply resegregating period through the 1980s. By one measure, about two-thirds of America is becoming less segregated by race, and about one-third is becoming more segregated. The bad news is that the progress is only in some parts of the nation and is only along some metrics, arguably not the most important ones. The more we break down the details, the more worrying the picture becomes. The worst problems are becoming worse, and schools are not integrating as much as neighborhoods are, a bad sign for the future, because on average disadvantaged students do better in integrated schools.[14]

First, most of the decline in measured segregation comes from more Asians and Latinos mixing in with African Americans. That is a positive development in the sense that it has broken up some formerly dysfunctional inner-city neighborhoods, but when it comes to blacks mixing into white neighborhoods, the trend is mostly in the negative direction. Barriers to white neighborhoods have remained, and in some regards they have intensified. For instance, in 1990, black households were in neighborhoods that had a 41.7 percent share of whites, on average, but that rate has since fallen to 39.8 percent.[15]

Second, if we look at school systems, racial segregation is also getting worse in some ways. In the South, if we consider the variable "percentage of black students in majority-white schools," that figure peaked in 1988 at 43.5 percent; as of 2011, it had fallen dramatically, to 23.2 percent. That is slightly *lower* than the integration level in 1968, a time when civil rights battles were close to their peak activity. I believe that most of America does not realize how much the South has retreated along this dimension, nor what a grim picture it heralds for the longer-run future in America.[16]

If we look at the country as a whole, and not just the South, the average black student attends a school that is about 27.6 percent white. Is that really a fulfillment of the integrationist civil rights dream of the 1960s? As mentioned above, residences, neighborhoods, and thus school systems with lots of black students now have many more Asians and Latinos; the average black student is in a school district that is 10.7 percent Asian, 10.9 percent Latino, and 48.8 percent black.[17]

There is some good news for the racial integration of schools, and that comes mainly in the suburbs. Depending on the size of the metropolitan area, black student presence in suburban American schools ranges from about 9 to 14.6 percent, and those numbers do show mostly good trends. In the 1960s, the suburbs often were considered the deadening, bureaucratic, and boring part of the United States. But easy suburban living, combined with commercial opportunities, decent public services, lots of immigrants, cheaper housing, and a general openness have turned American suburbs into the arena where racial integration has gone pretty well. There is less racial segregation in the suburbs, because it is harder to limit or choke off all possible sources of change, and thus the complacent class there is not (yet?) entirely in control.[18]

In suburban schools, however, there are still serious segregation problems, and, unknown to many, Latinos are experiencing more significant integration problems than are African Americans. For instance, in California, only 7.8 percent of Latino students are in majority-white schools. In part that is because California has large clusters of Latinos and in part because the fanciest white neighborhoods are difficult to afford, the latter again indicating a lot of economically enforced segregation rather than racist animus. The broader data on trends in Latino segregation also are not entirely encouraging, as, for instance, in 1990 Latinos had more residential proximity with whites than they did in the period 2005 through 2009.[19]

For the country as a whole, the racial integration of our school systems, especially in cities and in the South, is far behind what many people had expected—or at least hoped for—only a few decades ago. If you doubt that, consider the variable "percentage of black students in intensely segregated minority schools," because arguably the biggest problem with racial segregation comes in the most extreme cases. For all five major geographic regions of the country—South, Border, Northeast, Midwest, West—there is the same depressing result. Levels of integration were slightly higher in 1989–1990 than they are today. Most of these deteriorations are small, although for the Midwest, the figure has moved from slightly more than 20 percent to well over 30 percent.[20]

To return to the theme of how America is evolving, it is school systems that tell you what Americans care about and also where the country is headed. There is a common pattern of young, dual-earner couples deciding to live in cities and often choosing the funkier parts or mixed neighborhoods, in part to save money and in part because those areas may be interesting to live in. That is one factor driving down rates of residential racial segregation, and, to be sure, that is a positive development. Still, when they have children and it is time to send the kids to school, they often move to the suburbs, or to a more expensive part of the same city, or to a different city altogether. The integration is a kind of temporary experiment in white lives, to be reversed once the next generation comes along. It is good that so many people are willing to make this temporary experiment but bad that it doesn't have greater staying power or turn into a means of integrating young children.

To see how significant parts of America may be looking at a more racially segregated future, let's consider segregation in school systems in more detail. In 1980, in Maryland, 30 percent of black students were in intensely segregated schools. That same figure is now about 53 percent. If we look at the percentage of black students in what are called intensely segregated minority schools, since 1980, in Mississippi, that number has gone up 9 percentage points; in Tennessee, it has gone up 15 percentage points; in Texas, 9 percentage points; in Georgia, 16 percentage points; in Alabama, 10 percentage points; in Florida, 17 percentage points; and in Arkansas, it is up 21 percentage points. By the phrase *intensely segregated schools*, the literature usually is referring to white enrollment below 10 percent.[21]

Unfortunately, many parts of the North are failing as well, as the northern states and also California rank among the worst for many measures of educational segregation. For instance, let's consider the variable "% black in 90–100% Minority Schools."[22] That is a measure of levels rather than changes, and by that standard, the five most segregated states are:

1. New York
2. Illinois
3. Maryland
4. Michigan
5. New Jersey

That's hardly whistling Dixie. And if those numbers are not growing worse, as they are in many parts of the South, well, that is in part because there is hardly much room left for deterioration.

Again, American schools are a good measure of where the nation is headed, because that is where so many core attitudes are formed; school system choices also reflect the true attitudes and priorities of parents. A segregated, inferior, or otherwise dysfunctional school system will exert its effects for a long time to come, over multiple generations, most likely, including on the future degree of various kinds of segregation.

The future of the country looks troublingly similar on both coasts, as both New York and California perform poorly on segregation measures. In two of the three main measures of educational segregation by race, they are the worst and third-worst states in this regard, alternating those two positions. Again, the claim is not that New York and California are somehow especially racist or objectionable states but rather that segregation is being enforced by incomes, rents, home prices, building codes, how school districts are drawn, and a culture of sorting and matching. Racism does enter as a second-order phenomenon, in that racist feelings do lead some wealthy white elites to keep cheap housing out of their neighborhoods, out of an implicit or maybe explicit dislike of having to mix with lower earners or people with less education or, for that matter, people of color. But in any case, New York and California, two of America's most advanced and most progressive states, are dropping the ball when it comes to racial integration. Sorting and segregation are fundamental to the workings of modern America, especially cutting-edge, wealthy, and well-educated modern America.

Yet another recent study designated New York State as having the most racially segregated school system in the nation. New York City was worse yet. In 2010, only about 20 percent of the school districts in the NYC metropolitan area were considered racially diverse (more than 20 percent but less than 60 percent nonwhite students), and of that 20 percent, less than a third were considered to be racially stable, in the sense of being able to keep an integrated mix. Looking at charter schools within New York City, in 2010, 73 percent were considered to be what are sometimes called "apartheid schools" (less than 1 percent white enrollment), and over 90 percent were "intensely segregated."[23]

It has been estimated that for New York to become a perfectly integrated city (measured by residences rather than school attendance), 78 percent of the city's population would have to get up and move to some other neighborhood.[24]

It is discouraging to observe what happens when the possibility of greater racial integration approaches. In a recent case in Brooklyn, there was a population overflow in a gentrifying neighborhood known as Dumbo, short for Down Under the Manhattan Bridge Overpass. The growing population meant that some of the students from a predominantly white school district (P.S. 8) needed to be sent to a neighboring district, which was mostly black (P.S. 307) and overall 90 percent black and Latino. The white parents protested vigorously against having their children shipped to the other district. Furthermore, many of the African American parents also expressed concerns about how the educational environment for their children might change if so many white children were imported. Some felt it could mean more competition for their children but not fundamentally more resources. Eventually a rezoning placated many of the white and higher-income families, yet it is likely that the legal outcome will continue to evolve, due to parental pressure and the contentious nature of the issue. In any case, this episode is an example of how difficult it will be to achieve more school system integration. We've not only created a fairly segregated society, we've cemented it in.[25]

The negative trends for black-white racial segregation, by the way, are not driven by income alone. When it comes to residence, well-off blacks have only slightly higher proximity to white households than do poor blacks. As researcher John R. Logan put it: "Race trumps income for blacks." For whatever embedded cultural reasons, even America's hip and trendy neighborhoods just aren't that welcoming, including for wealthier African Americans, as we'll see in more detail below. In a lot of different parts of America, the older culture seems to have been more welcoming of racial integration, and mixing in general, even if direct racial prejudice has in some ways gone down.[26]

I found this Silicon Valley anecdote striking:

> She [Lena Alston, an African American woman] could see that Google wanted to foster a diverse culture, but, as the only African American on her team, she didn't feel she had much in common with her colleagues. "When I went out to lunch or something with my team, it was sort of like, 'Sooo, what are you guys talking about?'" she says. "It could be something as simple as, like, what they watch on TV or what kind of books they like to read. And those are just not TV shows that I watch or books that I read."
>
> "Back in the civil rights period, it used to be that lighter-skinned people were able to pass and be more acceptable, so they were able to get into organizations or get into companies," [Legand] Burge says. "Now it's a little bit different. It's about cultural fit. Do you laugh at the same jokes? Do you Rollerblade or whatever?"[27]

Even when it comes to Asians, the process of integration is not running nearly as smoothly as many people think. The standard narrative is of East Asian immigrants coming to this country and dominating the school systems and thus fully integrating into mainstream American society. There is some truth to that for specific groups, but the aggregate numbers for Asians are not as promising. Asians aren't nearly as segregated as blacks, but since 1990, their geographic integration into American society seems to have declined slightly. And Asian Americans still live in neighborhoods that, on average, have slightly lower resources than what is available for white neighborhoods. The integration records for many Asian subgroups, including Filipinos, Vietnamese, and Laotians, just aren't all that impressive.[28]

As segregation becomes worse in some ways, eventually it is accepted as the "new normal," to borrow a phrase from macroeconomics. And as many people see that many other people don't seem to mind this arrangement, they stop thinking of it as especially objectionable, and it begins to feel almost natural. In the longer run, that can make the tendencies for segregation stronger yet. And besides, there usually isn't a simple, up-front remedy to set everything right, as the underlying problems are quite deep and structural, rooted in some fairly fundamental features of America itself. Once the most obvious abuses of racial prejudice are eliminated, it can seem hard to find the proper righteous cause that promises an acceptable fix. And so environments can deteriorate, because, after all, no single individual can gain much from speaking out about the need to set things right.

Most of all, segregation of various kinds lowers the chance that some large group of individuals will achieve success in life: Those individuals on the losing end will have lower chances of happy marriages, higher earnings, well-adjusted children, and long and healthy lives. Furthermore, segregation's losers are often the poorest and most vulnerable individuals in America. Living in less salubrious neighborhoods, they have less access to resources, are socialized into less-beneficial norms, and end up with peers who in many cases encourage destructive rather than successful behavior patterns. There is good evidence that more integrated neighborhoods produce greater upward mobility in terms of income and education.[29]

You needn't consider this either a left-wing or right-wing point of view. The progressive left has for a long time emphasized the enervating effects of deprived environments, including segregated environments. Those on the right commonly observe that the worst thing about being poor in modern America is having to hang out with, and live near, other poor people, or in other words having to experience a culture of poverty on a regular basis. The rhetoric may differ in terms of whether poor people are portrayed as victims or blamed for purported cultural or character-related deficiencies, but in terms of the belief that segregation by class is a bad thing for the less-successful individuals, there is actually a fair amount of consensus. And just to show how far the problem has gone, there is now good evidence that black-white income convergence has pretty much stopped; in other words, blacks are no longer catching up to whites in their earnings.[30]

As I've already mentioned in the chapter on residential mobility, you might think that the people already living in the better neighborhoods will lose something from additional mixing, and maybe so. Still, as a moral judgment, it seems that well-off Americans are doing better and better, poor Americans are in some ways facing greater struggles, and we are moving farther along the scale of segregation in some significant ways. So a final judgment in favor of more integration, racial and otherwise, doesn't seem so difficult to defend, even though we don't have a comprehensive cost-benefit analysis of what the costs would be. We're seeing a lot of specific data-rooted signs that segregation is proceeding past the point we ever wanted to witness.

Finally, although I've focused on the traditional kinds of segregation by race, income, and education, America runs the risk that principles and practices of segregation will become common, accepted, and indeed entrenched more generally. The wealthier parts of the country will become wealthier yet, and the most talented individuals will entrench themselves in those areas, raising rents forever to very high levels. Prospects for mixing across incomes and social classes may recede all the more, to the detriment of the American republic.

Segregation has yet another negative consequence: It leads to more intense sorting along political lines, so that both Democrats and Republicans will be more likely to live in communities of politically like-minded individuals. That would lead to more polarization in Congress and to some extent governmental gridlock. A lot of what analysts call political polarization is actually the result of more intense sorting. To put it simply, a disproportionate share of liberals have decided they wish to live in cities, and many conservatives have decided they wish to live in suburbs and in rural areas. Those liberals and those conservatives also then may be exercising some influence over their immediate neighbors. That is, peer effects make cities more liberal and suburban and rural areas more conservative, and thus Americans are all the more tightly sorted, politically speaking and also by such variables as church-going behavior.[31]

Sometimes this tighter sorting is confused with greater political polarization of the *electorate*. Tighter sorting will make liberal areas more liberal and conservative areas more conservative, and our congressional representatives will reflect this more split division of opinion. Political debate will be more contentious, and it will be harder to find compromise; indeed, this has come to pass. Nonetheless, this phenomenon is distinct from the American people having become intrinsically more polarized in terms of their collective opinions. While I believe that political polarization has increased somewhat, the percentage of independents in the American electorate has not gone down and the percentage of Democrats and Republicans has not gone up. As political scientist Morris Fiorina has noted, "moderate" is still the modal political category for the United States.[32] Nonetheless, our federal government largely has fallen apart as a mechanism for solving economic and social problems, in part because Congress cannot agree on much, whether that is more regulation or less regulation or a liberal or conservative program to move forward.

The upshot is that segregations can have far-reaching and negative effects that we do not always see at first glance. And yet I still haven't discussed segregation in its most brutal forms. America's incarceration crisis, which has recently begun to be discussed as our great national disgrace, will not end anytime soon, given the length of the sentences handed out. America now has over 2 million of its citizens in jail, roughly a 700 percent increase since 1970. That is the largest jail population in the entire world and also the highest incarceration rate in the world. You may know that Alexis de Tocqueville originally visited the United States to study its prison system, noting that "[i]n no country is criminal justice administered with more mildness than in the United States." That has not been the case for some time, and the prisons with the gentlest reputations are often found in the smaller countries in northern Europe, not the United States.[33]

If we look at African American male high school dropouts, ages twenty to twenty-four, 19.2 percent are employed, yet 26.4 percent are in jail. By some (but by no means all) measures, America has become a much less racist country in the last eighty years, yet the use of jailing to segregate has risen. Compare the current numbers to the past, specifically to the black twenty- to twenty-four-year-old cohort born in the 1930s, when 68 percent were employed and only 6.7 percent were in jail. Even with a weaker ideology of racism in place, segregationist efforts continue and in some ways are being intensified. It is also worth noting that standard metrics of segregation do not count those who are in prison.[34]

The War on Drugs in particular has played a role in these processes. A mix of mandatory sentencing and an emphasis on stopping crack cocaine skewed the racial profile of arrests, whether intentionally or not. In 1974, narcotics arrests were 74 percent white and only 20 percent black, but by 1987, narcotics arrests were 63 percent white and 36 percent black. By 1993, African Americans accounted for more than 88 percent of crack cocaine distribution convictions, and often blacks were sent to jail at higher rates and received longer sentences, in some cases due to implicit racial profiling.[35]

This is a tragedy, and it shows that a lot of the orderliness of parts of the United States comes from various forms of intense sorting and segregation, and sometimes coercive forms at that. Very often the United States deals with its problems by sending them away to a different part of the country or a different part of town or, saddest of all, by sending them to jail. Being a "law and order" political candidate has been a winner for a long time; at the very least, being seen as weak on this issue has been a political loser.

It is often a puzzle for foreigners why the United States has such a dismal performance when it comes to murder, guns, and mental illness, all features of American life that, when compared to most of the other wealthy countries, are so awful they do not require further documentation. You might wonder how those bad results square with America's relatively strong performances on most social capital indices, such as trust, cooperation, and charitable philanthropy; on philanthropy, we even rate as the global number one. The truth is that those positive and negative facets are two sides of the same coin: Cooperation is very often furthered by segregating those who do not fit in. That creates some superclusters of cooperation among the quality cooperators and a fair amount of chaos and dysfunctionality elsewhere.

Whatever the temporary comforts and safeties of segregation may be, do we really want such an America, with so many parts of it segregated along so many new and old dimensions? But that is the America we are building right here and now, and the "cool" and trendy people among us are very often, and with an extreme complacency, leading the way.

4.

WHY AMERICANS STOPPED CREATING

Americans often point with pride to our role as the world's leading innovator. There are plenty of realms in which this is true, whether we look at lists of top universities, most important pharmaceuticals, or leading tech companies. And yet despite this leadership in innovation, if you compare America today to how it was forty years ago, the country seems to have lost its mojo. Apart from the tech sector, American innovation has underperformed since the early 1970s. This can be seen in sluggish measures of productivity, the slowing increase in living standards, the decline in the relative frequency of start-ups (contrary to what you usually read), and many other economic statistics. You also can feel it in the streets, so to speak. Politically, it was reflected in the rebellion against mainstream politics, as shown by both the Trump and Sanders campaigns. These economic slowdowns happened in conjunction with the social changes and other slowdowns studied in this book, and they are the clearest and perhaps the costliest manifestation of the fundamental shift in America's gears.

How did all this happen? Did the social changes lead or did the economic changes, and how did the two trends—social stagnancy and economic stagnancy—reinforce each other?

I think of the oil price shock of 1973 as the first negative shock in this broader sequence, and in that regard the economic changes provided the first link in the chain of events, even if they were not the most fundamental cause. In that year the era of cheap energy ended and the American economy slowed, and more generally the culture moved away from the idea of immediate and rapid transportation. Mentally, Americans moved from a world of moon shots to waiting in line to buy gasoline. The economic ramifications were far reaching too, as for most of the 1970s, American productivity stayed abysmally low. Social changes followed—for instance, Jimmy Carter put on a sweater and urged Americans to turn down the thermostat, representing a new era of lowered aspirations. In other words, the American response to economic adversity was to seek to restore comfort more than dynamism, and Americans pushed their culture in this direction all the more in the 1980s. President Reagan resurrected the rhetoric of dynamism, and Americans started to feel better again, but that was a time when dynamic economic growth was available only to a minority of Americans; in other words, it was the beginning of the age of income inequality. More successful Americans became determined to dig in and protect their privileged positions, and the rise of the complacent class as a phenomenon was under way. The beginning or intensifications of declines in residential mobility, job mobility, and integration cemented this dynamic all the more.

To be sure, the oil price shock wasn't close to large enough to have caused the complex chain of social and economic events that followed; it was simply their first visible sign and the first wake-up call delivered to the American population. If we are looking for ultimate causes of the succeeding stagnation, the most likely culprit, if that is the right word to use, is the dynamism and rebellion of the 1960s and early 1970s. Cultural energies eventually exhaust themselves or run down, people seek calmer times, and many Americans tired of the riots, the clashes with the police, the high crime, and the numerous social disruptions that attended this extraordinarily creative period of American history. I'll return to this theme of the cyclicality of history in the final chapter. But as the cultural slowdown operated in the 1980s and afterward, the fact that America is a relatively competent country enabled this quest for greater calm and security to be translated into results. American government and civil society, acting in conjunction, actually brought about a lower crime rate, more safety for most of our kids, no more draft riots, and more job and residential stability, among the many other changes that took place.

Of course, this portrait of a slowdown in dynamism is not usually what you hear from our business, political, and thought leaders. Bill Gates, for instance, has said that "the idea that innovation is slowing down is . . . stupid." He claims that new ideas are coming at a "scarily fast pace."[1] Or on Twitter, until recently, Marc Andreessen (@pmarca), Netscape founder and successful venture capitalist, would tweet up a storm at least once a week about the benefits of modernity, the progress of the American economy, and most of all the wonders of tech and Silicon Valley.

If the point is simply that today life is pretty good for many (but not all) of us, Gates and Andreessen are right. But still, by most metrics, as we'll see, economic opportunity is down and living standards, although they have advanced, are growing more slowly than in the past. For the most part, the American economy is more static than it was several decades ago, and that remains one of the most underreported stories of our time.

To look at one simple measure of both social and economic stasis, the rate at which business start-ups are forming has been declining since the 1980s. By one estimate, start-ups were 12 to 13 percent of the firms in the economy in the 1980s, but today they are only about 7 to 8 percent. That's right; for all the talk about Silicon Valley, we are less a start-up nation than before. By the way, this overall decline in start-up frequency is true for virtually every sector and every American city, and that includes San Francisco and even the legendary tech sector. In absolute terms, the number of new tech firms (younger than five years) peaked just after 2000, and in percentage terms, new firms in the tech sector have been declining since the 1980s. According to one of the standard measures of firm entry rates, only one American metropolitan area has seen an increase in corporate dynamism over the last few decades, and that is McAllen, Texas, probably a statistical blip rather than any proof of extreme Texas potency.[2]

If it feels to you like start-ups are on a rising pace, this is probably because many of today's most impressive new ventures are highly visible consumer-oriented companies, such as Uber and Airbnb, and also they receive a lot of media hype. You tap on your smartphone, and all of a sudden a vehicle appears at your door, ready to do your bidding. That's pretty cool, and it gives consumers a feeling of extraordinary power. But those impressions distract our attention from a more general slowdown in economic activity, including in the arena of start-ups.

Not only are there fewer start-ups, but a smaller percentage of them are succeeding. That means young firms are a smaller part of the overall market and so American corporations are increasing in average age, just as the American people are. In the late 1980s, 18.9 percent of the employment in the American economy was at firms five years or younger. This average had fallen to 13.5 percent right before the Great Recession; in numerical terms, that is a 29 percent decline over only seventeen years, a significant and rapid drop. New firms are also down as a share of total firms and also as a share of job creation, again since the 1980s. A big part of the miracle of Uber is that it is running *against* the prevailing trend, not with it.[3]

This corporate aging is slowing down the pace of change in American business, as older firms are less dynamic and more set in their ways. For instance, firms younger than five years old have a pace of job creation and destruction twice as rapid as firms six years or older, as the dynamism of the younger firms allows for more job turnover. But as American firms are aging, the job positions in our economy have become more stuck in place. Quarterly job creation and destruction is down in the measured trends, as is worker reallocation from one job to another. Again, that is good for those who already are well situated and bad for those who are trying to get ahead, similar to what I've already discussed in chapter 2. Having an older set of business firms means it is harder to switch jobs and also harder to switch where you live, and those trends reinforce each other in the direction of a more general stasis.

Employment at newly opened firms today constitutes 0.7 percent of all employment, while during the 1990s, it was above 1 percent; in other words, such jobs have declined by about 30 percent. We're coming uncomfortably close to that static, conformist caricature of 1950s oligopolistic business life where the relative status of the major companies just doesn't change that much over time and new jobs are increasingly rare. That description was in fact not true for the 1950s, but we seem to be approaching it today.[4]

If we pick apart this decline in dynamism into its component parts, the rate of starting new firms has gone down, and the rate of ending already existing firms has gone down too. In other words, it is harder for new firms to get up and running, but successful firms stick around for longer; both are signs of stasis. For instance, it is pretty hard to challenge the largest and most successful hospitals, and the dominant positions of those suppliers probably will not go away anytime soon. This decline in American business dynamism holds in every measured sector.[5]

Furthermore, not only are fewer new firms started in the first place, but the more successful new firms don't grow as they used to, and they are more likely to remain small than rise to prominence. That's again very different from the rhetoric pervading the rah-rah discourse, namely that start-ups are revolutionizing our country and business culture like never before. That's just not what the numbers show. Even when it comes to the information and related high-tech sectors, the growth in dynamism, as measured by the creation and growth of new firms, stops at about the year 2000 and then declines. For all of today's talk about "unicorns"—those celebrated, unique firms that take off and totally transform their markets—they are more myth than reality. Unicorns are not very visible in the data. Since 2000, there is also a declining propensity of young firms to turn into successful firms, including in the tech sector.[6]

Slower corporate turnover does mean greater job and financial security for those Americans who already have good jobs. It is an excellent deal for the privileged insiders, even though it is harder for the outsiders to enter the market and climb the ladder of success. Even four-year college graduates earned higher starting salaries in 2000 than they do today, by about seven to eight percentage points—assuming they get a job. This again points to the core theme that a slowdown in change will not comfort everyone to the same degree, and it will depend a great deal on where they start in life.

Some of the largest declines in dynamism, as identified by the rate of business turnover, have come in the construction, mining, retail, wholesale, and services sectors. In other words, the shops in the town square don't turn over as rapidly as they used to; some of this slowdown stems from the ongoing supplanting of mom-and-pop stores by major chains, which keep dominant market positions for longer periods of time. The dynamism declines are much smaller in transportation, communications, utilities, and manufacturing, which were more static to begin with. Overall dynamism rates seem to be converging, as the previously more-dynamic sectors in the American economy are falling to the change rates of the less-dynamic sectors. Just as people have traditionally expected their electricity company to be around for a long time, now a lot of retail chains seem to have taken on the same sacrosanct status.[7]

In 2015, I presented a version of this chapter at Princeton University, in suburban New Jersey. I first visited Princeton in 1978 as a teenager, and I can recall that the main street in town was filled with small stores, some of them charming, others crummy. These days it is filled with Ann Taylor and Brooks Brothers, upscale chains for wealthy students and their visiting parents, and maybe for the well-paid faculty too. Those stores sell a diverse selection of trousers and dresses and offer good and predictable service. Most of us like this, at least in our role as customers, and that is a major reason why the chains have advanced, a truth that my audience actually found somewhat disconcerting to ponder. As chain stores rise, there is also a loss of dynamism, competition, and market entry for new ideas and products. Keep in mind that today's major chain was once a small individual store on a street somewhere. A bit more economic chaos, even if it is inconvenient in the short run, actually tends to be correlated with higher rates of innovation.

Two of today's most rapidly growing sectors seem especially hostile to turnover and business dynamism, and they are not even counted in the standard business statistics. If we look at higher education, the list of top universities is barely different from what it was seventy years or even one hundred years ago, apart from having added some West Coast contenders, such as Stanford and UC Berkeley. The sociologist Kieran Healy made an explicit comparison of today's best schools using a listing of the best schools from a 1911 report by a Mr. Kendrick Charles Babcock. For the more mature regions of the United States, it's all a bunch of recognizable first-tier names, including Harvard, Princeton, Columbia, and, well . . . do I need to give you the whole list?[8] There has been considerable innovation in what has been taught and how universities are organized, but at the top, America's higher education sector does not have a whole lot of turnover; nor have innovative unicorn firms or schools taken over. For primary education, of course, most school systems are municipal, and they hardly budge for decades, although there is some dynamism from a recent wave of charter schools. As mentioned, low turnover in this sector isn't new, but education and higher education are taking on larger and more important roles in the American economy, and that represents an increase in stasis from a business point of view.

MONOPOLY POWER ON THE RISE

We can see signs of growing market concentration in a variety of industries. The United States has only two major cell phone carriers, and American cell phone markets are less competitive and more expensive than those in most of Western Europe. The American market also has consolidated toward four major airlines, a far cry from the 1980s deregulatory dream of a large number of small budget airlines competing fiercely across most major routes. Pending mergers are likely to bring the number of major health insurance companies, in the aftermath of the Affordable Care Act, from five to three, with hospitals undergoing significant consolidation as well. All of these corporate changes are yet another way of measuring a status quo that is pretty comfortable, stable, and inert.[9]

Those are only a few examples, and clearly some sectors have become far more competitive. Restaurant or grocery store choice is much better than in the past, and you can choose from many more computer games than ever before, to name just a few examples. Still, the data on the broader economy support the story that overall concentration seems to be rising somewhat. The best available data go up to 2007, and according to Deutsche Bank, the four largest firms then controlled half or more of the market in about 40 percent of U.S. manufacturing sectors, up from 30 percent in 1992. That is for manufacturing only, but still, it is one sign of decreasing competition and rivalry. In mid-2016, the White House's Council of Economic Advisers issued a report concluding, after scrutinizing the available evidence, that concentration in the American economy indeed was going up. It's fair to say those are relatively small changes, but they are moving in the wrong direction, and that is very much the opposite of what one usually reads or hears.[10]

There are yet other measures of growing economic concentration, but again the picture is not so cheery. A recent *Wall Street Journal* analysis of data from the University of Southern California found that, by federal antitrust standards, there is a high degree of concentration in nearly a third of all industries, compared to about a quarter of all industries in 1996. Or to cite another metric based on the same data, nearly two-thirds of publicly traded companies were selling in more concentrated markets in 2013 than earlier in 1996. Yet another measure is this: Of the more than 1,700 public companies in existence in both 1996 and 2013, 62 percent saw their share of the market go up over that same period of time.[11]

What is driving these developments? Most likely, some leading firms have the ability and intent to launch well-known national brands backed by extensive marketing and product development, and other, smaller firms cannot match their pace. The result is that some markets have a greater element of winner-take-all, as is suggested by the data on corporate valuations. If we look at the S&P 500 stock index in 1975, the category of "intangible assets" accounted for about 18 percent of the value of American capital. Most American capital was in physical assets, such as machines and factories, tangible items that can be purchased and replicated if need be. Today, over 80 percent of the value of the S&P 500 is due to intangible assets, including trademarks, patents, brand name reputation, consumer goodwill, and other factors. That's a big leap upward, from below 20 percent to above 80 percent for the value of corporate intangibles. It marks a fundamental change in the nature of American production, and in large part it stems from the long-standing shift away from manufacturing and toward services.

What do we know about intangibles? Well, for one thing, a big national or international brand is really hard to build up from scratch, and that helps the market leaders keep their dominant positions.

Second, many intangibles rest on reputation and image. If Google alienated most Americans with an ongoing series of offensive remarks and behavior, users would jump to Bing or to other search engines, just as many customers have left Chipotle because of its association with *E. coli* outbreaks. Furthermore, if Google lost its image as a cutting-edge place to work, it could lose its ability to recruit top talent. Once companies have ascended the mountain, they play it safe. They have no interest at that point in "disruption," and they try to offend as few users, or potential employees, as possible. There's nothing wrong with all that, and if those incentives stop some companies from being unsafe or offensive or perhaps discriminatory, so much the better. In 2014, the Mozilla CEO stepped down, basically for having donated to anti–gay marriage campaigns, even though at the time most Americans did not seem to favor the legality of gay marriage. Whether or not you worry about the constraints on speech brought by such firings, it's a sign that some kinds of risk-taking are over. We've also seen a lot of companies end or postpone expansions into North Carolina due to the 2016 passage in that state of a law perceived as hostile to transgender individuals. Again, the net result is that companies will obsess all the more over legal matters and public relations, sometimes at the expense of growing their business or focusing on the physical product or taking chances. We see corporate cultures stressing the law and also public relations, two inherently conservative corporate departments that are rarely sources of major innovations.[12]

Still further evidence for growing monopolization, and for that matter the social stasis it feeds, is what is sometimes called "the investment drought." That is, businesses just aren't investing as much as they used to. Net capital investment, as a share of gross domestic product, has been declining since the 1980s. An alternative measure of the value of capital services, a ten-year moving average which avoids the "noise" in the data for any single year, has been declining since the start of the millennium. It hit almost 5 percent of GDP around the turn of the millennium, but since then it has fallen steadily and is now hovering at about 2 percent of GDP. This again means that America is not replenishing its future sources of innovation, growth, and ability to pay higher wages because the future capital just won't be there to the same extent. Nonresidential investment is more than 20 percent below its long-run trend. Each of these numbers is hard to measure and interpret accurately, due to the difficulties in conceptualizing and operationalizing the notion of the value of investment, but it is hard to spin a positive story from the overall patterns in the data.[13]

During much of this period, and as I write, stock market indices have been relatively high. A high stock market means, all other things being equal, that the return on investment is high, which should mean more investment. And yet we don't see investment booming, as I already discussed. What's going on? The primary way to square these two facts is to consider that these days it seems to be harder to enter against established competitors and take them on and win. The winners do expand their operations a good deal, and a lot of new investment is indeed coming there. Still, those firms are relatively small in number, they have become establishment in their orientation, and they are not enough to drive a broader investment boom in the American economy.

Furthermore, many of the winners do not need more funds. In fact, not all of them invest dynamically what they have. Corporate cash holdings have shown a steady trend upward for decades, as companies are holding more funds in safe securities rather than investing them in new business opportunities. As of mid-2016, Apple had about $200 billion in cash sitting in very safe assets such as Treasury Bills. However, one investment that is quite popular is deal-making, and 2015 was a record year in this regard. When it comes to mergers and acquisitions, times have never been better. As early as mid-September 2015, the total value of large (over $10 billion) transactions reached $1.19 trillion, breaking the previous record from the dot-com bubble of 1999. So the cash piles of corporations are going somewhere, just not always into creating new ideas. Companies would rather buy up other, already established companies than try to succeed with new ideas or their own new product lines. That is another sign of how our contemporary business climate, like our broader society, is more about stability than most media stories let on.[14]

FEWER AMERICANS DIRECTLY INVOLVED IN INNOVATION

Another way of thinking about corporate innovation is to look at how much companies spend explicitly toward that goal, namely research and development expenditures. Right now a metric known as R&D intensity—the ratio of research and development expenditure to GDP—is about the same for America as it was at its early to mid-1960s peak. That's not a bad performance, but for most of the intervening period, it was down considerably, and that again represents a decline in the willingness of corporate America to spend on generating new ideas. There is hope in the recent rise, but again, we're just working back toward an earlier peak.[15]

Today, only about 8 percent of the American workforce is employed in the manufacturing sector, yet manufacturing accounts for about 70 percent of private business spending on R&D. That's a good sign for the creativity of the manufacturing sector, but it also means that fewer and fewer American workers have a direct connection to a sector engaged in a lot of fundamental change and innovation. These days manufacturing innovation usually occurs with few workers watching or working alongside because of automation, and indeed those innovations are displacing many workers. Factory floors have become much quieter places as more and more jobs have shifted into service sectors. Innovation thus becomes something more and more foreign to most American workers, embedded in tech devices but not something that most directly observe and participate in. Furthermore, virtually all analysts expect the percentage of the workforce employed in manufacturing to decline, further insulating American workers from direct experience of significant economic dynamism.[16]

If we adjust for increases in the American working-age population, the United States creates 25 percent fewer triadic patents per person than it did in 1999.[17] (A triadic patent is one filed in the United States, Europe, and Japan, and tends to be a relatively serious patent in terms of potential scope.) This measured decline comes in an age where an increasing number of trivial, ridiculous, or "trolling" patents are granted by an out-of-control patenting process; one-click shopping, however fun and easy it may be to do, should not be receiving patent protection. Patents may not be the best measure of our innovativeness, but they do capture one side of how hard we are trying to create the new, and again there is some decline. It's not that any one of these metrics proves so much, but when you put them all together, it is hard to avoid the impression of a less vibrant and dynamic American economy.

MEASURES OF PRODUCTIVITY INDICATE PESSIMISM

The most direct way to measure whether innovation has declined is to look directly at available measures of productivity. Economists have two primary measures of business productivity. One is called "total factor productivity," and the other is known as "productivity per worker hour." Unfortunately, both measures show the American economy to be underperforming, albeit to differing degrees.

Total factor productivity (TFP, for short) tries to measure how much new ideas add to national output, once we've adjusted for the contributions of capital and labor. This is a highly imperfect metric, in part because measuring the value of capital is not easy, but it is the single calculation that comes closest to measuring the innovation-generating capacity of an advanced economy. Sadly, the story embedded in the numbers is a depressing one.

During the period from 1919 to 1948, TFP averaged well over 2 percent a year, meaning that new ideas were contributing economic value at that rate, and in some particular years, TFP came in at over 3 percent. That represents the arrival of new ideas at a relatively high rate. Later, from 1948 to 1973, this measure of innovation still tended to average about 2 percent. But in 1973, TFP declined dramatically, often coming in below 1 percentage point a year, and for the most part, TFP growth stayed low until 1995, with an average of about 0.5 percent. The mid-1990s to early 2000s were a new golden age for TFP, which again at times ran at 2 percent or more. There is good evidence that those gains are largely due to the application of computers and information technology to business. TFP again slowed down, however, and in the most recent years, since the financial crisis, TFP has averaged well below 1 percent growth a year, only slightly above its disappointing 1973 to 1995 range. As productivity researchers John Fernald and Bing Wang put it: "Three out of the last four decades have seen business-sector productivity growth near 1½%."[18]

Overall, the history of this variable suggests the following story: America had a productivity heyday from the early twentieth century through about 1973. But then American innovativeness slowed sharply. The early years of applying IT brought a major rebound, but that dwindled as some of the low-hanging fruit from computer use, such as basic inventory management practices and email, was exhausted. Since the early 2000s, America has settled back into what is essentially a low-innovation mode of existence, with the exception of a few areas, such as social media. And as you can see from the earlier chapters, the slowdown story doesn't rely on just a single productivity number; rather, it is consistent with a broad array of data about many social and economic variables, many of them easier to measure than business productivity.

The story behind productivity per worker hour isn't as depressing, but still there is decline and subpar performance in recent times. For instance, from 1990 to 2007, this measure of productivity grew at over 2 percent. Since 2007, it has grown at only 1.3 percent.[19]

This somewhat brighter (but still declining) performance I don't consider so cheery, however. One big reason for the gains in productivity per worker hour is that American business has done a pretty good job of identifying which workers aren't producing much of anything at all and then firing them; this is euphemistically called "restructuring productivity."[20]

Similarly, American businesses decrease labor costs by outsourcing work to foreign nations with lower labor costs. Such decisions are sometimes necessary elements of running a business, and I don't mean to portray them as pure cold-hearted corporate villainy. Still, cost-cutting developments build America's productive future less than coming up with neat and new ways of doing things, such as harnessing electricity, developing antibiotics, or inventing automobiles. Firing lesser-skilled workers, or replacing productive but expensive workers with cheaper foreign workers, is, taken alone, basically a way of keeping the status quo in place—for some, that is—at lower cost to owners of capital and privileged workers who have kept their incumbent status.

Note that none of these figures attempts to measure productivity in American health care, education, the nonprofit sector, or government projects, four rather significant areas where America's productivity performance appears particularly doubtful. If we had better figures that incorporated American performance in these areas, I fear productivity measurements might show a greater slowdown yet.

A recent report by Wells Fargo showed productivity slowdowns in almost every sector of the American economy. Perhaps most strikingly, the sector "professional and technical services" showed no increase in the productivity of the average office worker at all. You might think IT and the wired office has boosted office productivity substantially, and it has in some ways, such as enabling rapid-fire communications across great distances or after work hours are over. But the evidence has yet to materialize for any kind of recent boost in office productivity. We don't yet know why this is, but maybe the time Americans waste on Facebook and texting and social media takes back some of the gains from all that added connectivity and greater ability to network.[21]

As some of the points mentioned have suggested implicitly, one way to think about much of America's productivity problem is as an average-is-over phenomenon or, as it sometimes is called, a "diffusion problem."

For instance, most of the rise in inequality is across firms rather than within firms. The ratio of the salary of the boss at the shoe company to the secretary's salary at that company hasn't changed much. What's new is the rise of a class of supercompanies—say, Apple and Google—at which lots of people get paid much, much more. But only a limited number of companies can achieve that kind of exalted status. It seems that cutting-edge American firms are not slower in their productivity growth compared to earlier eras. This makes intuitive sense if you think about the top tech companies, which are indeed examples of supreme innovativeness. What has slowed down is the ability of other, less-successful, lower-tier companies to bring productivity gains of the same magnitude. That fact is consistent with viewing America as having a still-innovative and restless Silicon Valley, with its top tech titans, embedded in a sleepier culture overall. Similarly, the top firms that use IT in dominant ways, in fields as diverse as finance, fracking, and health care, can open up significant leads over their rivals.[22]

There are different interpretations of this slow diffusion. In one view, the smaller, less-able companies just don't have the same mojo as the major innovators have. They lack the same level of talent, response speed, drive, or competitiveness, so they just won't catch up to the industry leaders. Under a second interpretation, the achievements of the major innovators are very often one-off projects. Google truly is a dominant firm in search—it is no surprise that "google" has become a verb in the English language. Google's smaller competitors may or may not mimic all of its innovations, but that doesn't so much matter because it is hard for the other companies to give users a reason to switch; most people don't much care if a Bing search is as good or nearly as good as one on Google. Today's innovators often produce unique, stand-alone silos. Modern Americans are perhaps not bad at diffusion, but they have created a world where diffusion is, at least for the time being, no longer so important as it was in the old days, when manufacturing was the dominant form of production. We're too often content with "one is enough" and not obsessed enough with the long-run dynamic possibilities from more immediately destructive forms of competitive emulation.

LIVING STANDARDS HAVE BEEN STAGNATING

The ultimate measure of technological progress is not the number of fancy gadgets we own but rather how much better our lives are. That is what we really care about, not the gadgets per se, not the patents, and not the productivity statistics. To the extent that new and useful goods and services are being brought to the market, this should be reflected in a general rise in living standards. But once again, there is some disappointing news, as the income of the median or typical American household is down since 2000, and unless wage gains are very strong in the next few years, this country essentially will have gone twenty years with wage stagnation or near wage stagnation for median earners.

Furthermore, when you zero in on male wages, the picture becomes truly disconcerting. *The median male wage was higher in 1969 than it is today.* That's a shocking fact, given earlier expectations of ongoing economic progress, and not many economists of that time, of any political stripe, would have predicted that to happen without a major catastrophe or global war. A big chunk of our economic gains have been driven by women getting better educations and working longer hours. That is good news for many women, but if the American economy were more dynamic, we would expect the males to have rising real wages just because so many technological advances have been dumped in their laps. Those numbers may to some degree understate real wages, because the methods of collecting inflation statistics do not capture all improvements in the quality of goods since 1969; those quality improvements, such as better-tasting chocolate, improve our lives but are not always easy to measure. Even so, a median wage decline over such a long period of time seems to go far beyond the bounds of what can be explained by statistical error alone.

Imagine Milton Friedman and Paul Samuelson sitting around a table in 1969, debating the future of the economy. In their lifetimes, they'd observed roughly a doubling of living standards every generation. Imagine they are assuming that there will be no nuclear war, that communism will fall, and that the world moves significantly closer to near-free trade. Now, we ask, what do you expect to happen to the male median wage over the course of the next forty-five or so years? Outside of the ups and downs of the business cycle, both economists would view ongoing growth in living standards as the normal state of affairs for a market economy.

Even the most recent trends are discouraging. If we take out the gains of the top earners, take-home pay for typical American workers has been falling since the Great Recession ended in 2009, an unusual path for an economic recovery. According to one good estimate, median wages for the American economy as a whole fell 4 percent from 2009 to 2014. There are also wage declines within a lot of occupations. For instance, median pay for restaurant cooks fell by 8.9 percent, and for home health aides, the median wage fell by 6.2 percent, even though the dining and health care sectors have been relatively robust in terms of both revenue and employment. Overall, given the wage trends within various professions, this decline in median wages doesn't seem to be just a composition effect from having more low-wage workers in the workforce.[23]

These wage problems are just another way of viewing or measuring the productivity problems discussed earlier. If American productivity growth had continued to rise at its pre-1973 pace, wages would be much higher today. In fact, the median or typical household would earn about $30,000 more. For purposes of comparison, if income inequality had maintained its pre-1973 trend, the gain for the median household would be about $9,000 in income this year, a much smaller figure. In other words, the growing stasis of America has hurt the living standards of large numbers of Americans and by significant amounts.[24]

If we look at how Americans are behaving (i.e., data on economic quantities rather than prices), the evidence still supports the basic story of a slower growth in living standards. For instance, the employment-to-population ratio is low and sluggish, which means not as many people are working as much as they used to, even if we adjust for America having more retirees. That's hardly what we would expect if the true real wage were much higher than it is being measured. When it comes to migration, the net flow of Mexicans is out of the United States, even though economic growth in Mexico is not much above 2 percent per year. Again, that is a sign that these are hardly boom times for workers here in the United States, especially at lower levels of education and skill. Finally, death rates and suicide rates are rising for white, middle-aged Americans. None of those statistics is what we would expect if there was a hidden, unmeasured dynamic productivity bonanza, leading to much higher standards of living than what the numbers seem to be showing.[25]

Another part of stasis has been stagnant income mobility—that is, the ability of individuals or households in one segment of the income distribution to move up into another segment, say, from the bottom fifth to the middle fifth, and so on. Nathaniel G. Hilger, a researcher at Brown University, has made one of the most rigorous attempts to measure the evolution of post-1940 income mobility, using education as a proxy. Hilger's main result is discouraging. He finds that upward mobility increased for each labor market cohort from 1940 to 1980, a time often thought of as a kind of golden age for America's middle class. But since the 1990s, income mobility in the United States has not been going up at all.

That's actually a better story than what you often hear, namely that income mobility has been declining especially sharply in recent times. Still, income mobility is no longer going up each generation, and that means Americans are more likely to "stay put" in their educational, social, and income classes than before. A further depressing part of Hilger's account is that the measured mobility gains are largely concentrated before 1960. Hilger's data point to high school enrollment and black-white income convergence—blacks gaining on whites in relative terms—as two important factors driving the mobility gains in earlier decades. But the high school graduation rate hasn't increased much since the late 1960s, and black-white economic convergence seems to be going in reverse, especially if we look at wealth rather than income.[26]

LOOKING BACK IS ALSO A BIT DEPRESSING

When you put all of these indicators together—low productivity growth, a sluggish labor force, fewer start-ups, greater business concentration, and a slower growth in living standards—the narrative about this period as being a time of unparalleled innovation simply doesn't hold up. And indeed, an intuitive look at history confirms this portrait.

Consider how Americans' lives changed in the period between 1900 and 1950. In 1900, only about 6 percent of Americans were graduating from high school, and the country had a standard of living below many parts of modern-day Central America. Most Americans lived on farms. Electricity and flush toilets were not to be taken for granted. There were no antibiotics and no vaccines, and clean water was a luxury.[27]

But what happened over the next fifty years? In the area of public health, vaccines, clean water, and antibiotics all became commonplace. In transportation, the car went from a rare sight to a commonplace part of American life, glorified in songs like those by Chuck Berry. Airplanes were flying across the country on a regular basis. A radio was in virtually every home, telephones were common, and just a few years later, television would be spreading rapidly. Computers were used mostly by the government, and they were slow and huge, but still they existed. Nuclear power plants were being planned and built as a new and useful source of energy, relatively clean in terms of carbon emissions.

And by the middle of the 1950s, the high school graduation rate was well over 50 percent.

In short, just about every area of life changed fundamentally over the course of those fifty years, including communications and tech.

Now, look at the period between 1965 and 2015. If you go back and watch a TV show from 1965 or thereabouts, the world you will see is a pretty familiar one. Homes look more or less the same. When it comes to transportation, cars today are safer and more comfortable and have better sound systems, but still they are cars, and their fundamental design and function has not much changed. We are still flying planes—like the 747—designed in the late 1960s. Medicine has made steady advances, but it is not clear we have matched the vaccine or the antibiotic for a fundamental new development of import. Genomics hasn't yet changed most lives, and due to accumulated resistance, some of our antibiotics aren't working so well anymore. Cancer was supposed to have been "fixed" decades ago, or so President Nixon had promised us. The high school graduation rate is up only slightly since the late 1960s, and it is debatable how much our high schools have improved since then. In all of these areas, we may (or may not) be on the *verge* of wonderful breakthroughs, and I'll return to that question later in the book, but still that does not overturn the portrait of the last few decades being a time of relative stasis.

To be sure, there have been huge and very definite advances in computers, the internet, and communications. There was nothing like the smartphone in 1965 or for that matter in 1995. That is a big, big deal. But still, compared to the advances of the earlier fifty-year period, recent progress has not been so broad based. A lot of our technological world seems to have stood pretty much still, albeit with a variety of quality improvements along the way.

The slowdown in progress is perhaps most evident in the area of transportation. The nineteenth century and much of the twentieth century saw travel speeds increase dramatically. Slow boats gave rise to fast clipper ships, and railroad tracks covered more and more of the world while trains became faster and more reliable, moving from steam to coal-fired engines. The trolley and streetcar, the automobile, and the airplane were all new and revolutionary. Starting in the nineteenth century, the humble bicycle, still an underrated technological innovation, boosted travel speeds for hundreds of millions. But since the 1970s, most travel around the United States has become slower—due to traffic—rather than faster. We've stopped increasing travel speeds and even have given up on supersonic jet transport. The Concorde, rather than proving to be the wave of the future, has been retired.

Entrepreneur Elon Musk stands as the most visible and obvious representative of the idea of major progress in the physical world. For all of his admirable confidence and unapologetic ambition, most of his projects have yet to succeed. The hyperloop talk seems like more of a publicity stunt than anything else, as we will not be transporting people by whipping them in capsules through reduced-pressure tubes, not anytime soon at least. We can't even get a new (slow) train tunnel built under the Hudson River to connect New Jersey and New York. Musk's most successful venture so far has been his satellite launches, and there he is basically providing security and a backup system for the previous, highly expensive and not totally reliable government satellite launch system. That's great, but again we see that the big success comes from the provision of security and reliability and insurance, not from the revolutionizing of our everyday world. Musk's electric car may yet prove it can make money, but that innovation is more protection against an impending series of problems—carbon pollution and climate change—than a vastly superior automobile experience. In the meantime, there are an increasing number of questions about whether Musk's ventures are financially sound.

The more general picture on transportation can be described with two words: less and slower. The number of bus routes has decreased, and America has done very little to build up its train network, even when additional or faster train lines would be profitable. Although American cities have growing populations and wealth, they haven't built many new subway systems in the last thirty-five years, with the exception of the partial system in Los Angeles. The Department of

Transportation has written, "All indicators show declines in personal travel for every age group, particularly among young people since the early 2000s. It is too soon to tell whether this decline is temporary or indicative of a long-term trend."[28]

Of course, these measures don't entirely reflect negative trends. To the extent that people are commuting less because they've moved back into cities, or using the subway less because bike sharing and bike lanes have made that form of travel more efficient and safer, that's great. And if video chat and Skype have meant that we have to travel less for business meetings, or to keep in touch with family and friends, there's certainly some good there too. Still, the overall picture on transportation does not suggest a dynamic economy. Slow, inefficient travel has made Americans less likely to travel, with the knock-on effect of removing political pressure to improve transportation systems. If I think of my own life, I've simply stopped taking most local car trips between 4 and 7 p.m., mostly because of pressures from traffic. I end up staying at home and clicking on Amazon and waiting for the packages to arrive.

One final way of thinking about progress, sometimes stressed by Silicon Valley venture capitalist Peter Thiel, is to ask whether the era of grand projects is mostly over. In the twentieth century, American grand projects included the Manhattan Project, which was highly successful, and cemented an era of Pax Americana. Two other grand projects were winning World War II and, starting in the 1950s, construction of the interstate highway system, both examples of thinking big and changing the world permanently on a large scale. The Apollo moon program was another grand project, and although its usefulness can be questioned, its mechanical success and above all its speed of execution cannot. At its peak it consumed over 2 percent of American GDP.[29] "Defeating communism" is perhaps too abstract to qualify as a specific project, but it is another major victory backed by a coordinated effort. Another potential nominee would be "construction of a social welfare state," although parts of this are politically controversial. In any case, a lot of these grand projects succeeded, often rather spectacularly.

If we look at the last twenty-five years or so, what do we have to count as grand projects? Some people might cite the environmental movement, but for all of its virtues, we are still living in a world where biodiversity is plummeting, carbon emissions are rising, and the overall human footprint on the environment, including from the United States, is increasing. So this is a possible contender for the future, but no, it hasn't happened just yet. Reforestation and cleaner air and water are major triumphs, but those happened much earlier in the twentieth century.

The most obvious and most successful grand project today is that virtually every part of the United States is wired to the internet and cell phone system. You can go to almost any inhabited part of the country and immediately access Wikipedia or make a phone call to Africa; sometimes this even works on hiking trails or in other out-of-the-way places, ensuring we are never that far away from communicating with any and all of our friends and relations or maybe business associates. Score one for the contemporary world—though, as I argue in the next chapter, this interconnectivity has come with a price.

The other potential grand project would have to be . . . reconstructing Iraq, making Iraq democratic, and bringing peace to the Middle East. On that project we have seen a miserable failure, and with the rise of ISIS and the collapse of Syria, the situation is becoming much worse yet. So the post-1990 era for the United States is scored at one out of two. I don't, by the way, count Obamacare on this list of grand projects. No matter what you think of it as policy, it provided health insurance to about 10 to 15 million of America's previously uninsured 40 million–plus population, with the exact number for new coverage still evolving. That helps many of those individuals, but it is hardly a game-changer in terms of a broader social trajectory, especially since many of those people already were receiving partial health care coverage and, furthermore, the Obamacare exchanges are experiencing some serious problems. If anything, Obamacare has locked in the basic features of the previous U.S. health care system rather than revolutionizing them.

On the issue of grand projects, it is wrong to think there is nothing to say on behalf of the contemporary world. Still, America seems to be producing major triumphs at a slower pace than before and also to be limiting some of our earlier grand achievements. Americans have shown little interest in pursuing nuclear power, even though it could significantly reduce carbon emissions. Communism is mostly dead, but Russia seems to be exerting nasty control over parts of Eastern Europe again and has invaded parts of Ukraine. We've stopped sending people to the moon (or beyond), and NASA is very far from the public eye, unlike in the 1960s. If anything, the agency is struggling to justify its existence to an increasingly skeptical public and to a Congress that is looking to further cut discretionary government spending. Even if you think that is for the better, it nonetheless represents a fundamental change in perspective. Millennials as a generation just don't seem that interested in grand projects, unless of course you count wired interconnectivity, at which they excel.

ARE THE PESSIMISTS UNDERVALUING TECH INNOVATIONS?

To close this chapter, I'd like to look a bit more closely at the link between our failure to innovate and our standard of living. It's commonly asserted that real GDP growth and real productivity growth are much higher than what turns up in the published numbers. Many of today's economic optimists cite a bunch of supposedly "free" goods that are making us much, much better off, though we do not pay for them. The most common examples of these goods are Google, Facebook, and Wikipedia. In each case, it is said that national income statistics do not pick up the value of these services, which typically we use for free.

But the values of today's free goods just aren't enough to make up for the productivity shortfall. Here is a simple comparison for imagining just how much the productivity slowdown has hurt living standards. Had the pre-1973 rates of productivity growth prevailed post-1973, household median income in the United States would be over $90,000 rather than in its current neighborhood of $50,000. Do the user values of Facebook and Google and other free services really make up for this gap? Another way to put the question is this: that $40,000 yearly difference amounts to more than $3,000 per month. If a web connection or smartphone costs $3,000 a month or more, how many people would be buyers? The wealthy would be, and some of the middle class would be too, but mostly because their jobs might require it to coordinate with others. It would not be because most middle-class Americans actually find those services to be worth more than 3k a month.

To make the comparison a yet more pessimistic one, when it comes to measuring the value of all of our innovations, it's a misconception to think that Facebook, Google, and other services are free, at least from the point of view of whether we calculate GDP accurately. Most people access Facebook, for instance, through a mobile device or a laptop or a PC. At some earlier point, they paid for the hardware and for web access, through a cable connection and smartphone contract, among other means. Those figures do go into the calculation for GDP. Furthermore, the more valuable Facebook is, the more people will pay for connections. In this sense, there is indeed a revenue stream that is picking up the value of web connections to free services, even if it does not measure the value of those services exactly. It's a bit like a buffet in an all-you-can-eat Indian restaurant. It would be wrong to say, "The Tandoori chicken is free—it's not counted in GDP." Instead, the tastier the chicken, the more people are willing to pay for the buffet. The internet too is like a buffet, with a lot of free goods but a price for accessing the bundle, and those transactions for access are counted in standard measures of GDP.

When we look at the demand for web access through cable connections and smartphones, we find what economists call "price elasticity," just like we do with most other goods and services. That is, when the price goes up, individuals buy a lot less of it. A counterexample would be insulin for diabetics; diabetics fare very poorly without insulin, and so, at least if they have the money, they will be willing to pay much more than they do. A higher price wouldn't much blunt their market demand, and that's a sign that the value of insulin is much higher for these people than the current market price indicates. The data for the internet don't indicate the same results; the value of marginal increments of internet doesn't seem to be much higher than indicated by current market prices, and that is another sign that the value of the internet is being picked up in GDP—imperfectly, of course, but it is by no means altogether absent.

Available studies do not support the view that mismeasured information technology can make up for the lost productivity in the American economy. For instance, countries with smaller tech sectors still have comparably sized productivity slowdowns, and that is not what we would expect if a lot of unmeasured productivity were hiding in the tech industry. Furthermore, the slowdown in productivity is too large to be explained by changes in the tech sector. Under one conservative estimate, outlined by Professor Chad Syverson of the University of Chicago, the productivity slowdown has led to a "missing" $2.7 trillion in GDP since the end of 2004. For the tech sector to make up for this difference, consumer surplus (consumer benefits in excess of market price) would have to be five times as high as measured in the industries that produce and service information and communications technology. That seems too large to be a plausible measurement gap. Or you can make the comparison this way: The productivity gap caused measured GDP to be about 15 percent lower than otherwise, again post-2004. For purposes of comparison, digital technology industries were only about 7.7 percent of GDP in 2004. Even if the free component of the internet has become more important in the intervening years, the unmeasured component of that growth is unlikely to make up for such a big chunk of GDP. Keep in mind that a lot of today's internet was very much up and running circa 2004.[30]

Other studies show that including the value of free apps and other online services in GDP has almost no effect on economic growth rates or productivity estimates. Apps are not only consumer products; they are also business inputs; imagine, say, using Google Maps to plan pizza delivery routes. If we were to assign prices and values to the apps rather than counting them at zero in national product calculations, in essence our measurement of business productivity would go down because suddenly those free inputs would be counted as costs. According to the best available estimates, valuing free apps explicitly therefore would raise true productivity growth by no more than a net of 0.004 percent a year.[31]

Sometimes I hear a quite convoluted argument in defense of the unmeasured productivity of the internet. It runs something like this: "True, *at the current margin*, the value of the internet is not that high for private consumers. For instance, another peek at Facebook just isn't that fun. But that is because our initial abilities to access the internet for those very first uses, which we have been doing for a while, are worth so much more; getting email really did change our lives in a fundamental way." Sophisticated purveyors of this critique will then dig out the technical phrase "inframarginal" gains, by which they basically mean the gains we reaped some time ago, and sum up this point by telling us that the inframarginal gains of the internet are very high.

This is a serious argument. But even if the chain of reasoning is entirely true, what does it mean? The rate of productivity growth, and also wage gains, was quite high in much of the 1990s, and a lot of those gains came from information technology. Those are also the years that a lot of productive people were using the internet effectively for the first time. They had fun, *and* the new technologies did a lot to boost growth in domestic production. Since then, we've been reaping lower marginal gains from IT. And that is very much in tune with the thesis of this book, namely that some earlier times have been more dynamic and innovative and full of fundamental change. When it comes to the economy, it really does seem like the years 1999 to 2000 are a kind of turning point, after which even more social and economic stasis sets in. Showing significant unmeasured economic gains from the internet since those years is much, much harder to do. I still think that the internet will *at some point* deliver very high productivity gains again, perhaps by connecting us with very high-quality artificial intelligence programs, as it is starting to do, but in very recent times we have not seen that progress.

So if Facebook and Wikipedia are at least partially counted in GDP, where might we find most of the unmeasured *current* economic gains from IT?

I submit it is from matching, which is the supreme skill of the complacent class. We spend our money and invest our time a lot better than before because of matching. Matching is in fact the new grand project of our time, and exactly how grand still remains to be seen. Still, it is likely the largest potential source of unmeasured gains in American well-being, so let's look at it more closely.

5.

THE RESPITE OF THE WELL-ORDERED MATCH:
LOVE, MUSIC, AND EVEN YOUR DOG

I sometimes say that I am a happiness optimist but a revenue pessi-
mist. I mentioned at the end of the last chapter that matching gives
people better access to what they really want, and that is an example
of how individuals can become happier without many of the core economic indicators, such as sales, revenue, or GDP, necessarily register-
ing big improvements.

That may all sound a bit cryptic, but anyone familiar with
music-listening in twenty-first-century America already has lived the
point. Revenue is down for the music companies and for some artists,
but the listening experience has never been better. Consumers are spending less for music and yet getting more in terms of aesthetic delight. To
cite one example, an advanced Spotify subscription for unlimited music
streaming costs only $10 a month, sometimes less with discounts. And
yet, circa 2016, the listener has access to about 35 million songs.

Spotify doesn't just measure "what you like"; the company also keeps
track of when you like it, how you like it, and where you like it. Some
listeners play ambient music at work, when they need to concentrate,
but rap or metal for their workouts at home, when they feel they can
cut loose. Ajay Kalia, who oversees the Spotify project of recording and
measuring taste, reports that the company appreciated early on the

distinction between what people listen to and what they really like: "A single music listener is usually many listeners, and a person's preference will vary by the type of music, by their current activity, by the time of day, and so on. Our goal then is to come up with a nuanced understanding of each portion of your taste." They've succeeded. By combining computer algorithms and human musical experts, Spotify understands taste in terms of the variety of musical "clusters" a person pays attention to. And these aren't just genres such as country or rhythm and blues, but also styles and moods, such as "wonky," "chillwave," "stomp and holler," or "downtempo."[1]

One measure counted 1,369 different kinds of music on Spotify, and growing. These categories include "black sludge," a combination of black metal and sludge, "unblack metal" (explicitly opposed to Satanism), "crustpunk," "deep filthstep," "mallet" (with mallets), "new weird America" (perhaps appropriate for this book), "vegan straight edge" (hardcore punk but vegan and antidrug), and "abstract" (it's like complextro, but more abstract than rhythmic). These are some of the data-based dynamic clusters spotted by Spotify's algorithms and data services, and if all those scare or intimidate you, just turn the channel to "vintage swoon" for some old-fashioned charm.[2]

Spotify is just one part of this broader musical matching market, and of course many listeners prefer to match their listening time elsewhere. YouTube offers many millions of musical cuts for free, and it is no accident that it is owned by Google, which means its search function is run by Google; YouTube is fundamentally about matching. There are also other venues—Amazon streaming, millions of artist websites, iTunes (still), and illegal download sites. Like most American music listeners, I can hear pretty much what I want, when I want, and in whatever version I want it. On the side, I still can buy CDs and LPs, but I use modern matching and search techniques, such as googling reviews, to decide what to buy. No matter what my mood or inclination, I can find the right song or symphony.

In the so-called good old days, people bought albums without always knowing much about the music. They might have heard a few cuts at a friend's house, but often the purchase was a risky one. Many purchased albums were heard once or twice and then allowed to lie fallow due to listener disappointment. Even the successful purchases often had no more than two or three good songs, or maybe just one; not every long-playing record was as consistent as *Sgt. Pepper's* or *Led Zeppelin IV*. How many songs can you name on Don McLean's *American Pie* album, other than the eponymous hit single from 1971? The scarcity of true creativity became all the more apparent when the seventy-nine-minute compact disc hit the market.

Classical music enthusiasts put great effort into finding exactly the right performance, knowing that sometimes pianist Artur Schnabel's fingers went off the rails, or Horowitz had a bad day, or, on the brighter side, Nelson Freire really was an underrated Chopin player. Who wanted to spend all that money on a mediocre rendition of Mozart or Beethoven? You could buy thick guides to the best classical CDs, but keeping up with all this stuff wasn't that easy—was the mono or stereo Otto Klemperer Beethoven recording thought to be best? (P.S.: It was the mono. Today you can use Google to confirm.)

All that has changed. You can listen for free, read web reviews until you are tired of staring at your screen, or text a friend for quick musical advice. Every few days I receive an email from a total stranger (typically a blog reader) giving me free music tips, requesting them, or most likely both at the same time. Usually I give it a try on YouTube or Spotify and follow up accordingly, or not. That's how I found out I like the jazz tenor sax player Kamasi Washington.

These days, it is hardly ever the case that people are buying music they don't like. Even before streaming and YouTube became so popular, the idea of a mistaken or unsatisfactory music purchase was on the way out. Listeners downloaded from iTunes, Amazon, or illegal sites. Almost always there was a way to hear the song at least once in advance and for free.

If you don't like what is playing, the main discomfort is the time

and effort cost of switching to another cut. In my new Hyundai automobile, I just speak to the satellite radio system and it changes the channel by itself, using voice-recognition software. I do that every time
there is a song I don't like or, for that matter, a song I consider less than
excellent. Music hardly ever disappoints, although paradoxically that
has led us to a world where in some ways music matters less than before, a theme to which I'll be returning.

We live in a setting where one part of GDP has gone down—GDP
for recorded music—while consumer satisfaction with music almost certainly has gone up. In the first decade of this millennium, revenue from
recorded music worldwide was about $60 billion, but now it is only
about $15 billion. Domestically, revenue from recorded music has fallen
by about 70 percent since 1999, even though the American population
has grown by about 46 million. Further declines may be coming, as
compact discs are still losing market share, and Walmart is cutting back
on shelf space devoted to recorded music. And it's not just the revenue
measures that are declining. If we measure individual tracks sold, that
number had fallen about 57 percent by 2010, and most of that decline
cannot be accounted for by musical piracy. Most Americans just don't
need to buy and own so many tracks anymore.[3]

And yet this new world is not so bad for the earnings of artists, especially for the ones who are willing to go out and tour. In 2014, over
60,000 Americans reported their primary occupation as musician, music
director, or composer, up from 53,000 in 1999; in percentage terms,
that's a bigger rise than for the American job market as a whole. The
number of self-employed musicians rose even more, going up 45 percent
from 2001 to 2014. (For comparison, self-employed writers went up
about 20 percent over those same years.) The earnings story is not
thrilling but also not bad. In 2012, musical groups and individual performers reported 25 percent more average revenue than in 2002. That
comparison is not adjusting for inflation, so it shows musical artists are
pretty much treading water as a sector, but keep in mind this is a time
when median wages for Americans generally have been falling. The bottom line is that revenue from recorded music plunged but the earnings

of the individual creator more or less held steady and the number of creators in the sector went up. Increases in revenue from live music made up for a lot of the decline in artist revenue from recordings. The big losers have been the music companies, not the performers, although many musicians do have to work harder these days, mostly through touring and added marketing effort, such as spending time on social media.[4]

The key point is this: By using better matching, the American economy is in some fundamental ways doing better than the numbers indicate. Our preferences are better satisfied, above and beyond how this might be reflected in GDP and other economic measures, and that is probably the cheeriest of the measures in this book. That said, "better matching," for all its pleasures and virtues, is also in some regards uncomfortably close to the concept of "more segregation," as we will see. Very often we match to what we already like, or what is already like us. Matching brings many new and varied delights into our lives, but in a lot of spheres, the like-to-like effects of matching outweigh the ability of matching to shake us up. That is partly *why* matching can make us so happy.

MATCHING CONTINUES TO SPREAD ITS INFLUENCE

Better matching has a big influence on many parts of American lives, not just music. As I mentioned in chapter 1, in the 1930s, one study showed that over a third of urban Americans married people who lived within five blocks. But for couples who married between 2005 and 2012, more than one-third of them met online; that number rose to nearly 70 percent for same-sex couples. No, I can't prove that these matches are better or happier ones, but at the very least we should be open to that idea. Some highly religious groups aside, I don't see too many of us going back to the idea of the arranged marriage or ceasing to use the internet as a way of communicating with potential or actual partners.[5]

For same-sex couples, the benefits of online connections appear to be much stronger, because their search and discovery problems are usually tougher. In earlier times, many gay people ended up marrying people of the opposite sex or didn't marry at all, if only because they didn't have enough freedom of choice and enough ability to find and make the right match. But with online matches, and of course also greater social tolerance, this situation has changed entirely. Regardless of sexual preference, the dating services and apps at our fingertips make it easier to narrow down the pool of people we meet online by religion, political affiliations, age, and geography and to date Jews, Muslims, Sikhs, liberals or conservatives, people in the right age group or geographic area, or those who simply want a quick fling.

Sometimes these matches extend to the ridiculous, but such possibilities of overreach show how far the new technologies have evolved and how much we have done everything possible to fill out the space of matching possibilities. Oscar Mayer, the food products company, is marketing Sizzl, a dating app that tries to pair people on the basis of whether they share a common taste for a preferred kind of bacon. Why date someone who prefers low fat when you opt for the maple-infused product? The marketing director put it pretty simply: "In love, as it is in bacon, it's important to be discerning when selecting your perfect match and to never settle for less than the best." Sizzl even allows you to press down on your phone for a length of time, which sends a signal about how much you desire the other person—the Sizzl-meter. This tongue-in-cheek app exists on the fringes of many more mainstream products, including apps for dating that match according to zodiac sign, taste in music, how you define sexy, taste in pets, and taste in marijuana, among many many others.[6]

By the time you are reading this paragraph, the offerings will have morphed to be even better synced to what users are demanding. The very latest I have heard about is the app called "Once." It connects to your Fitbit or Android Wear device and tracks your heart rate while you look at someone else's profile. The wearer receives the appropriate feedback, and in a planned update, the app will have the ability to send that data to the other person, if the wearer so desires. If both hearts are beating fast while the two are looking at each other's profiles, the app lets both people know; how is that for a credible signal? Right now, Once has 600,000 users in Europe, and it is slated to come to the United States.[7]

These services really do encourage a mentality of matching. There is experimental evidence that if you enter a speed dating room and just try to be nice and welcoming to everyone, rather than looking for "the right match," the other participants discriminate against you, and it is hard to come away from such events satisfied. It seems to work better to present some version of "who you really are" and then look for the person who will appreciate that, or in other words, it is better to try to match.[8]

For dating, there is also Lawyerflirts.com, JustTeachersdating.com, and FarmersOnly.com, if you wish to match by profession. Farmers, by the way, are especially likely to marry each other, in part because it's a tough job with unusual hours and in part because both members of the potential couple tend to live in rural areas with a smaller number of other professions around. If you are getting up every morning at 4:30 a.m., there is something to be said for marrying another person who does the same.[9]

"Assortative mating"—that is, the marriage of people of similar educational and socioeconomic backgrounds—has become more widespread than in the past. That phrase refers to matching generally, but it also refers more specifically to men of high education and income marrying women of high education and income. More concretely, lawyers marry other law partners, or perhaps investment bankers, rather than their secretaries. This in turn propagates inequality across the generations, as the money and brains become clustered in high-powered, two-earner families, determined to do everything possible to advance the interests of their children and endowed with the skills to see that commitment through. One study showed that family-connected decisions, including marriage, choice of spouse, female labor supply, and lower divorce rates for wealthier couples, accounted for a third of the rise in income inequality from 1960 to 2005. In other words, if you wish to understand income inequality, or for that matter the American economy, don't just study the *New York Times* business section; turn also to the Sunday marriage pages.[10]

The influence of matching spreads far and wide, so maybe sex is better too for many Americans. It's certainly easier to find, and if you have unusual tastes, or maybe just religious- or culturally based tastes, you are no longer confined to the circle of people you know from ordinary daily life. Online profiles, often backed by (initial) partial or complete anonymity, make it easier to reveal what you really want, without having to blurt it out to a group of people at a cocktail party or to a stranger at a bar. If your thing is S&M, you can more easily interact with others of similar interests, or if you don't use bondage dating sites, it may be less stressful to reveal that taste through an email than it would be in person. There are dating or sex services to find people of specific nationalities, religions, ages, breast sizes, preferred sexual practices, and various weight sizes, including for those who prefer the very obese. Facebook helps people hook up with their exes and their junior high school crushes—not always for the better, of course.

Some of this choice may encourage a narrowing of horizons, or too much choice may be alienating, or maybe the surfeit of choice makes it harder to settle down and be content. Or maybe some of you see all this matching as supporting too many "perversions," whatever you might define that concept to consist of. Furthermore, if you've ever tried to fill out an online dating profile, you know how hard it is to specify what you are looking for. As mere words, "intelligent" and "good sense of humor" just aren't very useful as practical or useful filters, even though when properly understood they may be absolutely essential.

Still, we need to seriously entertain the hypothesis that, on average, our sex lives and love lives are considerably better than they were a few decades ago. Effective matching makes it more likely that Americans will get what they want, and find it more quickly and more readily than before.

The evidence on online dating is fragmentary, but it does suggest some possible advantages to the practice. For instance, let's say you pursue online dates who meet your preferred cluster of traits as you express their relative importance; that is, if you prefer smarts over looks, you choose dates who rank well accordingly. Over time, those relationships tend to be more successful, at least according to extant studies. There is also evidence that individuals with similar attitudes and values tend to do better in relationships, and online dating may help people find such matches. On the downside, people are bad at specifying in advance what they really want in a romantic partner, and most generally, according to one comprehensive survey of online dating analyses, "there are inherent limits to how well the success of a relationship between two individuals can be predicted in advance of their awareness of each other." So online matching is probably useful for romance, but a lot of our contentment or even enthrallment with online practices may be based on an illusion of security, stability, and control, a theme running throughout this book. Unfortunately, information can be manipulated more easily than can reality.[11]

When it comes to information technology and matching, we are not just the hunters; we are also the hunted, and it is not just potential romantic partners who are looking for us. A given advertisement may follow you from your iPhone to your desktop to your tablet, all because of better matching, in this case matching of ads to people. Sometimes I feel like I am living in the supernatural dimension; for instance, if I buy a CD from Amazon, cuts from that artist start appearing on my YouTube page. Whether we like it or not, the characteristics of our phone, desktop, and tablet use indicate whether the same person might own all three. At the very least, probabilistic inferences can be and indeed are drawn. An entire company, called Drawbridge, specializes in connecting particular users to particular devices and then selling this information to marketers, who use it to target us with ads and promotions. As of mid-2015, Drawbridge connects over a billion users to more than 3.6 billion devices, and that number is growing. The bright side of this marketing barrage is that you are sent more useful ads than the network television staples of laundry detergent and Coca-Cola, but of course it is unsettling too. Sometimes the algorithms know what I want before I do.[12]

There is even a new method for tracking you and your web presence by sound, which I hope will be illegal or at least unpopular by the time you are reading this. Here goes:

> *The ultrasonic pitches are embedded into TV commercials or are played when a user encounters an ad displayed in a computer browser. While the sound can't be heard by the human ear, nearby tablets and smartphones can detect it. When they do, browser cookies can now pair a single user to multiple devices and keep track of what TV commercials the person sees, how long the person watches the ads, and whether the person acts on the ads by doing a Web search or buying a product.*[13]

EBay is another IT company that facilitates the well-ordered match, though here we are back to the more benevolent side of the practice. Some people own collectibles and others want to buy them. Before internet auctions, the garage sale, the flea market, and the antique shop coordinated the market, but usually you had to visit them in person. With internet auctions, you can buy and sell from anywhere, with buyer and seller reputations and guarantees to grease the wheels of trade. Whether it be Elvis Presley memorabilia, zero-gauge toy trains, or Panamanian molas (a kind of reverse applique textile), collecting is now feasible for more people than ever before, and even middle-class Americans have a pretty good chance to build up an interesting collection of some kind or another.

EBay and other contemporary institutions have so attuned us to favorable and most favorable matches that the Millennial Generation has rebelled against the idea of taking on parental possessions. Parents often want to hand down their leather sofas, their music collections, and their photo albums, if only to downsize. But American kids are not accepting these items from their parents as they used to. They seem less interested in possessions, less likely to own spacious homes, more interested in urban living, and more demanding that everything they own be matched exactly to their preferred styles. An entire generation of "stuff" is lying fallow in thrift shops and consignment stores and auction houses rather than being passed on through the generations. Scott Roewer, who works as a "professional organizer," put it this way: "They [Millennials] are living their life digitally through Instagram and Facebook and YouTube, and that's how they are capturing their moments. Their whole life is on a computer; they don't need a shoebox full of greeting cards." And the very fact that we now have "professional organizers" says at least as much as that quotation.[14]

In the early days of eBay, it was debated whether the service would cause the price of collectibles to rise or to fall. After all, eBay increased the demand to collect but also allowed everyone's attic and garage stuff to flow into the market. Both supply and demand went up, so what was the net effect on price? These days it is pretty much clear: eBay has lowered the price of most collectibles, after adjusting for inflation, and often even if we do not adjust for inflation. That is, relative to most people's wages, collectibles are cheaper than ever before, and that is because the "junk coming out of the attic" effect has outweighed the increase in demand for collectibles.

With respect to matching, I would say contemporary society has a lot more "happiness capital" than the available numbers indicate. Given that the prices of collectibles fell post-eBay, that means the previously higher price of collectibles was based on now-defunct artificial market barriers, most of all the difficulties of buyer-seller coordination across physical geography. Today a given collection may be less valuable in dollar terms, but probably it is of greater value in happiness terms, both changes being driven by better matching through the internet. This means that using market prices as a measure of value is undervaluing the quality of today's world relative to the past, because these days a lot of cheap stuff is appreciated quite intensely for its happiness value, more so than a traditional interpretation of the price numbers alone would indicate.

Or consider the used books for sale on Amazon. These days you can buy Tolstoy's *War and Peace*, or many other classic works, for only a penny, plus $3.99 for shipping. And it's not just classics; Jennifer Egan's Pulitzer Prize–winning *Visit from the Goon Squad* also sells for a penny plus shipping. These prices are the result of an intense process of sorting. The books often are donated to libraries and thrift stores, and eventually they find their way to large warehouses run by wholesalers, such as Thriftbooks or Discover Books, which may have bought the used copies for as little as 10 cents a pound. Automated scanners and algorithmic software then determine the worth of a book, where it should be put up for sale (Amazon or eBay or Alibris?, etc.), and how it should be priced. If all goes well, this culminates in a successful market transaction through which the buyer is one great book richer and one penny (plus shipping costs) poorer. That the price is so low is an indication of how many books are being matched to buyers rather than being pulped or sitting in a used book store barn somewhere in rural Pennsylvania, waiting three or four years for someone to come along and pay the $8 price inscribed in pencil on the inside title page.[15]

You can think of these accounts as broader parables for how matching gains are improving the world, but not always in a way that shows up in economic statistics. For instance, there is more consumer surplus from each book we buy, and thus more fun per dollar spent. Similarly, these blessings won't show up directly as an increase in the measured savings rate, even though better and more durable purchase decisions in essence boost savings through the medium of more effective consumer durables, more suitable marriages, and that breed of dog we really wanted all along. A counterintuitive way to put it is that the American economy has been deleveraging more than it appears, albeit in fairly invisible ways, namely improving the quality of purchase decisions. Informed stability is the new boon of modern consumer society, in America most of all.[16]

There is one other statistic that I find indicative of the new trend toward better and more powerful matching, and that has to do with how we treat our pets. When I was a kid, I remember that most dogs given away to shelters or to the dog pound ended up being put to sleep.

That is no longer the case. In New York City, the adoption rate for shelter dogs and cats now stands at 87 percent, compared to a much lower 26 percent in 2003. In San Francisco, the placement rate for shelter animals stands at 91 percent. The number of dogs and cats put to sleep has gone down by about 80 percent since the 1970s.[17]

And why is that? Well, shelters have become much better at matching pets to owners, albeit at the cost of some extra bureaucracy. The animal shelters profile both the pet and the owner when trying to arrange a pairing. After adoption, they also provide phone calls, visits to the home, and free veterinary care to help the match stick. Free spaying and neutering services make it easier and cheaper to keep the pet. Finally, the internet means that most potential pet owners know what they are in for, in terms of temperament and required care, before adopting a particular animal or breed in the first place. The end result is better matches, more matches, and happier owners, not to mention happier pets and more pets who manage to stay alive. These days, matching is for everyone, not just human beings.

And by the way, don't think that these days you have to *own* a dog to get the benefits. Just use the app Bark'N'Borrow, an Uber-like sharing economy service to help you spend some time with a dog—and then, when you are done, send it back to its owner. The dog's owner feels less guilty about keeping the pet in her apartment all day while she is working, the dog gets to go for a walk, your seven-year-old is delighted by the experience, and at the end of the day, everyone's carpet remains fully unsoiled. Don't forget to specify which breed you want.[18]

WHERE ELSE ARE BETTER MATCHES IMPROVING OUR LIVING STANDARDS?

Although Americans spend their money on music much more efficiently, that is a relatively small percentage of most consumers' budgets. The question therefore arises: Just how far does this better matching extend, and how much have our living standards gone up because of better matching? There aren't direct measures to answer this question, but common sense does suggest plausible hypotheses.

For instance, the dining and entertainment sector, like music markets, gives consumers much better information. It is easier for diners to find the kind of foods they wish to eat and to patronize the better restaurants rather than the worse ones, in large part because of the internet and apps. The quality of American dining, and also raw ingredients shopping, has reached all-time highs. The internet-based story there is pretty simple and transparent: It is now much easier to find and evaluate the better stuff, or the materials best suited to your particular needs. But again, dining out, like music, is a relatively small part of consumers' budgets.

If we look at the budget of a typical middle-class American, commonly the major items include rent (or mortgage payment), health care (if only indirectly through employer provision of insurance and thus lower wages), higher education, transportation, and food. Unfortunately, not all of these areas are seeing big gains in the quality of matching, and that is one way to understand why some big parts of the American economy remain somewhat stuck.

When it comes to residential decisions, such as matching people to areas, the picture is a mixed one, as I've covered in chapter 2. On the plus side, people seem to like their geographic areas more and more, and they are more likely to stay in them. More people live in areas with nicer weather and more sun than used to be the case. Yet we are replicating and indeed intensifying some patterns of undesirable segregation, as I considered in chapter 3. The decline in residential mobility also makes the American economy less dynamic and less able to adjust to recessions, again, as discussed earlier.

For health care and higher education, the results also seem to be mixed. It is much easier than before to discover who are the best doctors, or which are the best hospitals and colleges, mostly because of the internet and superior techniques of performance measurement. That said, these are not fully open markets for matching. Knowing that Harvard may be the best university doesn't mean you can go there, even if you are willing to pay full price. Similarly, appreciating the quality of the Mayo Clinic may not solve your basic health problem—what if you live in El Paso and are of limited means with no significant connections in the world of highly professionalized medicine? That's different from music, where everyone can listen to Bach and the Beatles—or whatever else is supposed to be best—without interference from others. You don't need Paul McCartney to sign off on your listening plan, and almost everyone can afford to access their favorite music.

To be sure, Americans nonetheless are seeing some matching gains in health care and education. What if your region has three community colleges, and you are trying to figure out which is best? Or maybe you just need to avoid the really bad foot surgeons to enjoy an acceptable recovery. Matching probably has improved in the middle tiers of the market and at the bottom, even if not many people can be matched to the very top in terms of quality. There is some evidence that patients are better matched to their hospitals over time, and in a way that is bringing slight improvements in life expectancy.[19]

Some of the benefits from better matching in health care and education are not apparent at first glance. Alvin Roth, an experimental economist now at Stanford University, won a Nobel Prize in part for using economic theory to come up with better algorithms for matching, and these methods are supposed to be robust across many realms in a quite general sense. His Nobel Prize was an especially deserved one, as it reflects the spirit of our times more than was recognized in 2012, the year he won.

Some of Roth's work focused on the allocation of doctors to medical residencies, which is fundamentally a problem of matching. At some point in the process of becoming a full-fledged doctor, candidates apply for resident appointments, but there are many candidates and many available places for service, and not everyone can get his or her top choice of venue or doctor. Given this complexity, what is the most efficient way to decide which candidates should be paired with which slots? The problem is to make the candidates as happy as possible with what they get, and also to make them as productive as possible. It's also desirable if hospitals end up with the doctors they want rather than those who do not fit into the needs or culture of that hospital. Roth came up with a scheme that asks both doctors and hospitals to present their rank orderings. His algorithm then uses this information to make the best possible allocation of doctors across residencies. Roth's matching algorithm now governs the national system of slot allocation. It's better for doctors and hospitals, and probably better for patients too, because happier doctors probably means higher-quality performance.

Roth's algorithms for matching are not just for medical residencies. Many colleges and universities, when they receive a new class of freshmen and must allocate them to dorms and roommates, draw on Roth's ideas to elicit preference rankings and then use mathematics to perform the optimal pairings. Again, not everyone can get his or her first choice, but the better matching makes as many students as happy as possible. In that context, better connections can mean more lasting friendships or business connections across an entire lifetime. So modern matching is improving our lives in many hard-to-see ways, not just through the immediately apparent world of the internet as you would find at Spotify or Match.com.

Although researchers are still pretty far from having a good overall estimate of how much the gains from better matching have improved our lives, there is nonetheless a useful generalization about the winners and losers in a world of matching.

OUR JOBS ARE ALSO ABOUT MATCHING

An additional lesson about matching comes from the two other economists who have won Nobel Prizes for their work on matching: Even small increases in the chance of a good match can have big effects on society. The power of matching is amplified by how different matches, as they interact across individuals, can amplify the power of each other.

Dale Mortensen and Christopher Pissarides, who won the Nobel in 2010, were obsessed with the question of why unemployment persisted for so long after an economic recession. In their minds, the problem of finding the right job was fundamentally one of matching; that is, how hard employers were searching for the most suitable employee and how hard workers were searching for the best job. Earlier economists, notably John Maynard Keynes and his successors, framed the question in terms of whether there was enough spending in the economy to sustain job creation. That factor remains relevant, but Mortensen and Pissarides asked some deeper and more fundamental questions about why it takes so long to reemploy workers laid off during a downturn. People are often laid off because they are locked into a wage agreement that the employer no longer deems profitable. But what about the workers who already had lost their jobs and who weren't tied into a specific wage bargain? Why couldn't they find new work quite rapidly at lower wages? Very often, this potential for rapid recovery just didn't happen. Mortensen and Pissarides's key insight for what went wrong focused on the idea that a good match is hard to make in the first place and even harder to make in a downturn. During a recession, employers, seeking to cut costs, which often starts with laying people off, are understandably less focused on finding *new* workers. Workers, for their part, take a long time to accept the proposition that they may have to take lower-quality/ lower-paying work. After all, once they do this, they fear, they'll be branded as lower-quality workers for the future. Better to hold on and search longer than to accept this downgrade. And so with both sides resistant to the notion of creating a new match too quickly, there are fewer good matches, and the whole labor market piles up more log-jams, so to speak. Some follow-up work on their model suggests these matching problems can account for up to one-third of unemployment during a recession.[20]

One thing economists have learned about matching from Mortensen and Pissarides is that small changes in the ease of a match—as measured by, say, the returns to search in labor markets—can have a big impact on the final number and quality of matches. Searching for a match, whether in work, love, or many other areas, involves a small chance that any possible sampled potential match turns out to be the right choice. And each act of search has a small but noticeable cost. So if you're using Match.com or looking at job want ads online, you don't apply for everything at once; rather, you build a sequential path through those options. You'll spend the rest of your time walking the dog, watching TV, or maybe exercising, because another act of search doesn't bring such a high expected yield. Yet if the (small) costs of search were to fall, you would walk the dog one less time and search more, perhaps ending up with a much better match.

Furthermore, better matches for you might make search better and more effective for everyone else, by clearing logjams in the market and speeding along the better overall allocation. If you find "the right mate for you," other individuals won't be distracted by that potential option (which maybe wasn't right for them to begin with), and the efficacy of their search will rise. You can think of better search as helping to clear up a coordination problem or a bit like fixing a traffic jam by getting enough cars past a bottleneck point. Not everyone wants to marry a guy who is a good dad but a fantasy sports addict, and if he is paired off successfully, that makes the search easier for other women, who will not waste their time considering him or dating him. Getting some successful matches done improves the search process more generally, just as clearing the broken or smashed-up cars from the road can help reopen a lane and restore traffic flow.

The simple truth is that a lot of searches could go better and lead to better matches than is currently the case. One recent economics research paper found that the "standard deviation" of the quality of a labor market match was worth about $9.75 an hour. That's statistical lingo, but basically it means that it is pretty common for one job match to be much better than another by that amount, if we translate the value of the different jobs' perks into dollar terms. In other words, there is still potential for information technology to further improve the quality of matches.[21]

A lot of our biggest social problems, such as unemployment, are in large part problems of matching. We haven't solved them all. Yet.

THE WINNERS AND LOSERS FROM ALL THIS MATCHING

That all said, the gains from matching are distributed very unevenly, and they accrue mainly to people who are better at using and handling information, a group whom elsewhere I labeled *infovores*. If you are completely wired, with a smartphone and good digital skills, and you're great at using Google, various apps, and knowing how to search for information, you'll improve the quality of the matches that you find on the internet a lot. In contrast, I've met people—smart, accomplished people in other walks of life—who are baffled by Yelp reviews and look only at the average number of stars given to a restaurant to form a judgment. It's much better to search out the longest, most detailed, and smartest reviews and see what those have to say. But not everyone knows this or is motivated to learn this. Some people are simply not so good at manipulating and interpreting digital information, so they don't gain nearly as much from the internet and the matching capabilities it gives us.

Another group that misses out from all these matching gains is those on the losing side of the digital divide. They are not well connected either at home or with smartphones, even if in a more just and less poverty-ridden world they might be superb at using the internet to improve their lives.

Finally, for all the benefits of matching, those benefits are distributed along class lines. Most of the matching I've outlined truly is beneficial, but still, it has helped to cement in a lot of segregation, stasis, and complacency of the successful. In economic terminology, it might be said that the world of good matches is a world of stocks, not flows. It is a world of accumulated and stable wealth and satisfied ownership rather than one of perpetual personal churn. It is a world of slower economic activity in some regards, because your good purchases and good personal choices last longer. But not all Americans have entered this new and stable world. Many poorer Americans appear to have much lower stocks of wealth and also higher divorce rates, so they haven't taken advantage of the possible shift to better stocks and smaller flows. A split in contentment, across some kind of socioeconomic class line, appears to have occurred, as is now widely recognized. As both the conservative/libertarian Charles A. Murray and the liberal Robert D. Putnam have pointed out, America seems to be evolving two sets of social norms: a high-stability set of norms for the higher earners and upper socioeconomic classes and less-stable social and marriage norms for many of the less-educated lower earners. Our pro-matching technologies are mostly evolving to serve the needs of the former, wealthier group, and it remains to be seen just how much they will help individuals in the less-stable situations.

The discussions of residential and labor mobility in previous chapters can also be read as tales of matching. To the extent that neighborhoods are more segregated by income, class, and sometimes race, it is because those in the better situations have improved their abilities to match into what they want. Those who have to live in less-safe neighborhoods with inferior school systems just don't gain much access to what they need from the better matching technologies.

In similar fashion, labor market matching may disproportionately benefit better-educated and more productive workers. A lot of America's matching goes on at the level of the firm—in the form of allocating the most successful workers to the most successful firms—and there we see the upside of matching but also its significant unintended effects. In chapter 4, I discussed how more and more of the top talent is being clustered in the largest and most successful firms. America's productivity problem is coming from small and medium-size enterprises, not the market leaders. Probably not all of Google's ideas will work out, but still, the company isn't just search. Gmail is pretty useful, YouTube is running and has been significantly upgraded, driverless cars and trucks seem to be on the horizon, and someday a version of Google Glass may even change our lives, even if Google Glass as we know it remains stillborn.

What is happening is that technology has made it easier for better corporations to identify those workers with stronger skills, more demanding work ethics, and higher intelligence, and vice versa. The more successful firms, having more to offer in terms of salary and prestige, are able to attract such workers, now that they can find them. This results in a kind of segregation of the skilled, hardworking, and smart, a negative in the sense of giving less-skilled workers a chance to learn from the best. But that segregation also constitutes better matches—a positive word if you are either a successful company or someone with the skill set to be desirable to such a firm. Americans with potent talents are working together, and more effectively, than ever before, and that is a kind of successful matching, an assortative mating of IQ and talent at the corporate level.

This new segregation has preserved the quality and cooperativeness of America's very best clusters, such as tech businesses in Silicon Valley. A troublemaker can't just show up at Google and set up a desk and start working and interacting with workers. The top American businesses enforce very selective standards for hires, taking the art of human resources management to new peaks—bureaucracy, excess credentialism, and standardized testing included. But of course it's not enough to be good at your job; if a job candidate is suspected of being incompatible with the prevailing culture, he or she faces a very tough uphill climb.

American businesses also go to great lengths to measure the cooperativeness of their workers with a common proxy being credit rating, which of course reflects how well borrowers keep their promises to pay the money back. (This is now happening for about *60 percent* of all hires.) Big data is also being used in other ways to ensure a compliant workforce: One recent study by Xerox found that employees who belong to one or two social networks are likely to stay in their jobs for a longer time period than individuals who belong to four or more social networks. That correlation is now part of how Xerox thinks about hiring and building a cohesive community of workers.[22]

As I think you already can sense, the downside is never far away. All the talk of "business morale" is very often code for a kind of profiling, that nasty cousin of segregation. Imagine you're someone whose previous job required you to sign up for every major social media account. Or you'd been stalked and had to cancel all accounts for that reason. I can assure you that the hiring software at Xerox couldn't care less, because it will never know or grasp the details of your individual case.

Companies, of course, can always find ways to use people who don't fit their ideal. If need be, the company can still buy things or services from those or comparable workers, but outsourced at a great distance and kept away from the prevailing corporate culture at home in the firm. Outsourcing is not just about the potential for lower wages, it's about not wanting to disturb a very tidy, neat, and somewhat conformist culture of highly cooperative and intelligent . . . nonconformists.

That's the other downside to all of this. For all the benefits produced by the elite tech firms, in the longer run, a lot of businesses will end up less innovative, as the best workers get pulled into a relatively small number of companies and sectors. That's been America over the last few decades, as the productivity of the country's small and medium-size businesses has been underwhelming.

While matching's downsides in the realm of finding music or restaurants may not feel like such a big deal—*who cares* if I don't discover new food or music if I like what I've chosen (and more on this later)—in the case of work, the costs seem to directly affect some human lives for the worse. There is one more positive attribute of corporate segregation by worker quality to weigh, however. It has helped to break down or at least weaken some other harmful forms of (previous) American segregation. The tighter that segregation for worker quality evolves, the more corporations will ignore a lot of other dimensions of traditional discrimination, such as race and gender. Today's major companies are a remarkable mix of progressive and indifferent when it comes to race, ethnicity, religion, and sexual orientation. If the company can measure the quality of the worker and control how the individual fits into the broader culture, those external markers do not matter because profit is more important; and besides, a lot of today's top entrepreneurs truly are tolerant. If anything, top companies will be eager to parade their diversity and tolerance in full public view, as their customers and potential customers are probably no less diverse. Credit Suisse, in addition to its tolerant hiring and promotion policies, has promoted an LGBT Equality Index, an investment product that focuses on companies with superior performance in supporting LGBT rights. As you might expect, Credit Suisse is such a company itself.

But neither has segregation ended altogether in all of its forms. America really is remarkably diverse in ethnic and religious senses, and you can walk into a company and find a Hindu from India, a Catholic from El Salvador, a Jew from Brooklyn and previously Russia, and a believer in voodoo from Haiti, all working together peacefully and productively. What you will not find so easily—in successful firms—is large numbers of slacking, untalented, destructive people who infest the prevailing corporate culture with ideas and practices of their own. "Matching" and "segregation" are indeed two words that are very well . . . matched.

WHAT ARE SOME OTHER DOWNSIDES OF ALL THIS MATCHING?

As I already mentioned in the discussion of love and dating, this notion of good matches is a little tricky, and pursuing a good match is not always the way to end up with . . . a good match. Very often the idea of a good match is driven by what we can specify up front, what we can see in a photo, or what we can divine from a single listen to a piece of music. Most YouTube clips are never viewed to the end, or even beyond the first thirty seconds.

I think many of us can see this in our own aesthetic histories. When I first heard Van Morrison's *Astral Weeks*, I didn't like the album. It sounded discordant and too jazzy for my taste. At fifteen years old, I put it aside. Still, I had bought the damned thing, and some guy in a book wrote that it was important, so a while later I returned to the purchase. Besides, at that time in the 1970s, I didn't have a free universal jukebox at my immediate disposal, so that was the music in the house and I didn't have the money to go out and buy all the albums I wanted.

But a funny thing happened—after five or so listens, I liked the album. Soon enough, I grew to love it.

In those days, good musical matches were harder to come by. Still, the aesthetic matches many of us bought and cherished were not usually based on a quick or superficial sample of the song or album. Those creations had a chance to settle into our minds, for better or worse. That process offered the potential for expanding musical horizons in an especially focused way that today's universal jukebox doesn't always manage to do. Listeners in the 1970s had a much narrower breadth of understanding, but often they knew and understood individual albums incredibly well. Arguably there was a greater commitment to the music, and in those days music probably was more important to a greater number of listeners. It signaled to others what the listeners had committed to, and it was not just another stop on the roulette wheel of making yet another temporary choice; rather, it was a core component of many social identities.

I've heard and read some related complaints about internet dating. The eternal possibility of finding a better match yet makes it harder for many people to settle down and make any match at all. Aziz Ansari relates the story of a middle-age guy, not rich or gorgeous or famous, who went through a list of ads from women and rejected them for one arbitrary reason after another. He didn't pursue one of the ads because *the woman was a Boston Red Sox fan*. He didn't hate sports or baseball; rather, it was the attachment to the Red Sox that turned him off. The prospect of the perfect match has become, for this person, the enemy of the good match.[23]

There is now an extensive literature in behavioral economics about how, under some circumstances, having more choice can make it harder for us to be content with our final selections. Maybe too many of us are always looking elsewhere, always wondering if we really ended up with what is best, and always noticing the other possibilities paraded before us all the time. All that choice can make us unsettled about what we have. There is even a phrase, Barry Schwartz's "paradox of choice," coined to cover this phenomenon. Nonetheless, we have to be very careful interpreting these claims. I know plenty of people familiar with these results—

that choice can confuse people and lower their well-being—and yet, as far as I can tell, they still all want the extra choice. It's not like smoking, where you tell people the truth and then many or most of them quit the habit, albeit with struggles. I don't see many people even trying to disconnect from the potent matching available through the internet, much less succeeding. I observe also that the migration of human beings is almost always to the societies with more choice, not less choice, and with more internet, not less internet. More choice and better matching have their problematic sides, but still they hold a great and probably permanent allure.

MATCHERS GAIN, STRIVERS LOSE

Finally, to understand some of the other distributional effects of a matching society, consider a distinction between those I label the enthusiasts and those I label the strivers, with the former being a kind of matcher. Of course, many people fall into both categories to differing degrees, but still these concepts allow us to pin down some regularities for how modern matching boosts some people more than others. In today's world, the enthusiasts have greater chances to bond with others, and that creates more possibilities for tribalism, especially outside of the mainstream conformist preferences. At the same time, more people will dare to be different, precisely because they can find online social support for doing so. This is again a way in which better matching can make us happier, yet in ways that are not reflected in the usual economic statistics.

OK, so let's work through these distinctions in just a little more detail. The enthusiasts have niche tastes, and some of their happiness comes from finding other people who share those passions, whatever they may be. They might seek friends with comparable collections of Motown 45s, or people who play the same computer games. They might look for a mate who prefers the same breed of dog. The enthusiasts are not trying to come out ahead of everyone else; rather, they seek to have some of their niche preferences fulfilled for the sake of their own internally directed happiness.

The enthusiasts have made major gains in contemporary America, and it is interesting to think about why, using a bit of contrast.

On the other side of this spectrum, the competitive strivers are driven less by their interests than by their drive to win in whatever context they find themselves. These are the people who strive to have the biggest office, bed the most mates, earn the most money, or climb whatever else the relevant status ladder may be. There is a finite amount of whatever they are striving for at a given moment, everyone knows more or less what it is, and lots of other people want it. Unlike the enthusiasts, the competitive strivers often face more intense competition for what they want because everyone else also can pursue it through online means. *The strivers are trying to win rather than to match*, and so the great matching facility of the internet doesn't improve their lives as much as it does for the enthusiasts.

The competitive strivers face yet another problem: The internet makes it harder for them to feel they have reached the top of the heap. Maybe two generations ago it was about marrying the most beautiful girl in town, but these days the standards for beauty are global. The pinnacle is now to marry a woman who is as beautiful as the sexiest Brazilian or Russian model on the internet, and that is difficult to accomplish, at least if you are wrapped up in this idea of a single-dimensional ladder of beauty and status.

So many of us now have seen or tried or maybe just read about "the best" that we either learn to be content with the matches we can achieve or we are perpetually discontented. The internet puts a stiff implicit tax or penalty on competitive status seeking, and it rewards those who are content with something niche and unusual. This may be one reason for the oft-reported diffidence that characterizes many of the Millennial Generation. They are not actually indifferent or lazy or lacking in enthusiasm—quite the contrary—but more and more of their passions take forms other than those of the old climb-the-social-ladder variety. Millennials might therefore appear to be lacking to the older generations who don't quite get the new terms of competition and satisfaction. In reality, the Millennials are doing pretty well with respect to the options the world has given them, and they are helping move that world toward more contentment and also less interest in grand projects or topping previous records of achievement. They too are part of the complacent class, and they are also its finest product and its most committed ideological carriers.

6.

WHY AMERICANS STOPPED RIOTING AND LEGALIZED MARIJUANA

In order to understand how peaceful America has become, we must consider what truly turbulent times looked like. Revisiting the recent past helps us see how the complacent class has shaped contemporary America and in turn has been shaped by it. The complacent class was itself originally a force of rebellion—it led an anticrime 1980s and 1990s movement against other dysfunctional features of an earlier America, such as unsafe cities and race riots. It is remarkable how far this country came toward greater calm and safety as a result. That is a lesson about the power and influence of the complacent class, but as we see later on, a historical perspective also warns us that perhaps not all of these gains will prove permanent.

With all of our fears of terrorism, the crime waves and riots of the 1960s and the early 1970s were much more destructive. During an eighteen-month period in 1971–1972, there were more than 2,500 domestic bombings reported, averaging out to more than five a day. Even though most of these did not involve fatalities, it boggles the mind to think of the number of people who dared to build or buy a bomb, plant it, and be prepared to live with the consequences of that choice. The most famous source of these bombings was the radical group the Weather Underground, but other bombers included anti–Vietnam War groups, student radicals, fighters for racial justice, and Puerto Rican independence groups, with plenty of amateur, homemade bombs circulating at the time. Yet it's today, and not back then, when the "security theater" to protect against bombs is so intense.[1]

And don't forget the riots. Starting with the 1965 Watts clashes in Los Angeles, the country faced a wave of intensely violent and often out-of-control social unrest. A police chief from the time remarked: "This situation is very much like fighting the Viet Cong . . . We haven't the slightest idea when this can be brought under control." A local CBS radio station reported: "This was not a riot. It was an insurrection against all authority . . . If it had gone much further it would have become a civil war." Four thousand people ended up in jail, thirty-four people were killed (mostly by the police), hundreds were injured, and about $35 million in property (1965 dollars) was destroyed.[2]

Or consider the Black Panthers. The Panthers were set loose to patrol cities, armed openly with guns in the places where that was legal, with the stated aim of defending black citizens from police aggression. Police aggression surely was a problem, and remains one today, as evidenced by the wave of unrest that occurred after events in Ferguson and Baltimore. But today's protests, at least so far, occur mostly within the law, with exceptions that are notable precisely because they are so rare. A disgruntled teenager might lunge at a cop in a moment of frustration and imprudence, a crowd might even burn down a pharmacy, but in neither case are participants likely to join a public group dedicated to a violent revolution to overthrow the capitalist system. "Black Lives Matter" is notable for avoiding any particular kind of political endorsement, and it is also more positive than destructive in its orientation. It favors inclusiveness, gender equality, and justice and peace rather than revolution. It's possible that the 2016 police officer shootings in Dallas may signal a change, but so far we've seen a pretty peaceful version of protest for a considerable period of time.

But in an earlier era, Black Panther Huey P. Newton, in his memoir, took a far more oppositional stance. Newton explained how much the Panthers stepped on traditional lawmaking functions: "Sometimes we got on a policeman's tail and followed him with our weapons in full view. If he darted around the block or made a U-turn trying to follow us, we let him do it until he got tired of that. Then, we would follow him again. Either way, we took up a good bit of police time that otherwise would have been spent in harassment." That's a more daring attitude than protest groups typically will express today.[3]

The marches and rallies of the 1960s and 1970s were often massive affairs. The group Mobilization Against the War in Vietnam put on a November 1969 rally with 500,000 people and a May 1970 event with 100,000 people, and the People's Coalition for Peace and Justice drew about 500,000 for its April 1971 rally at the U.S. Capitol. After the invasion of Cambodia and the Kent State shootings in May 1970, nearly 4 million students demonstrated and 536 schools shut down altogether, for at least a short period, with protests erupting on more than 1,250 campuses. During that single month of May, there were ninety-five instances of bombing and arson on college campuses alone, and thirty ROTC buildings were burned or bombed. Overall, whether it was on campus or not, the 1968 to 1975 period saw more instances of antigovernment violence than any time since the American Civil War.[4]

Campuses today are very different places, and they are among the segments of American society where the complacent class exercises its strongest influences. Universities massively overregulate themselves, and administrator appointments outpace faculty hires, so everything is set up to minimize the chances of something going wrong or becoming a public disturbance. When there are demonstrations, the student demands are often for "safe spaces" rather than violent overthrow of the government or the university administration. To the extent people today write of academia being disrupted, they might be referring to massive open online courses (MOOCs), which enable students to remain at home or in their dorm rooms, or to "competency-based learning," which, like a demonstration, can indeed shutter some schools, although for an entirely different reason, namely that some students can teach themselves at home more effectively and then take a test to prove they have done so. These developments are fascinating and perhaps promising innovations, but they are taking us ever farther away from the notion of the campus as a place of protest or social unrest.

To be sure, much of the chaos of the 1960s and early 1970s sprang from conflicts over the Vietnam War and the draft, events that dominated the evening news and took the lives of almost 60,000 American servicemen. But it's also no accident that the Vietnam War was intensified during that restless era. Today is instead a time of aerial bombing, drones, and minimal casualties, with extreme public scrutiny of every government decision and every possible error that comes to light, at least if it endangers domestic safety. Americans insist on their wars being near-zero casualties, on the American side at least, and something like the Vietnam conflict is inconceivable today, unless the direct security of the United States were to be involved. When it came, for instance, to Libya and Syria, the Obama administration so far has largely taken a pass, in part because the public simply wasn't interested in spending money and losing American lives for murky and perhaps unachievable goals. But the American public put up with the Vietnam War for quite a long time before support collapsed altogether in the early 1970s.

The struggle over gay rights shows the same contrast in restlessness between now and then. The seminal gay rights event of the 1960s was the Stonewall riot of 1969, when the police descended on a gay-oriented Greenwich Village nightclub, the Stonewall Inn, but ended up surrounded by an angry, rioting mob. Accounts from that time are hard to imagine in the context of modern, legally sanctioned gay weddings with expensive flower arrangements and officiating clergy. Here is a brief excerpt from Amm Bausum's study of Stonewall:

> *"Our goal was to hurt those police," explained John O'Brien, a gay man and activist who had joined the mob. "I wanted to kill those cops for the anger I had in me. And the cops got that. And they were lucky that door was closed, they were very lucky." [At one point only a barricaded door was protecting some cops from the crowd.]*[5]

As much as nonviolence was an essential feature of big parts of the civil rights movement, many blacks in the South, including many of the most prominent movement leaders, protected themselves with firearms, in recognition of what a violent and vindictive time they were operating in. Martin Luther King Jr. kept a gun at home and sometimes relied on neighbors to protect his home with firearms. Medgar Evers traveled with a rifle in his car and kept a pistol beside himself on the front seat; Evers later ended up being murdered.[6]

Almost impossible to imagine in today's climate of overprotective parenting, the civil rights movement even saw parents willing to put their children in the line of fire. The 1963 Birmingham Children's March paraded large numbers of African American children in front of potentially hostile armed police, police dogs, and also angry local, racist crowds. The worst-case scenario of violence against the children did not come about, but even the relatively calm course of the demonstration makes for harrowing reading today. This is from one newspaper report of the time: "The teen-agers, most of them 13 to 16, kept moving. Then the water hit them. Cowering first with hands over their heads, then on their knees or clinging together with their arms around each other, they tried to hold their ground." It's hard to imagine that being considered an acceptable course of action—from the marchers as well as the police—for the last few decades. Fortunately, at the time the police did hesitate to turn the fire hoses on the six-year-olds who participated in the march. And many African Americans were upset with their leaders for allowing it to proceed in this manner, yet it did, which is a reflection of how far that time was from the current safety-first mentality.[7]

It's worth noting that robust middle-class income growth does not predict peace and quiet, and sometimes general prosperity comes right before trouble and social unrest break out. The mid-1960s to early 1970s were the most violent and disruptive domestic period in America since the Civil War. Yet the 1950s and 1960s are considered a golden age for middle-class income growth in the United States. The same is true for black income growth, as the decades leading up to the 1960s saw the greatest gains in African American income in the history of the republic. Yet many of the 1960s riots were motivated by race, and many African Americans were prominent participants. In short, income gains are no guarantee of peace. If anything, income gains may raise expectations and increase the likelihood of social disturbances, a hypothesis sometimes associated with Alexis de Tocqueville's nineteenth-century analysis of the French Revolution. In the 1960s, Americans expected more, they didn't quite get what they had set their eyes on, and so they became more restless.

WHY DON'T WE RIOT ANYMORE?

Many of the seminal events of the civil rights movement could not happen today, most of all because society is more bureaucratized, more safety obsessed, and also less tolerant of any kind of disturbance or disruption at all.

Take the Selma marchers. It would be very difficult for a Selma-style march to happen today, and that is not because all civil rights grievances have been solved. In 1965, the Selma marchers had obtained the legal right, through petition, to conduct a fifty-two-mile, five-day march down an interstate highway. Of course, that blocked the highway, and for the most part such march permissions are impossible to obtain today, no matter how popular the political movement may be. Most motorists and truckers just don't want the highway shut down. Starting in the 1970s, the federal courts began to assert that public spaces are not automatically "fair game" for marches and demonstrations, and so local governments have sought to please users of such facilities rather than marchers.[8]

Linda Lumsden, a professor of journalism, put it succinctly: "The First Amendment right of assembly was the foundation of the civil rights movement of the 1950s."[9] That was true all the more of the 1960s. Those who led the movement often had to fight city ordinances that limited parades, protests, sit-ins, and marches, on the grounds that they might disturb public orderliness or breach the peace. The courts at the time sided pretty consistently with the protestors. Since then, however, there has been a lot of backsliding and less interest in seeing American public spaces evolve back into an outlet for volatile passions.

The disputes over a neo-Nazi march in Skokie, Illinois, made it clear to local governments that an undisputed de facto right of public assembly could be very costly. In 1977, a neo-Nazi group had petitioned for the right to stage a march in the predominantly Jewish community of Skokie. The number of demonstrators was small, but at the time many Skokie residents were survivors of Nazi concentration camps, so the issue took on an even stronger emotional hue than usual. The locality did not wish to permit the march, but eventually the Supreme Court intervened in favor of the marchers. Finally in 1978, a different version of the march took place but in Chicago, not Skokie, fortunately without major incident.

Nonetheless, local governments felt burned, in this case and in several others. If they could not prohibit undesirable marches, they would regulate them, if not out of existence, then into the less-visible and less-focal parts of their urban and suburban spaces. A new, slow war began, this one to make sure that demonstrators could not use the physical spaces they most desired. If arbitrary or capricious restrictions on demonstrations were not to be allowed, then regular restrictions, applicable to everyone, would take their place.

Along so many dimensions of American life, riots and protests have become more difficult to pull off, in part because of the increasing bureaucratization of daily life but also because of the bureaucratization of protest in particular. The NIMBY mentality limits high-density residential housing, wind power, and turbulent protests all the same. Which neighborhood these days wants trouble at its doorstep, especially when real estate values are at stake? This is all the more true when negative publicity is immediate and then amplified through social media. Back in the 1960s, the power of homeowners and businesses to coordinate, whether to stop a chemical waste dump or to deter a public march, wasn't nearly as high as it is today.

The application of management science to policing has been another reason why riots and rebellion have gone out of favor; their impact is too readily countered and defused. The police are better at managing, dispersing, and monitoring crowds in advance of any trouble, and at coordinating their own activities through rapid communications and information technology. If a riot was likely, more likely than not it would be defused by the deliberate application of crowd management techniques. Starting in the 1970s, police hired consultants, when necessary, for assistance in responding to extreme events. The result was that American public sector servants have nudged the citizenry closer to order in lieu of inflaming marchers with batons and tear gas.

To be sure, the recent trouble in Ferguson, Missouri, and Baltimore, Maryland, has represented cracks in this façade, a theme to which I return to later. In both cases, the initial police behavior was violent, and the subsequent police response to protests induced crowd violence, which then spiraled out of control, especially in Ferguson. The local police responded to protests with tear gas, helicopters, and smoke bombs, when they should have behaved more deliberately and taken steps to defuse the tensions. Management science, for once, did not govern the proceedings.

But in contrast to how matters might have run in the 1960s, this mistaken response did not translate into a large number of disorderly, violent protests elsewhere. On the side of the police, across the country, this was seen widely as a "lesson learned" kind of event, and vows were made to ensure it is not repeated. Even in Missouri, the State Highway Patrol was given control of the situation, and authority was taken away from the failed St. Louis County police. Soon Captain Ron Johnson of the Highway Patrol, an African American by the way, was leading a peaceful march rather than shooting or clubbing protestors. There was in Ferguson, in due time, some further trouble, again with complaints that law enforcement officers had instigated some of the violence. The response was a further deescalation, plotted very deliberately. Amnesty International was brought in to mediate.

Tensions have remained, but so far the lesson is how little of the trouble spread to other American locales, in part because the police around the country have taken a more measured and more professional approach than was initially the case in St. Louis County.

The legal authorities of the city of New York succeeded in defanging the Occupy Wall Street movement with a minimum of fuss. Rather than opting for outright confrontation, and perhaps some publicity victories for the protestors, a decision was made to wait for the winter to shut down the encampments and the protests. For instance, the New York City police kept a very careful watch over the main protest site, Zuccotti Park, once crowds started to gather there in the fall of 2011. They surrounded the site with police cars and set up a watchtower to keep a vigil over what was occurring. Various barricades were placed to keep pedestrians away from the site, and passersby were encouraged to "keep moving." Karen A. Franck and Te-Sheng Huang, who studied the event, noted: "The overriding concern appears to be the preservation of a high level of public order over all else, including the right to free speech." The protesters' original plan had been to occupy Chase Manhattan Plaza, but the police had prevented that altogether by the strategic use of barricades.[10]

As the "occupation" continued, city authorities threw new challenges at the protestors. But these were highly legalistic rather than a show of force. At first it was claimed that the plaza was dirty, and the protestors needed to be evicted to allow for a cleaning. The protestors in turn cleaned the plaza themselves. Nearby residents complained about late-night drumming, so the protestors negotiated a curfew on loud noise. The fire department then claimed that the gas generators being used by the crowd were a fire hazard, so the protestors switched to pedal-powered generators for much of their power. These struggles were legal and in part public relations battles, in contrast to the baton- and truncheon-wielding police tactics of the 1960s.[11]

The Occupy Wall Street activities did raise important constitutional questions, as the occupied space was in fact a private park, not a traditional public facility. The owner was Brookfield Properties, with the City

Planning Commission having a significant role in regulating the facility, in addition to a large body of applicable zoning law. One of these regulations was a twenty-four-hour access requirement, which is part of what enabled the occupiers to stake out a claim on the property. That said, tents and the storage of personal property were not permitted under the regulations. Nonetheless, the company and the city authorities worked together to ease out the protestors rather than to try to shut them down suddenly through forcible removal. This significant private-sector involvement made a violent attack on the protestors all the more unlikely, and it further regularized and bureaucratized the process of response to Occupy Wall Street. The underlying constitutional issues have yet to be adjudicated, but the on-the-ground reality is that Brookfield Properties and the City of New York ended up getting their way. Eventually the weather became colder, and Occupy Wall Street is now a kind of misty nostalgic footnote to history. If the ideas of that movement do take off, it likely will be through the educated and quite peaceful supporters of candidates like Bernie Sanders, not through public violence.[12]

Or consider the 2004 Democratic National Convention. As you might expect, there were numerous would-be demonstrators. They ended up being confined to a "Demonstration Zone," which one federal judge described as analogous to one of Piranesi's etchings of a prison. The zone was ringed by barricades, fences, and coiled razor wire. The demonstrators in the zone had no access to the delegates and no real ability to pass out materials, and no large signs were permitted in the area. Ultimately the protestors simply didn't show up in the Demonstration Zone. Where might civil rights be today, had the Selma protest been constrained in a similar fashion?[13]

The police strategies up through the 1970s have been described as a style of "escalated force." If the initial level of force didn't work in subduing the demonstrators, the strategy was to apply more force. Yet this often proved counterproductive, and it motivated further demonstrations and also a dislike for the police. Starting in the mid-1970s, the prevailing style has moved toward what has been called "negotiated management." In that approach, the police and protestors reach agreements in advance as to what kinds of actions will be permissible or not. And more recently, we've seen a new style sometimes called "strategic incapacitation," involving the creation of no-protest zones, the increased use of crowd-control techniques and nonlethal weapons, strategic advance arrests, and more surveillance and infiltration of the planned disturbance. Within that management style, the police often proceed by dividing up protest-vulnerable cities into hard zones, free-speech zones, and soft zones. In the hard zones are the targets of the protest, such as, say, the board members of the International Monetary Fund, and no protestors are allowed in or near these areas. The so-called free-speech zones are where the protests are allowed, but in a contained manner, and usually far away from the targets of the protest. The soft zones are near the hard zones, and entry is discouraged but not forbidden. These are the areas where conflict between the police and the protestors, if it does come about, is most likely to occur.[14]

Organizing and maintaining public opposition was tougher yet during the 2003 attempts to run New York City protests against the Iraq War. On February 15 of that year, the world saw the largest coordinated protests in history, with 30 million people demonstrating against the war all over the world. But in New York City things were not so simple. A quarter million people turned out to voice their displeasure, but the police had closed off the relevant streets and then used horses to chase people away from the protest sites. The city government also did not allow a march past the United Nations building, denying the permit on security grounds. In the end, a rally of 10,000 people was permitted in the Dag Hammerskjold Plaza, on 47th Street and First Avenue, about four blocks away from the UN. More generally, the New York City police had been denying permits for all marches for months, allowing only stationary demonstrations.[15]

Washington, DC, is in some ways even more restrictive. The National Park Service controls about 25 percent of the city, including many of the focal protest spots. For those locations, any protest of more than twenty-five people requires a permit. Furthermore, if the event is expected to be of any note, the protest organizers will be required to meet with the Park Police and possibly the Capitol Police to plan it out, accompanied by lawyers in many cases. Still further complications arise if the Secret Service is involved.[16]

And post 9/11, Washington, DC, protests face yet another problem: They are possible sanctuaries for terror attacks, or at least they are perceived as such. If the City Park Service or some other bureaucracy sees some possibility of a terror attack connected to a protest, or even believes that a facility or public locale may become slightly more vulnerable, it can deny permission for the event, very often with impunity. National security considerations usually trump all other arguments. The city has adopted a kind of bunker mentality. There are roadside and pedestrian barriers scattered around the city, restricting mobility, and they are not going away anytime soon. Those barriers both shape our society and reflect what significant parts of it already have become.[17]

It is by no means impossible to receive permission, but you have to work through the bureaucracy. There now exists a mini-industry of "protest planners," comparable to wedding or convention planners, and they charge fees to boot. They will help you coordinate with the police, set up stages and sound systems in the approved manner, and clean up after the event is over. These days, a DC protest is more of a bureaucratized event than anything else, and typically it is viewed by the media as such, or in other words it is ignored unless it has massive attendance. For better or worse, this whole process is a long way removed from the older custom of shouting and gathering an angry, demanding crowd in the local town square. When the Seattle antiglobalization protests broke out in 1999, the legal problems were not with the planned, registered assemblies but rather with the enthusiastic impromptu gatherings.[18]

Another change that favors stability over rebellion has been the greater likelihood of police, FBI, and national security establishment spying on those who are organizing domestic marches, following the passage of the Patriot Act of 2001. That makes many people hesitate before getting involved in protest activities, and, for the most part, the courts have not struck down this spying. There is also a much higher risk of protest activity being captured on closed circuit television, and in a way that may haunt individuals who plan later to go mainstream and succeed or maybe run for office. It is harder to get away with irresponsible behavior in public and harder to avoid being caught for any mistakes you might make in the heat of passion. These days, the truth about you is not so easily forgotten, and a lot of CCTV cameras, such as those on the National Mall in Washington, DC, are not too visible, so you never know when you are being watched.[19]

The federal government also has done its share to shut down protest. Even small protests are no longer permitted at the Jefferson Memorial, which was erected to celebrate a man who suggested that liberty periodically must be refreshed with struggle and "the blood of tyrants." In 2011, a District of Columbia Circuit Court of Appeals ruled that the Jefferson Memorial is not a public forum and thus not an eligible location for a political public gathering. There are now specified free-speech zones, often far from the main public venues, where demonstrations are to take place, and these zones do not usually include the spaces right next to presidential nominating conventions.

Americans perhaps have never had greater free-speech rights than today, as so many court cases have upheld the rights of the protestors. That's information space, so to speak. But when it comes to the geography or the physical breathing space for protest, matters are relatively grim. Protests and free-speech rights in actual physical space are more constrained than they have been in a long time.[20]

If there was any legal pointer in this direction, it came in the late 1970s and early 1980s, when the Supreme Court agreed that there could be rules limiting the geographic distribution of protest. The Court allowed for a categorization of places through what is now called the "public forum doctrine." It's not enough that free speech be "compatible" with a specified geographic area; that area also should be a properly designated forum for speech. Whether the full practical consequences of these decisions were foreseen is a moot point, but it seems voters and citizens are not screaming for a redo. The current state of tight physical restrictions on the geographical expression of free speech by protestors is popular and, most of all, not contested very successfully. After all, it keeps neighborhood nuisances, noise, and traffic jams to an acceptable minimum. It's NIMBY all over again—let them protest somewhere else.[21]

Compare this to the portrait painted by Harry Kalven Jr. in his 1965 classic *Negro and the First Amendment*. About the state of the law at that time, Kalven wrote: "[T]he speaker has a paramount claim to the use of the public forum which the state can subject to minimal traffic controls and to breach of peace limitations." The case *Edwards v. South Carolina*, decided by the Supreme Court in 1963, determined that a demonstration of African American students on state house grounds had the right to proceed, on the basis that it was in a public space that those same individuals otherwise had a right to enter. Justice Stewart, writing for all of the Court members but one, stated that the defendants were pursuing "rights of free speech, free assembly, and freedom to petition or redress of their grievances . . . The circumstances of this case reflect an exercise of these basic constitutional rights in their most pristine and classic form." That time period was a high-water mark for the freedom of assembly in American history. If you look at the major march scheduled for that year, the March on Washington, it enjoyed a freedom of movement that today would be very difficult to reproduce.[22]

It's not just the law that has changed; the incentives of the organizers are now fundamentally different. When a major public event is orchestrated, such as the Million Man March of 1995, it tends to be backed by a lot of organization and capital investment. That in turn requires a lot of mainstream support. Unlike the days of the Black Panthers, today's social protest can no longer be a shoestring operation based on cheap labor, a lot of walking, and some guns. For today's events, you need planners, operatives, and "nudgers"—on the side of the marchers—to make sure everything remains peaceful and to guarantee that the images on television are positive. More recently, social media consultants have been added to the mix, so there isn't that much room for the spontaneous throw of a brick. For the Million Man March, the whole point was to show public images of black males behaving peaceably and responsibly, and largely it succeeded. The police and security forces, in turn, also wanted to win the public relations battle, and that meant reacting peacefully to potential trouble rather than being ready to knock heads, as easily could have been the case a few decades earlier. If you look for the word *conflict* on the Wikipedia page devoted to this event, the relevant conflict was over the size of the crowd, as March backers wanted to argue they had a very large turnout, again for purposes of publicity. More recently, a viral video may do more for a cause than a very large demonstration, and of course it can reach a larger number of people.

This intensification and placidification of the publicity machine has been a major factor behind the calming of American participation and protest, which had been ongoing since the 1970s. (Later I consider whether this trend is being reversed today.) In the 1960s, the challenge was to capture the attention of America, given that the country was coming out of the staid 1950s, network television dominated the media landscape, and the core mindset was quite conservative. That system of centralized media favored relatively radical steps, including large marches and sometimes violence and extremist stances. In the new millennium, getting *some* attention is never that hard, and just about every group coordinates its followers through the internet. The new problem is taking your group's niche message and breaking through to respectability. Doing so encourages orderly, orchestrated events, based on a deliberate and calculated appeal to mainstream sentiment, and that in turn boosts the incentive for a peaceful, indeed sometimes soporific, event.

The very capital costs of having to run media and publicity teams turn demonstrations all the more in the mainstream direction. Those costs are much higher today compared to many of the ramshackle protests of the 1960s or early 1970s. This restricts most effective protests to groups that have a fair amount of up-front cash, which again serves as a moderating influence because it means the groups likely have to court some mainstream support. The complacent class very often has explicit bureaucratization on its side, but the most effective filters stem from the old-fashioned constraints of the pocketbook. As society and the law become more complex, many protest activities rise in cost, thus providing another channel for the encouragement of peace. Bureaucracy, whatever its other goals may be, is very much on the side of the complacent class.

HOW A DYNAMIC SOCIETY LOOKS AND FEELS

Through most of these chapters, I have been careful to rely on numbers and statistics, albeit buttressed by anecdotal evidence and also my own personal observations. In this chapter, I'd like to loosen up a bit and offer some more purely subjective impressions. These arguments are not as rigorous as those supported by numbers, but still they are an important part of why I believe we are living through a time of the ascendancy of the complacent class.

I have visited China many times over the past five years, for a different book project, and what I've observed there has made America's social stagnation increasingly clear to me. That was one reason why I came to write this book. Even with its recent economic troubles, China has a culture of ambition and dynamism and a pace of change that hearken back to a much earlier America. China, even though it is in the midst of some rather serious economic troubles, makes today's America seem staid and static. For all of its flaws, China is a country where every time you return, you find a different and mostly better version of what you had left the time before. Hundreds or thousands of new buildings will be in place, the old restaurants will be gone, and what were major social and economic problems a few years ago, such as unfinished roads or missing water connections, will have disappeared or been leapfrogged. That is what life is like when a country grows at about 10 percent a year for over thirty years running, as indeed China had been doing up through 2009 or so, with some years of 7 to 8 percent growth thereafter (and an unknown rate of growth today, due to lack of trust in the government's numbers). When a country's growth rate is 10 percent, it's as if a new country is being built every seven years or so, because that is how long it takes for such a nation to double in economic size.

The United States, of course, has a fully mature economy that lies on what economists call "the technological frontier"—that is, we can't just grow by borrowing from more advanced nations because in terms of technology there aren't any. America cannot grow at 10 percent a year, no matter what policies the country adopts, or even 5 percent a year. Nonetheless, just as previous generations saw America through the lens of Europe and European culture, so will forthcoming generations understand America through the lens of China and, to a lesser extent, the other major emerging economies, such as India. And such a contrast will draw attention to the relatively static sides of the United States.

Just as America's confrontation with the Soviet Union brought out its attachment to individual liberty and gave that quality greater importance on both the domestic and world stages, so will America's engagement with China and the other emerging economies shape how Americans perceive themselves and what kind of role the nation plays on the world stage. And so far that has been clear: America is the calm, safe-haven country, with clear blue skies, clean air, freedom of speech, and a reliable currency. That's great, but it is also a static picture of calm and predictability. On the global stage, safety is becoming more and more the American niche, and it is no surprise that America is now seen as one of the world's leading bank and tax havens.

Some brief biographies bring out the differences between America and China when it comes to dynamism, mobility, and complacency.

Jack Ma, who became the richest man in China in 2014, started off life really, really poor. He was born in 1964 into extremely unfavorable family circumstances. His grandfather had been an officer in the

Nationalist Party, and thus he was persecuted by the Chinese Communists. The whole family suffered at that time. His parents were musicians/storytellers, a profession banned during Chairman Mao's Cultural Revolution in the 1960s. These jobs were in any case not paths to riches, even in an economy where per capita income in the 1960s was perhaps no more than $200 a year.[1] Ma's childhood was one of the utmost material deprivation, and the political environment was insecure as well.

Ma worked hard early in his life, and he often got up at 5 a.m. to walk or bicycle to a nearby hotel so he could meet tourists and practice his English; this was later to prove very useful. But still he didn't get ahead. He was rejected for dozens of jobs, including at Kentucky Fried Chicken, a popular brand in China. He was rejected for university admission several times, although eventually he did graduate with a degree in English and went on to teach English at university level. He didn't touch a computer until he was thirty-three years old, and the first time he tried to load a web page, to try to prove to his friends and family that the internet actually existed, it took three and a half hours for half a page to come up.

Eventually he got his start building web pages for Chinese companies, with the help of some American friends. In 1999, he started Alibaba, and by 2014, his net wealth registered in the range of $30 billion, making him one of the world's richest men. (It has since declined but remains very high.)

In Jack Ma's original life setting, there was nowhere to go but up. Obviously most Chinese did not earn as much money as Ma, or even come close, but many of those who did also came from very humble backgrounds. Some of that phenomenon is simple logic: In the 1960s and 1970s, apart from a small Communist Party elite, just about everyone in China was poor.

Consider Liu Yonghao, who went around barefoot when he was young and worked carrying buckets of human excrement to serve as fertilizer. He later founded New Hope Group, one of China's largest agribusiness companies, and today is a very wealthy man, worth $4.8 billion by one estimate. He was very pleased, when he was young, to acquire a job as a government teacher. Eventually his family sold a watch and a bicycle to raise the funds to start a small poultry business. The rest is history, as they say.

Weng Wenyin was one of the casualties of the Cultural Revolution, and his family took a long time to recover. He reports that before the age of twenty, he never had proper shoes and was almost always hungry. When he started his first business, he was living out of a cement pipe. He later founded Amer International Group, which supplies cable and copper products, and he has been listed as China's fourteenth wealthiest man.

American rags-to-riches stories are much harder to find these days. You can certainly find riches—look at someone like Mark Zuckerberg. But he hardly grew up in rags. Simply put, these days not many, if any, Americans are starting out their lives in the kind of poverty that Jack Ma experienced as a kid. That sounds good, and indeed it is good, but it also means that wealthy, comfortable societies have less dynamism and churn, and that is going to mean much more complacency.

In the 1990s, it was a common view that with all of our new technologies—most of all the internet—income mobility would rise, including in the United States. The idea was that universal access to the internet would make it possible for more people to rise to riches, perhaps by lowering the cost of marketing new products, starting new businesses, or marketing themselves in new and unusual ways. And indeed we have seen such developments, but they don't seem to be that egalitarian. That is, internet marketing is helping people from wealthier families at about the same pace that previous advances had, and thus American income mobility is holding roughly constant, as I discussed in chapter 4. That is hardly a catastrophe, but it is a sign that America is not becoming more dynamic, at least not in terms of elevating poor people at a higher pace than before.

Commentators give plenty of reasons for the longer-term decline in American income mobility, including greater social stratification, competition with cheaper labor abroad, the increasing need for advanced skills and training necessitated by technology, the overregulation and ossification of the American economy, the decline of labor unions, and the increase in power for privileged elites. I won't go through these debates again, which I covered in an earlier book, *Average Is Over*, but many of these factors are indeed relevant. I'd like to focus on a more general point, namely that the basic tendency in a mature economy is for income mobility to eventually decline and then perhaps stay roughly constant. In other words, there is an underlying cyclicality to the dynamism of many societies. Societies that initially are dynamic, by the very nature of their ongoing successes, become less dynamic and more complacent over time.

Ongoing dynamism may in fact require a significant amount of strife and recurring troubles. To draw out a contrast with contemporary America, let's imagine an economy that has been ruined by war or communism or by a natural disaster, or maybe it is just starting out in a very poor place, like Jack Ma's China. In such an economy, almost everyone earns close to subsistence. That is true for the ambitious and the less ambitious and for the talented and the less talented.

Now imagine that such an economy reforms, improves, or otherwise moves onto a track with a lot of economic growth and opportunity. Over the course of the next generation, a fantastic number of people will rise from poverty to riches, as indeed we have seen in the emerging economies. In these economies, measured social and economic mobility will be extremely high, and that will correspond to some very favorable developments. In fact, measured mobility pretty much has to be high, because almost everyone who became rich came from a relatively poor family in the previous generation. As that country moves from poverty to wealth, it is unlikely that the basic income rankings of families will be preserved.

But think about these societies as time passes. In just about every case, we can expect cross-generational mobility to decline, even if these societies do everything right. The transmission mechanism here is that some of the qualities behind income success are heritable or at least passed down through families in some manner. For instance, intelligence, ambition, conscientiousness, and some personality traits all seem to possess some degree of heritability or at least intergenerational transmission. We have perhaps the best estimates for intelligence, and there the degree of heritability seems to run in the range of 40 to 60 percent, depending on which studies you consult. But even if you think those numbers are too high, it is pretty obvious that wealthier families pass along more education and better work habits to their children, even if genes have nothing to do with it. To put it bluntly, most successful social structures are pretty good at reproducing themselves.[2]

Given this fact, with each generation there will be pressures for mobility to decline, even if society remains fully open in terms of opportunity. The first generation of rich people—say, the Jack Mas—will have children, and on average their children will have higher levels of talent, ambition, and so on. Of course, Jack Ma's rather privileged children also will have greater opportunities. It no longer will be the case that all of the rich people of the next generation came from poor backgrounds. Some of them will have been born into Jack Ma's family or other wealthy families. Or maybe you think that the children of billionaires are lazy, spoiled brats (not my view), but even then there are today plenty of non-billionaire but higher-earning Chinese who will be producing the next generation of millionaires and billionaires. Those families are already working very hard to get their kids into Harvard and other very good schools, and those stories may be middle class to riches, but they won't be rags to riches.

As each generation proceeds, the most successful people will come more and more from pretty successful families, and that will be the case even if nothing corrupt or unfair is going on. Short of having another war or major catastrophe, there is just no way that, in this kind of setting, the third or fourth generation of wealthy people will all come directly from poor backgrounds. Matching and assortative mating—connecting one well-off family to another—may make this all the less likely. And thus we can see some very natural reasons why income mobility, across the generations, is often either stagnant or declining over time. To use the language of early twentieth-century Italian economist Vilfredo Pareto, over time, the "circulation of elites" will naturally decline, at least compared to earlier situations of poverty and chaos. And indeed in China today, the special privileges held by children of prominent Communist Party members have become a major social issue and source of complaint.

In other words, the richer, more stable, and happier your society is, the harder it is to generate high or rising levels of income mobility over time. Mobility itself becomes immobile, and that too is an ongoing source of stasis.

We typically think of income mobility as something desirable, and in some key ways it is—who doesn't like the idea of a hardworking but poor kid getting ahead? Isn't that the American dream? That said, a very high level of measured income mobility can be a symptom of some very unfavorable developments, such as that a society recently experienced a catastrophic crisis or leveling event. Similarly, a lower rate of intergenerational income mobility can be a symptom of social and economic stability, and such stability, whatever its limitations, is something a lot of us are working pretty hard to achieve.

For a clearer look at the downside of high mobility, consider international comparisons of mobility across countries. It can be difficult to get good data on income mobility for previously poor or chaotic countries because of problems with data and record keeping. Nonetheless, I know of one fairly good index of educational mobility across a wide swath of countries, including many with checkered pasts, and it confirms that high mobility can be a symptom of trouble. The countries with the least educational mobility have some serious problems in their fights against poverty, and those places include (in order) Peru, Ecuador, Panama, Chile, and Brazil. The three regions with the greatest educational mobility, however, have generally lower living standards, and they are rural Ethiopia, rural China, and Kyrgyzstan. To some extent, the high mobility in these places is a sign of almost everyone in the earlier generation having started off from a bad status quo, and therein we can see that high intergenerational mobility is not always something to be envied.[3]

There is yet another way of thinking about American mobility, mostly optimistic, and that involves international comparisons from a different angle, namely that of immigration. The very good news is that America's income mobility is in reality much higher than standard measures indicate.

There is one key area in which virtually all statistics on income mobility are misleading: They evaluate within-country mobility only, considering, say, the difference between the income of my father's household and the income of my household. They then estimate how well one variable predicts the other. But imagine that an individual moves from Mexico to the United States, as so commonly happens. The Mexican income of that person's father will not show up in these studies, which capture data on American incomes only. Yet that migration brings about a big step up from one Mexican generation to the succeeding Mexican American generation. Since a poor Mexican household might only be earning a few thousand dollars of income a year, even a move to a "mediocre" U.S. job paying $22,000 is a lot of upward mobility. And indeed there are plenty of Mexican Americans earning about 22k a year who also are sending money home. On top of that, many immigrants to the United States come from countries poorer than Mexico, including much of Central America and many parts of Africa and Southeast Asia.

The data do not indicate how large an effect that is likely to be, but according to one estimate, 40 percent of Fortune 500 companies were founded by immigrants or their children. Eighteen percent were founded by immigrants themselves. That's a lot of upward income mobility that isn't being captured by the available numbers.[4]

Any country with a lot of immigration will have much more upward mobility than its published numbers indicate. And if you look at the United States today, about 13 percent of the population is foreign-born, the highest level since the 1920s. For the most part, these people came from poorer countries, and thus that is a lot of unmeasured upward mobility.

So if you read a comparison between, say, the United States and Denmark claiming that intergenerational mobility is higher in Denmark, that comparison is either wrong or at the very least misleading. Denmark hasn't elevated nearly as many immigrants, in either absolute or percentage terms, as America. At most Denmark has more income mobility for its ongoing domestic generations who are staying within the country. When it comes to international comparisons of income mobility, the United States gets a bad rap because, whether you like it or not, this country specializes in upward mobility for immigrants.

What is the broader lesson here? It is not, I think, that migrants are stealing all of the upward movement away from Americans. If you look at America's earlier period of very high immigration, early in the twentieth century, domestic intergenerational mobility was probably high too, from what we can tell. Quick question: If your family has been in America for a few generations, and you are ambitious, are you really considering moving to a region of the country with very few immigrants? How about West Virginia or eastern Kentucky? Probably not.

I would put it this way: Upward income mobility is something Americans are leaving to foreigners and migrants more and more. Good for them if they can take advantage of these opportunities and along the way create more opportunities for others, as Sergei Brin did by helping to build Google.

But still there is a downside, namely that those who are rising in income are less culturally central to the United States than might be ideal. As we'll see, this instance reflects the general pattern that America is outsourcing a lot of its dynamism. Americans who have lived here for a few generations or more are probably culturally more central and more influential than recent arrivals, at least on average. They are more likely to be citizens, more likely to vote, and more likely to participate in civil society, including running for office. I don't intend any criticism of the immigrants on those points; it's understandable that they are spending their energies on providing for their families. A lot of the immigrants aren't citizens yet, and many are working very hard to get ahead and have less discretionary time to devote to volunteering and the local bake sale. In fact, their greater focus on earning more is part of what boosts their dynamism.

So overall, America is building its core culture and norms and politics more and more around people and families who just aren't that mobile across the generations and who have a relatively static and stratified sense of how things work, which indeed is a pattern they see in their own lives. In other words, we are building our core norms and culture around the complacent class, even though some very different tendencies exist in the America of today.

THE SPREAD OF THAT STATIC FEEL

What I find striking about contemporary America is how much we are slowing things down, how much we are digging ourselves in, and how much we are investing in stability.

In intellectual terms, I feel lucky to have been born in 1962, because that year straddles two very different times and perspectives. I very well recall the turmoil of the early 1970s, the riots, and the Vietnam War, in addition to the Watergate scandal. I grew up in a New Jersey and New York world of political turmoil, the dominance of the car, and a sense that safety was never entirely guaranteed. At that time, few people expected that America would end up as such a calm place again. If I really wanted to find out a piece of information, I had to drive to a library, or sometimes I would telephone a library and ask a librarian for assistance. He or she would have to call me back, because finding out the information—if that was possible at all—would involve looking at physical books, or maybe even ordering books from another library. My intellectual ambition was to read as many of the Western classics as possible: mostly big books that required sustained, repeated attention and a lot of careful study. In the meantime, I drove around visiting used book stores in Washington, Philadelphia, New York City, and other spots in the Northeast.

Since then I've evolved into a work life spent largely in information space. I've blogged every day for over twelve years, am active on Twitter, and write for many online outlets. I can go for a month without visiting a physical library, even when I don't have my research assistant around to make book-carrying trips for me. If need be, I find books online and click to buy used copies on Amazon, and I visit used book stores only every now and then. I can stay at home and all of that information will just come to me.

I feel very lucky to have lived a significant number of years in each world; in fact, I am likely part of the last generation to be able to say this. As you well know, the dominant influence on kids growing up today is information space. We've all seen that (online) video of the three-year-old holding a copy of a magazine and trying to swipe it with a finger as if it were an iPad or smartphone.

That said, I do not regret the passing of the world of my youth. I am very much enjoying this new America, in part because I feel my dynamic upbringing put me in a position to be relatively successful, both financially and in terms of knowing how to access information and resources. I enjoy the greater safety of the current world, compared to the Manhattan I grew up with, where even the Upper East Side was not a sure haven. I also can see just how many people are benefiting from today's greater access to information, and in this world, in part because information is so freely available, there has been a spread of rights to many different kinds of minorities.

This relatively recent emphasis on security pops up in so many forms, many of them extremely beneficial for our lives. For instance, the acceptance of gay marriage has proved a big (and to me pleasant) surprise. As recently as 2008, neither Barack Obama nor Hillary Clinton would endorse national gay marriage, and they both openly expressed reservations about the idea. Of the two parties, the Democrats have been much more pro–gay marriage than the Republicans, but still, the two candidates for their party's nomination seemed to think the nation just wasn't ready. They, like I, had underestimated how strong the appetite of the American public was for bundled mixes of justice and stability, as was manifested in the legalization of gay marriage. As you probably know, in 2015, a Republican-majority Supreme Court voted to make gay marriage legal across the nation and basically settled the entire issue.[5]

Public intellectual and blogger Andrew Sullivan had been advocating for gay marriage since the 1990s. But even within the Democratic Party, the reaction was often to discourage Sullivan or to view him as having a futile, quixotic obsession. The view was that the idea was too far away from reality, it could hurt the Democratic Party electorally to be too closely associated with the "gay cause," and perhaps other discrimination issues, involving women or African Americans, should receive more attention. At that time, it seemed that the gay marriage idea just wasn't going anywhere. In reality, gay marriage was the cause most closely connected to stability, and it rose to a fairly rapid triumph, most of all relative to expectations.

Even within the community of gay and LGBT intellectuals, the gay marriage movement was not entirely popular. Michael Warner, for instance, a leading "queer theorist," argued that marriage was too conservative an institution and what the gay community needed instead was a radical liberation from the idea of shame. Warner wanted straights to learn from the sexual practices of gays at the time, including the idea of promiscuity as it had been attributed to the male gay community. Most of all, he disliked the idea, promulgated by Andrew Sullivan and also Jonathan Rauch, that full legal marriage would in some sense tame or civilize many of the gay communities in the United States, and for the better. Like Barack Obama and Hillary Clinton, Warner underestimated the hunger of Americans for comfort and stability. Now the debate is over and the views of Warner have almost disappeared, as the conservative defenses of gay marriage have become so common and universal they don't receive much of a second thought in most liberal circles.[6]

I've found more and more that, in modern America, whenever we argue for doing something virtuous—and I don't mean this in a cynical way—we will find something deeply calming, stabilizing, and risk-reducing beneath the surface.

I also see the new and more static America showing up in our physical infrastructure. I see it in building styles, town layouts, and home interiors. All stay within a pretty staid range of styles—gone are the days of modernist rebellion, as had marked earlier parts of the twentieth century. Hardly anyone sets out to shock these days, because at this point that's almost impossible to do, given how long the avant-garde and the rebels have been part of the mainstream in the worlds of art, architecture, and visual design.

I also observe an essentially calm and soothing aesthetic in how people dress. Some of the stasis in American mobility has come—counterintuitively—through American individualism, American comfort, and, believe it or not, its increasingly casual culture. The more casual culture of dress while at work is one example of this. The relaxation of dress codes in many companies and social settings is one striking way how today's America generates a mix of extreme tolerance, relative immobility, and extreme segregation—or shall I call it matching?—according to talents and skills. The less strict the dress code, in fact the harder it is to look good and to fit in, and that disadvantages those who are not from well-educated and successful backgrounds.

Fashion is but one example of how the American wealthy have been redefining social status through a practice known as countersignaling. Countersignaling is when you go out of your way to show you don't need to go out of your way. The boss doesn't have to wear a tie or even dress up. If he did, that would suggest he had something to prove, which would be a negative rather than a positive impression. The next step is that the vice presidents also don't have to dress up, and soon enough most of the company doesn't have to dress up.

Similarly, titles such as Dr. and Professor are no longer thrown around with such force, and their excessive use comes off as an overstatement or an embarrassment. Country clubs seem passé. Jackets and ties are now anachronisms in most of Manhattan's top restaurants, and if anything, they are likely to reflect the relative poverty rather than the wealth of a visitor to Le Bernardin—maybe it's a very young man trying to impress a date or a middle manager dressing up so as not to offend a Japanese client.

Americans at the top have become the experts in countersignaling, because they don't feel they have to impress anyone. Everything is now casual, because the new aristocracy of talent enforces all the conformity that is needed. The wealthy have set this tone, most of all in America's highest-glamour Silicon Valley tech sector. Americans were never a culture of monocles, war medals, and dapper moustaches in the first place; in his day, Alexis de Tocqueville noted a strong American skepticism toward the practice of the duel.

But don't be fooled—this new form of status-seeking is no less oppressive than older practices, and in some ways it is less conducive to upward mobility. The problem is this: If everything is casual, what exactly do you do to show your seriousness? Bill Gates wears khaki pants and enjoys McDonald's, but he has achieved renown as the world's richest man and one of its most influential philanthropists. He can countersignal all he wants, and he is still Bill Gates and obviously so. A variety of other billionaires and millionaires, or Nobel laureates, carry their reputations with them too. Recognition is never more than an act of Google away, and so the American notion of class is based all the more on what a person already has done, and the class distinctions are enforced ultimately not by snobby matrons who run social circles but rather by the act of Googling itself.

If you're twenty-four years old and looking to get ahead, it can be tougher. There isn't such a simple way to visually demonstrate you are determined to join the ranks of the upwardly mobile. Looking smart on "casual Friday" may get you a better date, but the boss will not sit up and take notice. In other words, a culture of the casual is a culture of people who already have achieved something and who already can prove it. It is a culture of the static and the settled, the opposite of Tocqueville's restless Americans.

In an art gallery or some other high-end retail outlet, the dealers and directors know that very often the biggest spenders walk in the door wearing jeans and sneakers. Those who show up in the suit and tie are less likely to drop $10 million on a Basquiat, as the choice of formal garb signals they still have something to prove. But if you're just hanging out in a train station and watching travelers pass by, you probably won't think the same lofty thoughts about those people in the jeans and sneakers; instead, you would sooner assume that those with the suits and ties have more money. The upshot is this: When it comes to signaling and judging status, significant parts of America are becoming more like the art gallery and less like the train station.

Since the 1960s, the cultures that have produced the most upward economic mobility include Japan, South Korea, and China, due to their supercharged rates of economic growth. It is no accident that these are the same cultures obsessed with business cards, stereotypical blue suits, submission to hierarchical authority, and bringing the perfect gift, among other customs. The young and ambitious really can set themselves apart from the slackers, even if doing so looks conformist and stifling when multiplied and observed on a larger scale. Societies of upward mobility, when based on large and growing business enterprises, look and feel somewhat oppressive. Much as many of us might not want to admit it, the casual and the egalitarian are closer to enemies than to allies.

Good matches are lots of fun, but in a country with so much social stagnation and extremely good matching, eventually we become aware that we too are most of the time being turned away at the gate.

8.

POLITICAL STAGNATION, THE DWINDLING OF TRUE DEMOCRACY, AND ALEXIS DE TOCQUEVILLE AS PROPHET OF OUR TIME

Anti-establishment insurgent campaigns were the talk of the 2016 presidential campaign, and both Donald Trump and Bernie Sanders were legitimate anti-establishment candidates. But a peek beneath the surface reveals that much of the fear and anger that drove their campaigns was based not on a hope for change in Washington but on a hope for a return to the past. Trump's rhetoric about "making America great again" was, when you looked at the fine print, mostly a promise that in electing him, voters could avoid the forces of change that are sweeping over the rest of the world, whether it be the loss of manufacturing jobs, an increasing dependence on immigrants, or the loss of the political and cultural dominance of white men. His argument for making a better deal on behalf of America was little more than a recipe for de facto stasis, supposedly funded for free by better trade deals and rooting out fraud and waste.

It's easy enough to single out Trump for his campaign promises, but it's important to recognize that stasis has been the defining characteristic of our government for some time now. And that begins with the way our spending is allocated. The basic problem is that so much of the money gets allocated and locked in to programs that are politically untouchable and that grow more or less on automatic pilot with rising enrollments and costs.

More and more of the budget is consumed by Social Security, Medicare, and Medicaid, which are far more likely to grow in their expenses than shrink. (Trump, by the way, promised not to cut these programs at all.) Congress sets the core content of these programs and then expenditures rise as the population ages; inflation increases, thereby activating indexing provisions; and health care costs increase. Those three programs, taken together, now constitute *49 percent* of the federal budget, and this number is slated to continue to rise over the next several decades, no matter which political party wins the next few rounds of elections.[1]

Short of major tax increases, only half of our budget is left for everything else, including defense spending and paying interest on the national debt, two categories also characterized by significant lock-in effects. What remains is taken up by so-called discretionary spending— that is, programs subject to regular political decisions based on priorities. Two examples of discretionary spending are federal government support for the arts (e.g., the National Endowment for the Arts) and for science (e.g., the National Science Foundation). Naturally, given the inflexible nature of spending on Medicare, Medicaid, and Social Security and locked-in expenditure growth, politicians typically have to cut discretionary spending in their budgets—this has been true even for the budgetary plans of President Obama, a relatively left-leaning president. It's not that President Obama has been personally opposed to government discretionary spending; rather, the pull of the automatic spending is too difficult to resist, and those parts of the budget eat up more and more of government revenue every year. Since politicians are also reluctant to raise most taxes or to significantly boost the budget deficit for too many years in a row, federal government discretionary spending has ended up on a downward trajectory.

These political realities show up in concrete numbers. For instance, the Steuerle-Roeper Fiscal Democracy Index measures how much of American fiscal decisions are being determined by current democratic procedures as opposed to automatic pilot. As C. Eugene Steuerle defines it: "This index measures the extent to which past and future projected revenues are already claimed by the permanent programs that are now in place (including interest payments on the debt). The fiscal democracy index is neutral; it favors neither a liberal nor conservative agenda."[2]

The index presents a sobering picture. In 1962, about two-thirds of all federal government expenditures fell under the heading of fiscal democracy, namely they were not predetermined by permanent programs. In the mid-1960s, this number started falling steeply, and by 1982, it was below 30 percent. The low point for this index came in 2009, during the recession, when it turned negative. For that year, every dollar of revenue coming in the door—and then some—already had been committed by previous decisions of Congress. Of course, to make ends meet, the federal government had to borrow more money. Circa 2014, the index stood at about 20 percent, and it is slated to fall well below 10 percent by 2022, given projected demographics. It is hard to see how the United States might escape this dynamic.

If anything, the problem will become worse. For instance, the U.S. federal budget would be even less free for discretionary allocation if current interest rates were not so low, as the low interest rates mean U.S. government interest payments on its debt are very low. Under plausible projections from the Office of Management and Budget, which consider the possibility of higher interest rates in the future, interest payments on the debt would go from their current 6 percent of the federal budget up to about 13.5 percent of the budget. That would represent a further loss of fiscal democracy because there is no real choice about whether to pay that interest, and so even less money would be left over for other choices.[3]

On one hand, this loss of budgetary control can be considered a democratic outcome. One could argue that entitlements are consuming more of the U.S. federal budget because our representatives are voting for what we collectively are demanding, and that seems to be true.

But the problem is in the longer run. Overall, a low level of fiscal democracy is a sign of stasis and a lack of investment in thinking boldly about the future. Over the next few decades, the world is likely to change a lot, but the U.S. federal budget much less so. So if we think about that mix for a moment—a changing world and yet a government and also a budget of stasis—what kind of dynamism can we expect from the country as a whole? Keep in mind that government is both a cause and a reflection of broader social priorities, and so the notion of a government on autopilot should not come as a total surprise in a society where so many other things are static too.

Yet all along the way, a locked-in budget will not seem like a disaster to many of the most influential Americans. For the more successful members of the complacent class, their incomes are rising due to their own efforts, and social order seems to be staying in place. They may regret that things are not "better yet," and very often they themselves are the most vociferous advocates for greater discretionary spending from government. Still, it just doesn't seem that pressing compared to, say, how the 1960s radicals responded to the Vietnam War. It does, in fact, seem that most of the country is getting along OK, an impression that has been dented only lately with the surprise political ascent of Donald Trump or in the United Kingdom the Brexit movement. And so this process has continued, because the lock-in effects are much stronger than the forces seeking to break from this pattern.

This process ultimately becomes a malfunction of democracy. The standard arguments for democracy stress system flexibility and also error correction mechanisms. Even if democratic governments do not start off with the right policies, they are supposed to be able to shift to those policies over time, based on feedback and ultimately accountability to the electorate. That makes sense, and it reminds me of Winston Churchill's famous adage, "You can always count on Americans to do the right thing—after they've tried everything else." Yet how much can this argument count for when we observe democratic budgets, and thus such a big chunk of democratic policies, simply repeating year after year? What we've lost is in fact the ability to "try everything else" and so we never get to Churchill's "right thing."

Another way of measuring this stasis, and lack of flexibility, is to consider the share of federal government expenditures as part of the economy. If we look at the time period 1965 to 2014, the historical average is that federal spending is 20.1 percent of GDP and federal revenues average 17.4 percent of GDP. And how do things stand today? Well, federal spending in 2014 was 20.3 percent of GDP and revenues were 17.5 percent of GDP, both remarkably close to their historical averages. These may or may not be the numbers we ought to have, but they seem to have hit pretty stable levels.[4]

Furthermore, Americans are using most of this government revenue to make their lives safer and more predictable. It's a common view that the Western European nations have well-developed welfare states while the United States enforces a kind of cutthroat social Darwinism. That caricature is far from the truth. It is true that often the United States deploys social welfare funds wastefully or inefficiently, but the American government still spends plenty relative to Europe on protecting its citizenry against risk, or at least the American government is trying to do so, and that is unlikely to change.

Consider a simple comparison: The American government spends more on Americans' health care (per capita) than the French government spends on their entire health care system (again in per capita terms). It is a fair criticism that some individuals are left out of this coverage, or perhaps too much is sent to doctors and hospitals, but using some very plausible metrics, the American government is more involved in health care than is the French government.[5]

Alternatively, consider some measurements of the social spending of various developed nations. If you just add up direct government expenditures on social programs as a percentage of GDP, the United States comes out toward the lower end of the scale, with France, Finland, Belgium, and Denmark leading the way. That fits in with the traditional picture of America being a social welfare laggard of sorts. But if we look at what are called tax expenditures, the picture shifts radically. Tax expenditures refer to the use of the tax system to induce individuals or corporations to take one set of decisions rather than another, and they include tax-favored private charity, tax-favored pensions, tax-favored health insurance, and a variety of other benefits that the American government has a large *indirect* hand in encouraging. Here is the bottom line, according to the OECD (again in per capita terms): "In the United States public social spending is relatively low, but total social spending is the second highest in the world." In other words, American governments go to great lengths to make their citizens feel safe and protected; they are just more likely to use the tax system than direct expenditures. And if you add in defense spending as a kind of broader social protection, against both foreign aggression and terrorism, the American government invests in safety all the more, in this regard more than any other country in the world, including in per capita terms.[6]

In the 1990s, the federal budget also was somewhat static, though less so than today. Yet state and local governments expanded their spending a lot, and so American government was pretty flexible at some of the lower, less centralized levels. More recently, rising health care costs and thus rising Medicaid costs have put a big crimp in most state budgets. It's also expensive to keep so many people in jail, and K–12 schooling expenditures are politically popular and in any case hard to avoid. State governments are experimenting less at the policy level, and very often the main state-level budget question is either (a) How do we deal with the excess promises we made through our pension system? and/or (b) How rapidly should the state colleges and universities be losing state funds? Those are some pretty depressing questions.

It is not just the budget where American politicians are running away from accountability and clear votes for their decisions, it is also that most fundamental function of government: war and peace. When it comes to foreign policy, Congress typically prefers to avoid voting on military actions abroad. For instance, the United States undertook a limited engagement in Libya, starting in 2011, without official congressional approval. President Obama did discuss this matter with congressional leaders, and he had enough support from both parties to proceed with the intervention without creating major pushback from Capitol Hill. But after the highly unpopular Iraq war, representatives did not want to be burdened by a "war vote," instead preferring plausible deniability. This is a far cry from the post-Vietnam 1970s, when Congress stipulated that the president could not act abroad without explicit authorization. Congress is walking away from its constitutional and democratic responsibilities. "Creative ambiguity" is often a much easier game to play than taking a publicly recorded and registered stand. The resulting lack of accountability means that if something goes wrong, well, not that much in politics has to change in response.

While some people do protest this situation and call for more engaged debate, most do not. At the end of the day, there is a complacency about this issue, because in the meantime life in the United States just doesn't seem that bad. It doesn't feel like this is an especially pressing issue requiring resolution *today*, and so we pile up more and more issues of this kind, namely ones not requiring resolution just right now. The end result is likely to be that we lose our capacity to resolve them at all, whether today, tomorrow, or any other time in the future.

Since Libya, we've seen a similar logic play itself out in Syria and Iraq: again, some U.S. military involvement on uncertain terms and with uncertain explicit authorization from Congress. Across the broader world, how many drone strikes in Pakistan or Yemen does the American government have to run before it might be the case that, at least by the standards of an earlier America, a congressional vote would be required for an explicit declaration of war? My guess is we'll never find out. It's not that we're too divided, as in some cases of government gridlock; rather it's that we, taken collectively, just don't seem to care enough to force a definite resolution.

Again, in one sense these procedures are highly democratic. Voters, after all, could elect representatives who would refuse to shirk on their voting responsibilities, but they don't. Congressional incumbents are reelected at high rates, often at or above 90 percent, and that is even when approval ratings for Congress are abysmal. In other ways, however, the process is not very democratic at all. The normal link between political decisions and accountability has been broken, and voters have responded by giving the U.S. Congress a 7 percent approval rating, possibly headed lower. Voters have an abstract desire to end the congressional flight from accountability, but on so many particular issues it just doesn't seem pressing to the complacent class, in spite of whatever complaining they may be doing in the meantime. The practice thus continues, even though most voters do not seem to like it.

Elections these days often seem more about who is to blame than who is to govern. New governments end up unpopular rapidly after their ascent to power, and very quickly the debate focuses on who or what is to be voted out rather than who is to be voted in. Voters are less inclined to see their selection as a long-term contract with a candidate or party and more likely to see it as resembling a transaction with a used car salesman. If you don't run out the door screaming for an alternative, it is because you expect the same treatment from the next merchant down the road. So just stay put and stick with the party or the candidate you're already voting for. In other words, you can add "less voter mobility across competing politicians" as another way in which mobility in American society has declined.[7]

The evolution of thinking in political science has reflected these fundamental changes in how American government works. Political scientists used to favor ideas known as Downsian competition and the median voter theorem, two different names for the same notion of dynamic political competition, to a greater extent than they do today. Those constructs postulate a world where politicians from both parties compete vigorously to win the allegiance of the voter who sits most squarely in the middle of the political spectrum. And maybe that theory was a reasonably good description of an earlier America; perhaps not coincidentally, Anthony Downs, the main driver of these ideas at the time, first published them in the 1950s. But that approach seems increasingly distant from American politics today. Core government programs still are backed by most voters, but political change at the margins seems to result from complex battles among lobbies, interest groups, financiers, political maneuvering, and who can win public relations campaigns fought in the media. The ideal of the perfectly centrist voter as the ultimate adjudicating force just doesn't appear that relevant for thinking about a lot of those changes we do observe.[8]

This world is a pretty far cry from the one envisioned by the classic theorist of American democracy, Alexis de Tocqueville, who saw American democracy as an active process, a spirit, a way of being, of feeling, of thinking, and indeed of living. Tocqueville was a French aristocrat who visited America in the 1830s and wrote *Democracy in America*, perhaps the most famous book on American modes and mores.

What is striking about Tocqueville is not just his observations about antebellum America but how much he anticipated America's current predicament. If there is any primary theorist for the decline of American restlessness, it is Tocqueville, who understood that a static America might in the longer run have trouble maintaining the democratic spirit of the country and that an ongoing stasis was not the same as perpetual stability.

Whatever his fears for the future, Tocqueville's basic portrait of the United States was of a land perpetually in motion. *Democracy in America* details a nation in ferment, in the process of becoming, and full of energy and ambition. Tocqueville noted that Americans were far more restless than the English, and furthermore this restlessness came from a great awareness of what they always were lacking. In his view, "[Americans] never stop thinking of the good things they have not got. It is odd to watch with what feverish ardor the Americans pursue prosperity and how they are ever tormented by the shadowy suspicion that they may not have chosen the shortest route to get it." As I interpret Tocqueville's discussion, men are insecure in their standing, yet they can observe the situations of many other people who are more or less on an equal plane. There is no natural aristocracy, so people become acutely aware of how they differ from others, of what they are lacking, and of how they might possibly obtain a better state of affairs. They are thereby driven to a restless pursuit of both wealth and higher social status.[9]

Among other forms of restlessness, Tocqueville was struck by the degree of geographic mobility in America, most of all in the westward direction. In the nineteenth century, he wrote: "[M]illions of men are marching at once toward the same horizon; their language, their religion, their manners differ; their object is the same. Fortune has been promised to them somewhere in the west, and to the west they go to find it." He didn't just mean the Far West, as he noted how rapidly the state of Ohio moved from being empty to being full of capital and settlers, and that many of the residents of Ohio were then moving on to Illinois.[10]

Yet while the dynamism, egalitarianism, and democratic spirit of America provided the foundations of Tocqueville's book, those qualities were not the end of the longer story. Through a deep study of the classics and the long arc of human historical development, he understood that current historical trends were by no means guaranteed to be permanent, and American restlessness might contain the seeds of its own demise. Tocqueville feared that human beings, including Americans, would, precisely through the process of their sluggish satisfaction, fall "into a complete and brutish indifference about the future."[11] Rather than being too restless, a future America might be too complacent, too self-satisfied, and above all too unwilling to regenerate the energies that once made it great, and thereby might fall into mediocrity.

He stated his fears bluntly:

People suppose that the new societies are going to change shape daily, but my fear is that they will end up by being too unalterably fixed with the same institutions, prejudices, and mores, so that mankind will stop progressing and will dig itself in. I fear that the mind may keep folding itself up in a narrower compass forever without producing new ideas, that men will wear themselves out in trivial, lonely, futile activity, and that for all its constant agitation humanity will make no advance.[12]

Ever spend too much time answering work email? But of course that is looking very far ahead. For Tocqueville, who was not even observing the use and spread of electricity, how might this spiritual and cultural decline come about?

For Tocqueville, the philosophy of "pantheism" helps drive this fall from grace. Tocqueville uses the word *pantheism* in a special way, so don't associate it exclusively with the theological doctrine that God is represented by the material universe as a whole. For Tocqueville, pantheism is as much a social construct as a religious perspective. It promotes the merging of man and nature and thereby attempts to remove the idea of the transcendent from human discourse. The transcendent is no longer something man ought to strive for, and that surrender is for Tocqueville the essence of pantheistic philosophy. The creator is no longer distant from man, giving people something to look up to, and so there is a lost source of inspiration and therefore a death of enthusiasm. There is instead a search for unity, resulting in a lazy pride and contentment and a forgetting of the striving and heroism that can make men great. In Tocqueville's view, pantheism puts the mind to sleep and soothes it, thereby allowing citizens to slip unknowingly into a boring and mediocre stasis. Pantheism, like socialism, is a strong tendency for the human mind to rest and stop searching, and, in the words of Peter Augustine Lawler, it can "lull the human mind into forgetting what it really does know."[13]

To be sure, *pantheism* no longer seems like the right word for what Tocqueville was describing. Few Americans subscribe to explicit pantheism. And while the environmental movement has had some implicitly pantheistic tendencies, that does not account for the general slowing down of American social life and social change, even if it has stifled commerce in some regards. Furthermore, Christian and Protestant beliefs have proven robust in the United States, although they are on a slight downswing at the moment. Still, the identification of pantheism with a kind of social stasis nonetheless captures a significant insight. Think of Tocqueville's invocation of pantheism, and the disappearance of the transcendent, as a general stand-in for the phenomenon of self-contained contentment and complacency, which I think is what he was really getting at once you cut through the awkwardness of the now-obsolete nineteenth-century terminology.

Given the technological limitations of his time, Tocqueville probably could not understand how far this phenomenon would spread. It never occurred to him that you could sit at home for a week, read the internet, watch Netflix streaming, and have groceries delivered to your door, all in lieu of striving for greatness. Nor could he have grasped that these services might in some ways *free up* our time to reach for some kinds of greatness, such as producing a wonderful start-up firm to serve millions and boost the quality of their matches. Still, Tocqueville understood that the very restlessness of the American spirit would produce so much wealth, and so satisfy our needs, that Americans eventually might run the risk of moving to a philosophy of less striving, less heroism, and less emulation of greatness. Americans might turn their backs on comparing themselves with similar others and striving to do better, and settle into their comfortable cocoons. After all, how many Americans these days really track whether the Chinese economy might be passing the American in terms of total GDP? And is that GDP as measured by market exchange rates or by purchasing power parity metrics? It's mostly the Chinese who seem to care.

Tocqueville did not think the American system of government would prove permanently sustainable, and this again stemmed from his views on restlessness. He thought American governance was effective because the country was relatively compact and small, but he also knew that was unlikely to last. In *Democracy in America* he wrote:

> *I think that before that time has run out [the next hundred years], the land now occupied or claimed by the United States will have a population of over one hundred million and be divided into forty states . . . but I do say that the very fact of their being one hundred millions divided into forty distinct and not equally powerful nations would make the maintenance of the federal government no more than a happy accident . . . I shall refuse to believe in the duration of a government which is called upon to hold together forty different nations covering an area half that of Europe.*[14]

Of course, Tocqueville's prediction of the collapse of American government was wrong. The United States did emerge intact from the Civil War, albeit severely damaged. And since then, the American federal government has not left the scene and it shows no signs of doing so, even though the United States now has fifty rather than forty states and the country surpassed the 100 million population mark in the 1920s. What Tocqueville did not see was that extreme federal stasis was an alternative to federal dissolution. If what the federal government does simply cannot change very much, then all those states and all those diverse and numerous people can't have such a destructive fight over the content of policy, and, thus, for that reason among others, the republic will not collapse. That gridlock may be depressing in some ways, but it has kept America going for some number of decades in recent times. In other words, Tocqueville underrated the self-stabilizing properties of a complacent and not-so-restless democratic America.

Nonetheless, some of Tocqueville's other predictions about democracy have come to pass. He argued that the new kind of "tyranny" will not resemble the despotisms of antiquity but rather will be based on the conformism and mediocrities of Americans of the future: "[I]t would degrade men rather than torment them." That's Tocqueville describing his version of the complacent class. Stable is better than unstable, for the most part, but that doesn't mean we are going to be very pleased by the choices American democracy will put before us. American democracy was originally a system combined and consistent with restlessness, striving, and rapid change. Tocqueville understood that America would one day be overtaken by a version of democracy mixed with stasis and that such a future would cease to inspire us politically.[15]

The very insistence of Americans upon their own democratic character will become part of this stasis, as Tocqueville foresaw:

> *Centralization is combined with the sovereignty of the people. That gives them a chance to relax. They console themselves for being under schoolmasters by thinking that they have chosen them themselves.*

*Each individual lets them put the collar on, for he sees that it is not
a person, or a class of persons, but society itself which holds the end
of the chain.*

*Under this system the citizens quit their state of dependence just
long enough to choose their masters and then fall back into it.*[16]

IS DEMOCRACY DEAD?

At some point, the complacency can set in so far that a snap back is
due. In recent times, that has happened most prominently in the United
Kingdom, where the elites were shocked that the electorate voted decisively to leave the European Union. Unemployment was only slightly
above 5 percent, a recovery was well under way, and London is one of
the world's most remarkable cities, so to Britain's complacent class,
it just didn't seem things were so bad or so requiring of such a radical
connection. Of course the broader population did not agree, and the
vote for Leave was motivated by, among other things, the view that the
increasing encroachment of a less-than-accountable European Union
bureaucracy could cause British democracy to wither away. The final
denouement of Brexit remains uncertain as I am writing this, but nonetheless, this is a case of democracy realizing its own fragility and striking
back, even if you think Remain was a better way forward for the United
Kingdom.

Although dozens of countries are nominally democratic, it's not
always appreciated how precarious actual democracy is in today's
world. And keep in mind that democracy isn't just a method of governance; rather it is an entire philosophy of government whose effective
functioning requires broader social preconditions, such as beliefs in
individual liberty, the rule of law, and some notion of accountability,
even if the exact content of those notions varies across distinct nations
and cultures.

Let's consider the world split into its three largest economic and political units: China, the European Union, and the United States.

China is not a democracy, and it seems unlikely to become one anytime soon. If anything, the country has been moving toward more censorship and more state control in the last few years. Democracy appears quite far away, and yet on the global stage China has never been more influential.

The European Union (EU) is comprised of democracies, but actual governance has taken a strong nondemocratic turn. First of all, the EU itself is much more of a technocracy than a democracy, and EU institutions have achieved increasing sway over economic policy and even over national borders, including borders for immigration purposes, albeit with a great deal of recent pushback from the level of the nation-state. EU regulations now control many different aspects of business in its member nations, although many observers see this as a quite fragile state of affairs, precisely because the popular legitimacy of the EU is not always so strong.

Is this arrangement truly democratic? EU officials will rush to assure you that it is, but that is far from obvious to the typical European voter, who is by far most interested in purely national elections. There is a European Parliament, a European Council, and an EU president, but they are not seen as having much of a democratic stamp of approval. Their elections and appointments just don't map very well onto the concerns of voters at the national level or the issues that voters debate and relate to. The EU president is selected by EU national leaders, in conjunction with the EU Parliament, and in that sense it claims democratic legitimization. Again, it hardly feels that way to a large swath of European voters. It is more like democracy several steps removed, with few steps in the hands of voters for actual recourse or accountability.

Sometimes expansions of EU powers require the exercise of formal democratic procedures in the member states. For instance, the Irish constitution requires a referendum for certain kinds of political changes, and the core EU Lisbon Treaty required Irish approval through such a referendum. On the first go-round, the Irish rejected the change, which would have meant a failure for the entire EU, since unanimity was required. So what happened? The Irish were given a chance to vote again, and next time around they "did the right thing." What could be more democratic than to keep on voting on issues until the citizenry gets them right? As I write, there is plenty of talk that perhaps the United Kingdom won't go through with Brexit. Whether they do or not, the very fact that this is a live option, at least for the time being, shows the democratic deficit in the system as a whole.

Since 2011, the spread of financial crises around Europe has meant a dominant role for "the Troika"—the European Central Bank, the European Commission, and the International Monetary Fund—in setting national budgets and defining austerity targets. It also seems that Germany has de facto veto power over any proposed solution, and Angela Merkel more than the national parliament, even though the latter has a final veto. That doesn't sound very democratic, and if national budgets and national borders are being controlled by nondemocratic forces (the Troika and the Schengen agreement, respectively), are these really still democratic nations? To be sure, people still vote, but that's not a guarantee of democracy as a living process for improving policy and governance arrangements.

The European Union is also relying increasingly on its central bank for macroeconomic management rather than on the national legislatures. For better or worse, the same has been true for the United States. That may be an entirely good and practical decision, but it also represents a step away from democracy as the concept traditionally has been understood.

In recent times, there have been some extreme manifestations of democracy in the European Union, most notably the independence referendum in Scotland and the possibility of such a referendum, or some modified or proxy version thereof, in Catalonia. That's direct representative democracy for sure. But even in those cases, an absolutely central question is whether the new national unit would be accepted into the European Union. Without EU acceptance, the democratic decision to secede probably isn't possible and won't happen. And that EU decision is made by unanimity among EU member nations, and then we are back to there not being so much democratic decision making after all. The veto rights granted by unanimity rules are in a sense an opposing force when it comes to the possibilities for democratic change.

In regard to Europe, I worry that nondemocratic arrangements are ready to fall apart or at least dramatically weaken. The recent refugee crisis has mobilized public opinion in many European nations, and typical citizens are opposed to the relatively pro-migration policies of the EU. More and more people are asking why the EU should have such authority over national matters in the first place, and the Brexit vote may be just the beginning of a broader rebellion against the supra-national powers of the EU. We'll see how that goes, but arguably this is another example of how an initial political stasis, and the appearance of staid bureaucracy, can give rise to rebellion and possibly even a legal counterrevolution, followed by a fair degree of chaos.

The one part of the world where democratic decision making and democratic discourse most apply is—oddly enough—Latin America, a region that was democracy-challenged, to say the least, only a few decades ago. And that democratic progress says a lot, because on the bright side, it shows the possibilities for true, dynamic human improvement. For all of their problems, most of the Latin American countries now have free, (relatively) fair, and open elections. Their parties and leaders run on distinct platforms. Those platforms are debated. The winner of the election has some chance—with checks and balances—to put policies into action. Those policies represent a real change and alter the allocation of governmental budgets across priorities. If citizens don't like what they have voted for, they can vote those leaders and parties out of office next time around. Over time, policy changes quite a bit, as we've seen in Mexico, Brazil, Colombia, Peru, and many other countries in the region. Furthermore, in most of these countries, the size of the middle class generally has been growing, which creates a dynamic toward even greater support for democratic procedures. If that isn't democracy, what is? And who would have predicted that turnaround in the 1960s, when Latin America hardly had any democracies at all? Of course, it is entirely reasonable to conclude from this example that greater democratization does not by any means solve all problems, and that is a big reason why the forces for democratization are not always as strong as the political rhetoric of (partially) democratic nations might indicate.

One simple way to get a good read on "democracy in America," circa 2017, is to ask what America's main rival on the global stage, China, thinks of the American system of government. I have found that many Chinese admire and indeed envy America greatly, pointing to its much higher standard of living, freedom of speech, and relatively clean environment, among other positive features. Still, even those Chinese who admire America find it hard to praise our government. The constant refrain is that American government isn't very good at getting things done. And you don't have to take that remark in any kind of left-wing, liberal, or interventionist light—you might think the thing Americans are failing to do in politics is to deregulate or to cut taxes or otherwise shrink government. America is simply stuck for the time being, in its government most of all.[17]

So static America has a static government, and that is ultimately unsustainable. I'm now going to look at why that is the case in more detail, and that discussion will prove to be part of a bigger picture of why the complacent class will not be getting its way forever and in all things.

9.

THE RETURN OF CHAOS, AND WHY THE COMPLACENT CLASS CANNOT HOLD

I've discussed a number of main elements driving the trend toward a more static, less risk-taking America. These include the collapse of fiscal freedom and democratic process, lower residential mobility, less building in America's most productive cities, more segregation by income and status, a much greater concern with safety and risk, the coddling of our children, and fewer start-ups and slower growth in living standards, among others. These forces have led to an America that is calmer, safer, and more peaceful, at least in the short run. But it is also an America that is losing the ability to regenerate itself, reinvent itself, and create new sources of dynamism. And as the years pass, it seems increasingly obvious that the social and economic stagnation of our times is more than just a temporary blip; instead, that stagnation reflects deeply rooted structural forces that will not be easy to undo by mere marginal reforms.

We also are seeing more signs that the beneficial features of peace and calm cannot stay in place forever; rather, eventually they will trickle away with the dynamism. Ultimately peace and stability *must be paid for*. They must be paid for with real resources, with tax revenue, and they also require the support of people. If relatively high mobility goes away for too many Americans, perspectives will turn against the established order, and, furthermore, there won't be the money to pay for it. Right now Americans are failing to regenerate sources of future progress, and thus they are borrowing against the future rather than paying their bills.

If the system is still plagued by a lot of underlying troubles, what should we look for as signs of those troubles and how will they evolve? As Norman Cousins, the political journalist and world peace advocate, once put it: "History is a vast early warning system." But what exactly are today's events warning about?

IS DOMESTIC ORDER UNRAVELING?

I think of the unrest that began in 2015—of Ferguson, Baltimore, and the campus rebellion at the University of Missouri (and whatever other stories have come along since)—as the signals that something deeper is going wrong in today's America. They are warning signs that not all is well, not just with those particular communities but in American society at large. Those particular incidents may or may not continue to reverberate, but they are signs that some comparable set of forces will. To see this, let's look at an economic analogy: the Great Recession. Where did it start? It started with subprime mortgage holders, many of whom were lower-income or minority borrowers. Was it the case that the subprime borrowers *caused* the Great Recession? Absolutely not. Rather, they were (again) playing the canary-in-the-coal-mine role, and if you look at the numbers, you will see that the losses in subprime were just one small part of a bigger story of broader economic overextension. If everyone or almost everyone is overextended in terms of risk, who will run out of money first and thus end up in the first set of headlines? Well, usually that will be the poor, in this case the subprime borrowers, and of course a disproportionate share of those individuals were African American or Latino.

Consistent with this framing, the economic downturn came absolutely last to the contemporary art market, where it takes the longest time for the buyers and potential buyers to feel the pinch because they are so well off and so flush with cash. Even right after the Lehman Brothers failure in 2008, which was a grave event for the global economy, there was still a mostly successful major auction of numerous works by British artist Damien Hirst, most famous for his dead animals preserved in formaldehyde and displayed in boxy glass structures. The proceeds exceeded $200 million, even while a lot of the world's financial infrastructure was falling apart. Subprime was the first sign for later, broader collapses, and for a long time, most observers did not see how far-ranging and systematic the problems would prove.

Right now, in the United States, there is increasing discontent among some segments of the poor and among some ethnic minorities, most of all African Americans. Those discontents are significant enough to make the evening news and to be major events in American race relations. They are not yet significant enough to affect aggregate variables, such as crime rates, incarceration rates, GDP, and other social and economic indicators. (There is fragmentary evidence that murder rates may be edging up again, but as I write, this cannot be considered confirmed.) But I am asking you to consider the possibility that these events are in some ways like the subprime defaults.

Whether or not you agree with all of their complaints and grievances, the protesting groups of African Americans are among the most vulnerable elements of American society. They respond first and complain first and exhibit signs of dissent from the complacent class. They are, in varying ways, trying to renegotiate or secede from the current deal, and that is a sign that something is deeply wrong beneath the surface. I read and hear many critics alleging that these complaints are not serious enough, not practical enough, and do not reflect real hardships, given that Americans, even poor ones, live in a time of such great plenty. There is lots of talk, not all of it on the surface, that the complainers have been spoiled or coddled. I think those responses are missing the point, whether or not you agree with all of the complaints on the table. Most of all, the complaints are a warning signal that the current system is in some ways broken and that the complacent class, for all its good intentions, has in some ways failed America. It's better to debate that issue straight on rather than trying to take down the complainers by finding possible holes or hypocrisies in their arguments.

Finally, the themes that brought Donald Trump to the top of the Republican ticket and propelled Bernie Sanders's strong challenge to Hillary Clinton have finally caused the media to realize that something about American life has fallen off the tracks. An increasing segment of Americans no longer extend unconditional trust to the "expert" technocrats running the country. We don't yet know when that line will crack, but as with the vote in favor of Brexit, the electorate just doesn't seem that impressed by experts anymore, and one even wonders if a lot of people aren't voting against experts and elites just out of spite or a desire to show them up.

I believe that the decline of American restlessness will not in the longer run bring total calm and stability to our lives and that America is in for some additional surprises. In 2016, Trump got most of the attention because of his vivid personality, his outrageous statements and beliefs, and his manipulation of the media. That is an important surprise in its own right, but we should not forget about the more fundamental causes—an ongoing disruption of the previously stable patterns of complacency and stasis, and at levels that are social, economic, and political all at once.

In other words, maybe this is a process that will spread more deeply, just as the subprime crisis did. Maybe these incidents are just the beginnings of some deeper fissures in American life, fissures that will in due time rip open our sense of calm and tranquility. Fissures that will show the American quest for safety is not "foolproof," fissures that will bring a "great reset," and fissures that in some fundamental ways will make the pot boil over. If Ferguson was step one and Trump was step two, what then will be next? Keep your eye on these issues. They won't be going away anytime soon, and they are heralding the beginning of a new phase in American social life.

Let's consider some further angles on the forthcoming return of instability through a few more granular levels. I'll start at the campus level and then consider crime, government, and finally foreign policy and global affairs, which is in fact the most worrying dimension of the broader problem.

The Return of Instability to the Campus

The last two years have seen the surprising return of open protest and racial discontent on American campuses. Arguably, the events themselves show that the discontent never really went away, but at least for mainstream media coverage, it had not been a focal topic for most white Americans, including well-educated, well-informed white Americans.

Yet what has happened? A movement at Princeton to rename the Woodrow Wilson School of Public Policy, because of Wilson's horrible history as a segregationist, showed considerable staying power, far more than anyone would have expected a year earlier, even if it did not eventually win. A rather complicated series of events at Yale, first coming into public view with an email about potentially offensive Halloween costumes, expressed and intensified African American alienation at that school. Again, the issue isn't going away quietly.

Perhaps the most startling story, however, has come at the University of Missouri (Mizzou). The most powerful public incident was when the football team went on strike, demanding the resignation of the president of the university. Among the grievances of the football team, which included many African Americans, were claims that the university was full of racism and that it was a hostile rather than supportive environment. Amazingly, or so it seemed at first, the university president did in fact step down, thereby affirming the power of the football team (and of the media) and creating future headaches for other university presidents around the country, who now must tread very gingerly around these kinds of issues.

As press coverage of the story developed, it turned out that Mizzou had been the site for a wide array of ongoing racial insults and slights. The "N word" was deployed as an insult more than infrequently, a swastika with feces was smeared on a wall, and numerous anonymous threats were directed against minorities, including threats of violent physical harm, on social media sites. The ultimatum of the football team in fact was preceded by a series of protests and also by a quite serious hunger strike. Overall, it seems that racial tensions had become a pretty typical and also deeply entrenched part of the status quo ex ante, even if most outsiders weren't paying much attention to these trends. Behavior at some of Donald Trump's rallies, and by some of Trump's supporters online, has brought similar truths to the fore, namely that undercurrents of racism may have been silenced for a while, but they never really went away.

The overall demographics of Mizzou are pretty typical for American higher education. Blacks are 8 percent of the student body, which is lower than their percentage of the American population (about 13 percent). Furthermore, blacks are graduating at a rate of about 55 percent, compared to 71 percent for whites. White and black students at Mizzou have markedly different experiences at the school, and you can think of that just as another manifestation of resurgent segregationism in American life. The campus has been described, quite simply, as "very segregated." But arguably this university is no longer part of the country as it has been envisioned by the complacent class. The school suddenly is undergoing a lot of change, toward what ends we do not yet know.[1]

My point in raising these incidents isn't to take sides in what are often quite complex disputes. The point is that we have seen—once again—that apparently peaceful environments are often not so peaceful once you scratch the surface. And once the apparent peace of these environments is disturbed, those disturbances tend to spread, and the grievances become amplified.

Mizzou and the other campus episodes also reflect a common pattern for how segregation can become a kind of norm, festering under the surface but receiving relatively little public attention. Without a discrete event to put in the evening news, the media typically do relatively little reporting. After enough time, the segregation ends up being accepted as pretty normal, and a lot of people don't give it much thought. After all, we all segregate ourselves with relatively "similar" or "like-minded" others, so if some kind of similar process goes on at a lot of campuses, it doesn't have to seem that sinister. The long-run losses of opportunity and dynamism—however real—just aren't that visible, at least not in ways that can be shown, reported, and easily proven to casual observers.

By the time these campus brouhahas hit the news, the publicity itself can make things worse rather than better. Many of the protestors learn, by seeing the number and strength and passion of the other protestors, just how many other people are unhappy and how deeply they are unhappy. That revelation of support raises the numbers and consciousness of the protest movements. Critics in turn charge that the complaints are from "spoiled, overprotected babies" who don't know what real problems are. By the time that matters come to a head, a lot of the resulting dialogue is inflammatory rather than healing, and so campus polarization and also segregation can worsen. Suddenly it becomes an issue "what stance" you take on the hunger strike, the football team, the president, the memo from the dean, and many other matters. Students and faculty and administrators can end up divided along these lines, and, all of a sudden, yet another form of segregation has arisen.

When it comes to American campuses, the pot is likely to continue boiling over, because the more people on campus talk about these questions, the more they seem to polarize themselves. In the short run, the good news is that most of these campus events won't disrupt the rest of the outside world very much, given the somewhat insular nature of the academic world. The bad news is that these events represent key and sometimes legitimate grievances, even if their on-campus manifestations are often silly or overstated. Often those grievances come to campuses first because students have more free time, they are gathered together physically (the ongoing relevance of physical location, even in a world obsessed with information technology), and more educated people tend to have a greater number of detailed political opinions. The key question is when and at what pace those disturbances will spread to other segments of American society. Details of the racism and the unruly behavior in the Trump campaign suggest this may be a lot quicker than most people had thought.

The Return of Instability to Crime Rates

Many Americans take today's low crime rates for granted, and maybe even expect them to fall farther, but I think those expectations will turn out to be a mistake. In fact, based on what is now years' worth of headlines, I'd say we are on the cusp of another big crime wave, and probably it is already under way.

I am not predicting the return of the kind of crime we saw in the 1960s through the 1980s. I don't expect a repeat of those same patterns of student bombings, antidraft vandalism and riots, murder rates, auto windows being smashed in to steal sound systems, and later the crack-driven street robberies, to name just a few forms of crime that probably will not be making major comebacks. It is sometimes said that history does not repeat but it does rhyme. I think we are seeing new kinds of crime, ones that don't enter into the "decline of crime" statistics which are so frequently cited. Of course I am referring to the internet.

I don't know of any vaguely reliable figures for internet crime as a whole. Nonetheless, just a few of the magnitudes that are thrown around are pretty sobering. I've seen reports of 10 to 15 million cases of identity theft a year, tens of millions of phishing attacks, millions of successfully consummated fraudulent pleas for cash, but tying such crimes to specific nations is not always possible. I've seen one estimate that Nigerian internet scams alone are pulling in over $12 billion a year (globally, not just from America). Tens of millions of Americans have had their personal data stolen, with what results we do not yet know, or perhaps the authorities won't tell us. Millions of fingerprints have been stolen too, which may someday compromise security systems. Most episodes of cyberextortion and cyberespionage are not reported, and the internet is used with growing frequency for illegal drug transactions. There is also the estimated $20 billion of lost time each year from the proliferation of spam, not necessarily an illegal act but unwelcome none-theless. Illegal online pornography, often involving minors, is rife.[2]

It is hard to know how much cyberwarfare is going on, but it was used against Iran, with some success in the form of the Stuxnet vi-rus, and it has become a major issue in U.S.–China relations. China has stolen a great deal of intellectual property from American companies, and who knows what the Americans might have done in return? Com-panies are investing more and more in their cyberdefenses, and they are reluctant to publicly admit those breaches that do happen, if they are even aware of them. Recently we learned that it was probably Russia that hacked into Democratic National Committee emails and voice-mails, ostensibly for the purpose of influencing an American election toward Trump.

Another disturbing story came in early 2016, when it was revealed that hackers stole $81 million from Bangladesh Bank through SWIFT, which is part of the international payments network. To date most of the money remains missing, and it is sobering that the same hackers tried to steal as much as $1 billion. The entire global economy rests on the presumed safety and integrity of payments systems, but we don't have a good sense of how robust they really are, especially as hackers' capa-bilities increase over time.

Again, such crimes won't be counted in figures that look at declines in traditional metrics, such as murder rates, assaults, or thefts of autos or bicycles.

If you think about it, none of this should come as a surprise. If we are living more of our lives through the internet, we should also be see-ing more crime through the internet, and indeed we are. Just as more of our matching comes through the internet, so do we see the match-ing of criminal and victim as an increasingly internet-based phenome-non. Just as we already have lost a lot of trust in government, we may end up losing trust in the internet, or at least significant parts of it.

Internet crime of course starts picking up as soon as internet use does, so that means the uptick begins in the 1990s. In other words, internet crime started rising at more or less the same time that other crimes began to fall. For that reason, the overall amount of crime hasn't gone down nearly as much as many people think.

There are also many internet "activities" that may or may not translate into formal legal crimes but that distress people nonetheless. I am referring to the threats, the stalking, the insults, the harassment, the social media campaigns, the shaming, and the wrecking of reputations that go on every day. Even the threats—which *are* illegal in the technical sense of that term—only rarely stand much chance of receiving police attention, much less enforcement of the laws against them. The reason for that is pretty obvious: There are so many of these threats, and they can be hard to trace. But even getting the police to try to follow up on them doesn't usually yield much return. It's basically millions of unreported crimes each year, with varying degrees of distress attached, and again it is mostly unmeasured.

To be sure, internet crime has some pretty big advantages, if that is the right way to put it. You can't murder someone over the internet (yet?), although you can threaten them, stalk them, intimidate them, and harass them. For that reason, internet crime usually takes the forms of fraud, identity theft, misrepresentation, and various swindles, in addition to threats and harassments. You could say that internet crime is a calmer kind of crime than more traditional crimes, at least on the whole, and indeed that characterization fits the broader portrait of modern society in this book.

That said, those calmer crimes bring some special problems precisely because they are calm and also because they are relatively invisible. The outrage against cybercrime doesn't have much of a chance to build up in public spaces. The victims don't ever come together, coordinate, or vote as a bloc on crime issues. In the United States, starting in the 1970s, being "tough on crime" became a big vote winner and forced many beneficial changes, such as more police patrolling in the streets. We don't see the same kind of movement for cybercrime, nor do I expect that soon. Many cybercrimes are quiet, gentle crimes, and if you make movies about them, the vigilante is a programmer nerd rather than Charles Bronson or Clint Eastwood; the screen will show a lot of frantic typing on keyboards, with various cinematic tricks tossed in to make the film feel somewhat suspenseful. People just don't feel that outraged—yet—by the very high levels of cybercrime and internet fraud.

Anyway, my prediction for the next crime wave is pretty simple. The next crime wave is going to break the internet, or at least significant parts of it. Most likely, the growth of Amazon and Facebook (or the next generation of their competitors) will continue unabated, because those companies and some others will have enough money to invest in making their systems secure. But most people will not think of the open internet as a safe space. It will be viewed as a place to be abused, insulted, and harassed and to have one's identity stolen. We will move more and more to walled-off, regulated apps, and the former utopian dream of the internet as a true intellectual and commercial free-for-all won't ever come to realization. A mix of crime and a slack online advertising market will take that from us. In this regard, the bad guys will win, and you can argue they already have won. American cocooning through the privatized parts of the internet will continue, to the benefit of many, but the most open and vulnerable part of our society—the open internet—is already losing out. Again, if you are looking for signs of future trouble, look at the most vulnerable nodes of a network first. Yet, because many internet crimes are so isolated, so lonely, and so outside the public eye, this festering sore can build up for a long time before it boils over as a truly major problem to the public.

Most generally, we should not expect that peaceful or low-crime periods will continue. In 1960, the famous sociologist and cultural commentator Daniel Bell asserted that there was no big crime wave in the works and that there were just a few class problems and also some "social rebellion." He assured his readers that "in the personal lives of Americans, in the day-to-day routines of the city, there is less violence than a hundred or fifty or even twenty-five years ago." Of course, Bell was wrong, and the country was about to experience its biggest crime wave ever. The point is that this change was not very visible or obvious until it was well under way, once again a sign of a "great reset" as they typically occur.[3]

One of the striking features of the decline in crime rates is how difficult those declines are to explain. Not long ago, the Brennan Center for Justice published a very serious, very scientific 131-page survey paper entitled "What Caused the Crime Decline?" by Dr. Oliver Roeder, Lauren-Brooke Eisen, and Julia Bowling. A lot of the features behind the crime decline are pretty well known, including increased incarceration (although that is a smaller feature than most people think), increased police numbers, aging population, growth in income, decline in alcohol abuse and some drugs, changing economic conditions, and decreased lead exposure among children and thus fewer developmental delays. But by the time all of the known factors are added up, for 1990 to 1999, almost half of the decline in crime remains fundamentally unexplained. For the years 2000 to 2013 in particular, over half the decline in crime remains fundamentally unexplained. Furthermore, the decline in American crime rates, as measured by *changes*, almost exactly mirrors a corresponding decline in Canadian crime rates, albeit at different *levels* of crime. All that indicates the change in America isn't just about changes in American policies and laws; rather, it is something more ineffable. The mood of the times really matters, and those moods can, if enough pressure builds up, flip fairly suddenly and set off new dynamics and unfavorable and unseemly trends.[4]

I suggest that most of those unexplained crime residuals are "declines in American restlessness." Or, given the Canadian parallels, you could call them "declines in North American restlessness," based on a common change in social mood. But that is a subjective factor, and unlike, say, the aging of the American population, we cannot be assured that it will remain in place. We don't understand it, we can't measure it except as a residual, and most likely we can't predict it. So let's not be so quick to extrapolate from the recent status quo and assume crime rates only can fall. The reality is that we understand the causes of crime fairly poorly, and the reasons we give for expecting crime rates to continue to fall are far from decisively correct. Let's not be totally shocked if the next set of significant innovations among the American professions comes . . . in the profession of crime.

The Return of Instability to Government

No matter what you may think of the content of current policy, America's government has been run pretty stably for the last few decades, as I discussed in chapter 8. Nonetheless, a problem will arise as more and more funds are preallocated and locked into preordained uses. At some point this country will face an immediate crisis, and there won't quite be the resources, or more fundamentally the *flexibility*, to handle it. Imagine, for instance, military crises in the Baltics and the South China Sea at the same time. To resolve such a messy situation, America probably would need more resources, more cooperation across government, and more public support for involvement than we currently have.

Of course, that is just an example. I don't know what this crisis will be or when it will come. If not a foreign policy problem from a two- or three-front conflict, it could be an environmental catastrophe requiring immediate attention, a major terrorist attack, or perhaps something entirely unexpected, a true "Black Swan," so to speak, in Nassim Taleb's use of that term.

Ramping up government spending to respond to that crisis won't be so simple. It could require higher tax rates and higher government spending—and bigger cutbacks elsewhere—than the American economy could sustain or the American people would be willing to support. In any case, it is not just a question of raising money; institutions for handling the problem have to be built as well—how long has it taken to turn the Department of Homeland Security into a well-run organization? Are we there yet? Building good institutions and capabilities very quickly is no longer something the American public sector is very good at, perhaps not since the days of the moon-landing program, which from announcement to fruition took well under a decade.

Until that big policy crisis comes, everything will seem fine and will be pretty peaceful. Government will proceed as it has been doing, albeit with a slowly corrosive increase in the level of public cynicism and a slow decline in America's ability to ramp up public sector institution building. But at some point, governmental flexibility will have so eroded that when policy changes have to come, the required changes will be very big indeed, and the ability of American government to respond to those needs will have been hampered for many years on end.

There is no particular clock governing this process of institutional failure. It simply depends when the next big crisis will happen—big, that is, relative to America's ability, and most of all fiscal ability, to respond to it. That timing and thus the associated response capacity will be partly a matter of luck, a truth not entirely reassuring for America's fiscal planning.

Along these lines, another way to think about the erosion of stability in government is to look at trust, and whether trust in American government is rising or falling. When trust is rising, the ability of government to respond to a crisis is relatively high because the support of the citizens is there. When trust in government is low, we see phenomena such as the widespread unwillingness of parents to vaccinate their children, which has now become a slow-burning public health crisis of sorts.

The data are not so cheery. For instance, a recent Pew poll found that only about 19 percent of Americans feel they can trust the government always or most of the time. Only 20 percent describe the programs of government as being well run. And a majority of the public believes that "ordinary Americans" would do a better job running the country. Those are some of the most pessimistic responses found in the last half century. It's not that voters and survey respondents are so stupid; rather, low trust creates self-fulfilling prophecies whereby government is not sufficiently well run to earn the public trust.[5]

Trust in the American government peaked in the late 1950s—in 1958, by this measure—when it ran at 77 percent of respondents basically trusting the government. But high levels of trust in government are by no means so entirely set in the distant past. From the mid-1990s to the early 2000s, measured trust in the federal government rose steadily and reached almost 60 percent. What is striking is how much trust has fallen, in spite of the fact (because of the fact?) that the core functions and competency of American government just haven't changed all that much as of late.

This erosion of trust eventually will limit the effectiveness of American government; indeed, in many ways it already does. As long as the feds are just sending checks through the mail and making electronic deposits, through transfer programs such as Medicare and Social Security, lower levels of trust may be manageable. But as soon as Americans have to rely on their government to do something new and concrete—whether at home or in the realm of foreign policy or public health or the environment—low levels of trust will make that more difficult. Americans are not just all going to get behind new initiatives the way they did with the moon program or the interstate highway system or even the Reagan military buildup. The better-run governments in the world tend to be trusted by their people. They can announce what they want to do, be believed, proceed with concrete steps, and at the end of the process be evaluated by voters in a more or less fair way. In contrast, the untrusted governments usually have to resort to subterfuge, lies, and trickery, and that tends to come bundled with corruption, economic distortions, and a general lack of transparency. Think of, say, Sweden versus Argentina.

By the way, there is another method for measuring declining trust in government, and that is in terms of how much members of one political party dislike members of the other. These days Republicans are more loyal to Republicans (Trump aside), and Democrats are more loyal to Democrats, but it's not that either side trusts its own politicians more. Rather, it is that each side trusts the politicians of the other party less than it used to and also trusts the members of the other party less than it used to. For instance, Republican parents don't want their children marrying Democrats, and vice versa, much more than used to be the case. Again, that hasn't stopped the smooth operation of a lot of government transfer programs, but Americans are eating into their future capacity for governance and also their ability to respond effectively to future crisis situations.[6]

A final sign of the erosion of trust in government is the election of Donald Trump as president. It's pretty clear that a lot of Republican voters no longer trust "the system," as evidenced by how criticisms of Trump didn't much seem to stick with his supporters; it seems those people just want to be contrary. As I write this, the election has only just occurred, and people are still trying to make sense of how Trump was able to ascend to our highest office, using the stealth tactics of his celebrity persona, grabbing media attention through insults and outrageous statements, and boldly stating that the proverbial emperor, namely the American political establishment, has no clothes. But as with the financial crisis of 2007–2008, this is often how resets work. Everything seems calm and fine, until one day it is not. That is because the buildup of social and economic pressures can be fairly invisible until a crisis situation comes along, in this case the appearance on the scene of a candidate—Donald Trump—with some pretty special talents for appealing to the disgruntled.

Very commonly it is suggested that income inequality is behind these growing dysfunctions in our politics, and that is one of the most common memes you read in the press today or hear on television. But for all the popularity of this view, it doesn't have enough evidence behind it. For instance, if we look at those who voted for Donald Trump in the Republican primaries, they had an average income of about $70,000 and also education levels higher than the American average. No matter what you may read or hear, that is not exactly the revolt of the have-nots. Furthermore, a lot of Trump's campaign presentation stressed his wealth and his luxurious and glamorous lifestyle. Whether we like it or not, the rise of Trump is centered fundamentally in the complacent class. In the absence of a dynamic and compelling vision for America's future, people will, in fact, turn to less-positive visions, and more likely than not, they will get those visions from the elite. If you listen to Trump on China, it's not all that different from how Paul Krugman was advocating tariffs on Chinese goods just a few years earlier.[7]

More generally, the other social science evidence indicates that income inequality often gives rise to political disengagement rather than unrest. That is what one major study of the topic found, drawing upon European experience because the greater number of countries in Europe creates more data to work with. For all those people except individuals in the top quintile of income, greater inequality is correlated with a reduction in protest participation, and that result holds across a data set of twenty-five different European democracies. Political interest, the frequency of political discussion, and participation in elections also all tend to be lower in situations with higher income inequality. Similarly, a global study based on the World Values Survey found that support for democracy was relatively low when inequality was high; thus, engagement also might be low under those conditions.[8]

I've heard many a question about when the next revolutionary Thermidor is coming to the United States, but the data suggest a different story. Since 1970, American survey respondents show no greater preference for government redistribution. Furthermore, two notable groups show considerably weaker support for redistributive ideas and policies over time. The elderly decreased their support for redistribution by an amount that is more than half the distance between Democrats and Republicans on this question. Perhaps more surprisingly, African Americans also have decreased their support for redistribution, with almost half of this change coming from decreased support for race-based forms of government aid. This is in spite of the fact that the black-white wealth gap has been widening rather than narrowing. A lot of African Americans think race relations in America have worsened, but economic redistribution does not seem to be at the center of these concerns.[9]

I don't consider these studies close to what might be called "slam dunk" empirical evidence, but still they puncture the myth that more inequality necessarily leads to riot, rebellion, and revolt. It's not even clear that higher inequality leads to stronger calls for redistribution. The basic story is instead that inequality breeds disengagement.

So what then is happening with the Trump phenomenon and other indicators of political turmoil? I would put forward an alternative hypothesis to the continued stress on the politics of inequality. As I see it, the complacent class has ceased to outline a truly compelling reason to believe in the dynamic properties of the status quo. The complacent class has lost the ability to inspire an electorate with any kind of strong positive vision, other than some marginal adjustments. Witness the sluggishness of so many voters in the United States, including Democrats, to evince true enthusiasm for the candidacy of Hillary Clinton, and in the United Kingdom, the inability of the Remain forces to build a glorious case for their preferred option (resorting instead to relatively ineffective scare tactics about leaving the European Union).

The complacent class itself has ceased to believe in the regenerative properties of the world we all inhabit. So it's not that lower-income groups are rebelling against their wealthier overlords, but rather that so much of society, at all levels of income and education, has lost faith in the system. And without a strong ideology and a strong belief in the future, the vacuum can be filled by other, worse ideas, and again that will happen at various levels of income and education. In fact, it is members of the privileged segment of the complacent class who seem to be leading the rebellion. It is no accident that Donald Trump came from a very wealthy family, and we can expect further "rebellion into a vacuum" from the privileged class in the years to come.

ONE SCENARIO FOR A MORE DYNAMIC AND MORE CHAOTIC FUTURE

When will the individual Zeitgeist in the United States become one more of change and dynamism—both good and bad—and less one of comfort and stasis? This is the hardest question to answer, and it might seem that the general aging of American society will limit any trend toward greater dynamism. Older people really are, on average, more set in their ways, and they are also calmer. But imagine this picture of an America say ten, fifteen, or twenty years hence.

- Antidepressants as we know them have fallen out of favor; they have been replaced by alternative medical processes that address problems of depression without "tranquilizing" Americans so much.

- The differences between America's wealthy and less well-developed cities and suburbs have become big enough to resurrect economic motives as a reason to relocate, so rates of residential mobility rise again, leading to a new pioneer class. Driverless vehicles and better transit systems make these new commutes bearable.

- Artificial intelligence, smart software, robotics, and the "internet of things" have come together to bring significant productivity gains and lots of disruptive change. You walk around your house, or the store, and ask for things to happen, and they do. You can ask any question just by talking to yourself, and a good answer comes immediately.

- Cheap, clean energy has become a reality, enabling a lot more ambitious physical projects in physical space. Americans become interested in exploring outer space again, if only through robots, and a new generation of robot-manned probes will help us map and understand the entire solar system, possibly finding life in the oceans of the moons of Saturn.

- Ongoing world crises, and a continuing uptick of domestic terror attacks, convince Americans that "living for the moment" deserves a lot more attention. Life won't feel so calm any more.

- Growing wealth, automation and automated home chores, combined with changing customs, mean that families of three or four children will return to favor. That is already the case among the very wealthy, who can afford it, and America is already at the point where better-educated women do not choose to have fewer children. Over time, American society becomes much younger again, and in the meantime, the adults start thinking more about the dynamism of the future.[10]

- Spurred by the growing prominence of racial incidents in the headlines, the ongoing cultural marginalization of African Americans turns around, and African Americans play a greater role in many parts of the national scene, including American intellectual life. Furthermore, a new wave of African immigrants revolutionizes the prevailing racial dynamic, and for the better, but with a lot of change and remixing of core categories along the way. Those African immigrants also help the country feel young again, because Africa has a very young skew to its population and also older people are less likely to leave.

These are some of my picks for how America is likely to become a more dynamic nation again. They are deliberately speculative, but overall, is this such an implausible picture? In this world, Americans' internal sense of themselves, their nation, and their future will be more restless, less static, and more forward-looking in mostly beneficial ways, but it will also leave a trail of partial chaos in its wake.

Now let's turn to the most dangerous feature of our future: foreign policy and global affairs.

THE RETURN OF INSTABILITY AT EVERY LEVEL, INCLUDING THE GLOBAL

As we look to the global arena now, more than fifteen years into the new millennium, a lot of the optimism from the 1990s has vanished. Much of the Middle East has been destroyed, Russia has invaded Ukraine and broken down the old international order, China is newly assertive in the South China Sea, and terrorism is a major news theme in many parts of the world. Europe seems unable to deal with its refugee problem in comparison to the rather smoothly handled Yugoslavian refugee crisis of the 1990s. Both Russia and China seem to be less free, and to be resorting to more censorship, than ten or fifteen years ago. In Turkey, democracy seems to be collapsing altogether. European growth remains sluggish, and it is far from obvious that European Union governance mechanisms can meet current challenges, including problems with the eurozone and the need for a more coherent refugee policy in light of an inflow of millions of North Africans, with more likely to come. The United Kingdom voted to leave the European Union altogether, even though this appears contrary to their economic self-interest. These international events may seem outside the purview of this book, but the broader point of relevance to foreign affairs is that a country cannot forever afford to stand still if the rest of the world is in dangerous flux.

Behind these particular issues is a bigger question, and it is a question of the principles that govern the world. In particular, the most disturbing idea to have reattained prominence in the last ten to fifteen years is the notion that history may be cyclical rather than involving monotonic, ongoing progress. That is, the very logic of good times may tend to bring some bad consequences upon us, no matter how hard we try to hold such problems at bay.

Consider recent world history. During the 1990s, the degree of optimism in the United States and around the world was extreme. Productivity growth was high, information technology seemed to hold all kinds of promise, and in some years real wages grew by 3 percent or more, including for the middle class. Everything seemed to be moving in the right direction. The attacks of 9/11 had not yet happened, and terror attacks did not dominate the news. Just about every country seemed to be embracing good liberalizing reforms, including India and Russia and China; there was even talk that Russia might join the European Union in due time, and it seemed Russia was now a democracy, albeit an imperfect one. The Middle East was hardly ideal, but it was nothing like its current conflagration. Overall, it was an age of reform, democratization, and rapid economic growth. And, in the United States in particular, life was stable too, unless you happened to be one of the many black people ensnared by our criminal justice system. It was as if we had the best of all possible worlds, dynamic growth and stability all rolled into one happy picture.

This legacy is hardly gone, and much of it has continued through the present day. For instance, if we look at absolute levels, more of the world is middle class or richer than ever before. And there is a lot less extreme poverty in the world than there was fifteen years ago, including poverty for children, most of all in Africa and South India and China. But if we look at some of the changes in trend, it no longer seems they are all so positive, not compared to the 1990s at least. What is even scarier is that the new troubles, in many cases, seem to be derived, albeit indirectly, from the old patterns of growth and stability. More and more hints are coming that perhaps cyclical theories, with nasty kicks on and after their turning points, are the ones that apply.

The return of the cyclical perspective is perhaps clearest in macroeconomics. Throughout most of the 1990s and considerably beyond, until about 2008, most economists believed in something called "the Great Moderation." It was believed that the business cycle was, if not quite dead, defanged, due to better monetary policy and financial regulation. It was believed that the advanced economies could enjoy both growth and a kind of stability more or less forever, at least if our central banks would follow some textbook-level advice. And indeed, for many years the United States, among other countries, demonstrated fairly smooth economic performance with low unemployment. But it turned out that the very stability of the system had destabilizing properties, and in some key ways it contained the seeds of its own destruction. The more stable that investors and homeowners, thought things would be, over time, the more willing they became to take risk and pile on excess leverage. Americans borrowed more and more, and eventually thus arose a real estate bubble and an unstable banking system. By now the story is well known and I won't repeat it all here. But by the end of the financial crisis, economic opinion had shifted in the direction of the ideas of Hyman Minsky, an earlier theorist of cyclical economic crises. Minsky had argued that periods of financial stability contained the seeds of their own destruction, because eventually all that stability would cause investors to let down their collective guard and take too much risk. We saw a version of the same happen in the eurozone, where, following the creation of the euro, there were many very positive expectations and a major flow of capital to the economy in the periphery, including of course Greece. But eventually these positive expectations started to outrace the reality, and so those capital flows culminated in a financial explosion and crisis starting in 2011, followed by intermittent flare-ups and generally low economic growth and, in many countries, massive unemployment.

These days, few macroeconomists are predicting that we have beat the business cycle forever. The current and wiser view is that business cycles and also deep recessions eventually return in a cyclical manner. Long periods of stability sooner or later give rise to excess risk-taking and some kind of overextension, leading to a later correction (and typically a bumpy rather than a smooth one). In fact, the stronger and more durable the initial period of calm, the more of a doozy the eventual downturn might be.

The thing is, we've learned that about the business cycle, but only now is it starting to sink in that such patterns have a lot of power to explain cycles in other realms as well. Americans have dug into their comfortable cocoons with greater skill and acumen than they protected their shadow banking system or than how they tried to redo the Middle East. But the big domestic and social question of the next few decades will be this: **When it comes to ordinary, everyday American life, how quickly will matters turn chaotic or disorderly again, and what forms will that implosion take?**

Commentators have used a number of words or phrases to describe this general process of a period of peace or calm leading to subsequent volatility. Richard Florida coined the term "the Great Reset" in a book of the same name, mostly about the evolution of North American cities. Greg Ip, an economic reporter at the *Wall Street Journal*, wrote a book called *Foolproof: Why Safety Can Be Dangerous and How Danger Makes Us Safe*, about how the obsessive quest for safety can be self-defeating, because risk does eventually accumulate. Nassim Taleb titled his 2015 essay with Gregory F. Treverton "The Calm Before the Storm: Why Volatility Signals Stability, and Vice Versa." So these ideas are in the air, but they haven't burst forth to dominate the discourse. Therefore, I wish to say it again: **The biggest story of the last fifteen years, both nationally and globally, is the growing likelihood that a cyclical model of history will be a better predictor than a model of ongoing progress**.

A lot of today's stories, while significant in their own right, can be understood properly only in terms of that larger risk. Or if you wish to use the language of financial economics, the possibility of cyclical patterns in history is right now the single biggest source of systemic, undiversifiable risk.

There is in recent times a sneaking suspicion that similar kinds of cyclical patterns may hold in global affairs and foreign policy as well. As Steven Pinker demonstrated in his best-selling book *The Better Angels of Our Nature: Why Violence Has Declined*, most measures of conflict have been falling since the end of the Second World War. That's great, but should we expect such a trend to continue? Pinker's tale is that peace begets more peace, as peace brings prosperity, which in turn encourages peace all the more. Who wants to give up a comfortable, happy lifestyle for the uncertainties and pains and expenses of war? For many of the world's citizens, violent conflict becomes unthinkable. Who now expects France and Britain to fight a war against each other, as in fact they have done many times in past centuries? Once people have prosperity, democracy, and security, it seems they want to keep those features in their lives and for all the right reasons. This is one big, big way in which modernity has been all to the good. Most Americans, and indeed most people throughout the developed world, have enjoyed a remarkable era of peace; the same is true for many of the emerging economies, at least outside of the Middle East.

Yet the processes favoring cumulative peace no longer seem as strong as they once did. Even a casual glance around the world reveals significant signs of slippage. The more the well-off countries desire peace and stability, the higher are the returns for some of the nastier autocrats to grab territory or resources using violence or the threat of violence. Again, it is like how macroeconomic stability eventually gives rise to excess risk-taking, thereby dissolving the previous stasis. In a general atmosphere of safety, risk builds up nonetheless, like simmering pressure under a volcano. To be sure, most countries still prefer the continuance of peace, and maybe more strongly than ever before, but that doesn't mean all countries will play by these rules. A small number of countries and their autocrats will take the widespread desire for peace and stability as an invitation to grab something. And so in this new world order, Putin's Russia has seized part of Ukraine and sent active troops to Syria, in both cases disrupting previous norms. Even the future of NATO now seems open to serious question, in part from Donald Trump but more generally because enthusiasm for the alliance has waned and most of the member countries are not spending on the military what they had pledged. Various fighting forces have destroyed much of the Middle East and North Africa, without expecting much in the way of a decisive foreign response. That expectation may well turn out to be wrong, but as I am writing in late 2016, reluctance to get involved in another Afghanistan or Iraq has kept American ground involvement in those conflicts to a relative minimum, compared to the scale of the violence being perpetrated. In any case, the world is no longer becoming more peaceful each year; whether this should count as a longer-run break in trend remains to be seen.

In none of these cases can it be said that the response of "the free world" has solved the foreign policy problem or pushed back the prior aggression. And so we have to consider the possibility that such breaches of the peace will continue and perhaps even accelerate, thereby introducing a cyclical pattern through which a previous peace proves unstable and eventually leads to subsequent conflict.

It is far too early to conclude that global peace is collapsing. It remains a possible scenario that today's hottest trouble spots patch up their problems and the world returns to a calmer state of affairs. Nonetheless, confidence in ongoing progress toward ever-greater peace has been shaken—badly shaken, I would say—even if things have calmed down by the time you are reading these words. If Syria can be devastated as a country, surely some other place can follow and maybe will follow. How many more? If Russia can get away with seizing Crimea in Ukraine, what other territory transfers might prove possible? Are all of the Gulf

States so stable? Might the Saudi–Iran proxy war explode? Will the North Korean tyrants really stay bottled up in their impact on the broader Asian continent? As I write, no one knows, but it is far from obvious that the net trend has been toward ongoing improvements when it comes to these questions.

In fact, most measures indicate the world is now becoming more conflict-ridden and less free. The number of conflicts has been increasing for about six years, much of the Middle East is up in flames, Syria has produced the world's greatest refugee crisis since the Second World War, and illiberalism and political autocracy have been on the rise, by the best available measures, since early in the new millennium.[11]

These days the path toward ever-greater peace doesn't look as sure as it once did. The higher the benefits of peace, the more gun-shy and war-shy the prosperous and peaceful countries will become. And thus the greater the incentives for some smaller number of brutes to seize territory or start wars or otherwise behave in an aggressive manner on the international scene. And once one brute shows it is possible, some number of other brutes may follow. **All of this can happen even if you think the majority response will be a greater and greater love of peace**, as indeed I do think. Only a few rotten apples may be enough to upset the entire equilibrium once the lid is lifted, so to speak. And so the cyclical story here is not an entirely encouraging one.

The ancient Greeks very commonly viewed history in cyclical terms. They had seen so many territories, city-states, and empires rise and fall that they knew not to believe in either ongoing progress or in perpetual doom and decline. What they saw was a pendulum swinging back and forth. I was struck by this passage I read recently in a work on ancient history:

The economy of Greece is in shambles. Internal rebellions have engulfed Libya, Syria, and Egypt, with outsiders and foreign warriors fanning the flames. Turkey fears it will become involved, as does Israel. Jordan is crowded with refugees. Iran is bellicose and threatening, while Iraq is in turmoil. AD 2013? Yes. But it was also the situ-

ation in 1177 BC, more than three thousand years ago, when Bronze Age Mediterranean civilizations collapsed one after the other, changing forever the course and the future of the Western world. It was a pivotal moment in history—a turning point for the ancient world.

That is from Eric H. Cline's *1177: The Year Civilization Collapsed,*[12] but as Cline himself points out there is a striking parallel between the distant past and present times.

Perhaps at our peril, the insights of antiquity into the potential cyclicality of history were swept under the carpet with the coming of the Western Enlightenment in the eighteenth century and the flowering of the Industrial Revolution in the nineteenth. The dominant narrative became one of extreme and enduring progress, for reasons that corresponded to some pretty splendid evolving events on the ground. Even most of the dissidents believed in some form of ongoing progress, at least once the right social switches were flipped. For Karl Marx, for instance, communism would bring a final, utopian, and fully peaceful state of affairs. The classical economists viewed commercial society as the end product of a long period of historical development, and Georg Friedrich Hegel portrayed history as marching toward civil society, commercialism, and the modern state as he saw it embodied in Prussian bureaucracy.

Cyclical theories lived on in a kind of intellectual underground, such as in the writings of the eighteenth-century Italian philosopher Giambattista Vico. These ideas were neglected in part because, at least for a while, they didn't seem to fit the historical data being generated, and so the cyclical perspective on history remained on the periphery of Western thought. That made it harder for people to understand the import of temporary slowdowns and how they might herald the building up of greater pressures.

The two world wars threw these progress-based views for a considerable loop, and for a while, cyclical views of history returned, especially to Europe, as exemplified by some of the writings of historians Arnold Toynbee and Oswald Spengler. Nonetheless, from the late 1940s onward, most of the Western world again seemed to go in a pretty splendid way, Europe most of all, and so progress again became the dominant narrative. In some ways the progress narrative was stronger than ever. After all, if two major world wars could not dislodge the ultimate march of economic progress, social progress, greater tolerance, democratization, and fine August vacations, what possibly could?

There is the distinct possibility that, in the next twenty years, we are going to find out far more about how the world really works than we ever wanted to know. As the mentality of the complacent class loses its grip, the subsequent changes in attitude will be part of an unavoidable and perhaps ultimately beneficial process of social, economic, and legal transformation. But many Americans will wish, ever so desperately, to have that complacency back.

AFTERWORD TO THE 2018 EDITION

Given the nature of the publishing process, I wrote almost all of *The Complacent Class* before the 2016 U.S. presidential election. There are some mentions of Trump beating Clinton, but as last-minute fill-ins rather than integral discussions. Given that absence, I thought I would add a few thoughts on how the election, and its subsequent unfolding, relate to the core themes of this book. In reading this, however, keep in mind there is another production lag, so in fact much more has happened—quite possibly some major developments—since I drafted this afterword.

I think of the 2016 election campaign as a backward-looking debate reflecting two visions of America's past. The two candidates were among the oldest who have run for the presidency, and neither counts as a fresh face. Trump's fame is rooted in the 1980s, and Hillary Clinton's in the 1990s.

Hillary Clinton campaigned on the basis that the Obama administration was essentially a success, had worked out well, and that we would get more of the same, though perhaps with more social welfare programs at the margins. She also was happy to rely on the successes, or perceived successes, of the earlier Clinton administration run by her husband. At times her campaign toyed with slogans such as "It's her turn." The campaign felt rooted in a sense of entitlement, and although there were detailed policy briefs on all or most of the major issues, she didn't do a very good job articulating to voters her vision of where America should be headed or why she wanted to be the president. It felt to her, and to many of her supporters, as if she deserved it.

Ultimately, I think she and many of her supporters realized that her election might not have made America a much more inspiring or different place. But for the complacent, this was OK, and she promised to her supporters—with some credible arguments behind it I might add—that electing her opponent would lead to something far worse.

Trump also campaigned on a backward-looking vision, though he looked further back to the past than Hillary Clinton did. "Make America Great Again" refers to an earlier albeit ill-defined period of time; the slogan was not, but could have been, something more like "Bring a New Greatness to America." After all, John F. Kennedy had "The New Frontier," Lyndon Johnson promoted "The Great Society," and Ronald Reagan spoke of a "new morning" for America. Trump made a deliberate decision to do otherwise.

The core features of Trump's campaign promises in fact hearkened back to the 1950s. He imagined an America with many more manufacturing jobs, less reliance on foreign allies, higher tariffs, fewer immigrants, much less political correctness, and more sharply divided distinctions between male roles and female roles in society. Those views to me sound broadly like the Eisenhower years, except this is to be for 2017 and later.

The actual presidency of Trump, so far, has differed significantly from the campaign promises. He has focused mostly on undoing various Obama-era changes, on issues such as regulation, the environment, and foreign policy, with a (so far) failed attempt on the health care front. No matter how many of these policy changes you might agree or disagree with, they seem strikingly unambitious for a president whose party controls all major branches of the government. For all of his outrageous rhetoric, Trump is essentially a presidency of stasis.

I find it striking that many of Trump's supporters don't seem to mind very much. They understand full well that Trump is not going to bring back the past, or some mythical version of the past. Instead, many of his supporters are happy enough to have someone in the White House voicing a particular set of cultural sentiments and offering them some recognition.

In an essay I wrote for the periodical *The American Interest*, I referred to Trump as the "placebo President":

> *Trump's main policy* is his rhetoric, *and his very act of promising to restore control to the "deplorables" is a significant signal of control itself. In essence, Trump supporters are diagnosing America's problems in terms of deficient discourse in the public sphere, as if they had read George Orwell and the Frankfurt School philosophers on the general topic but are drawing more on alt-right inspirations for the specifics of their critique.*[1]

In other words, the Trump presidency isn't actually about getting things done. Insofar as Trump relates to voters, it is about giving them a sense of motion and a rhetoric, while keeping many things the same, or if anything, promoting policies that will enhance the interests of traditional wealthy Republican elites.

In the meantime, America is not really moving forward. In *any* direction, except perhaps for increasing disorder within our politics, one sign of what I called in this book the Great Reset: a concept referring to the implosion of certain kinds of order that we previously took for granted. Again, I think this is the correct diagnosis regardless of your particular degree of like or dislike of the presidency of Donald Trump (I myself have never been a supporter).

I also find the opposition to Donald Trump striking in its complacency. Again, put aside your personal views on how good or bad Trump's proposals have been; we all can agree that many of Trump's opponents regard his presidency as a crisis and an unmitigated disaster.

As of July 2017, you can debate what the Russia connections really mean, but again it is clear many people think they signify something quite terrible, illegal, and irresponsible.

Given this background context, I am struck at how subdued the response to a Trump presidency has been. One might have expected that every weekend there would be major public events in Washington, or other major cities, calling for his impeachment or at least to put some of his associates on trial for conspiring with the Russians. Imagine sit-ins, marches, vigils, or maybe even riots. So far we haven't seen much of those, although there have been a fair number of campus protests about safe spaces, political correctness, and supposedly objectionable conservative speakers. In the 1960s or 1970s, I think the pushback against the Trump administration would have been very different and also much stronger and more effective. But those days are long since gone.

I do see that social media have sucked up a lot of the opposition to Trump and other controversial political figures. People tweet against Trump all day long, or they post missives on their Facebook pages. No matter what your political point of view, this just doesn't seem to be helpful, and sometimes I wonder if it isn't outright counterproductive. Social media seem to have become the opiate of the masses, another sign of complacency.

Ongoing polarization has enabled this complacency to continue. If you imagine the Russian revelations coming in, say, the America of 1963, the immediate outcry would have been staggering. There was more or less a common agreement on what America should be, and if one party had been more guilty than the other, the common vision would have kept us on track and Russian interference would not have been so much a partisan issue. Everyone would have rebelled against it rather quickly and decisively. These days, an America more segregated by ideology and income turns the issue into an ongoing debate between Republicans versus Democrats. That makes it much harder to solve the underlying problem of preventing Russian interference from happening again, or punishing the wrongdoers in the first place.

The Brexit referendum and its unfolding also illustrates some core themes of *The Complacent Class*. Like the Trump candidacy, the desire for Brexit reflected an urgent feeling that something had to be changed, combined with a complete unwillingness for people to give up any of their actual concrete privileges. Whether you favor or oppose Brexit, the result has been a political gridlock. The United Kingdom doesn't actually have much bargaining power with the European Union, and yet its citizens, post-Brexit, have been dreaming of alternatives that still give them open market access and most of their previous European Union rights. Instead of a coherent negotiating process, the conservative government has lost its grip on power and it is far from obvious how anyone can steer a Brexit process with any degree of order. There is now the risk of a "hard Brexit," whereby the United Kingdom is pushed out of the European Union without receiving any kind of new deal in return, with a big and immediate negative shock applied to British business and London as a financial center.

I view the Brexit movement as having promoted a backward-looking vision, unrealistic in terms of what it promised. And after the Brexit vote, it was revealed there had been absolutely no preparations for how to proceed in a positive direction. The British simply had lost the ability to imagine themselves as shaping a future very different from the present they already had; for instance, there hasn't been much of a movement to follow up on Brexit by moving Britain in either a socialistic or libertarian direction. Mostly the Brexit advocates were thinking in terms of cherry-picking the positive aspects of EU membership and simply proceeding as if there were no actual trade-offs to be faced. I find that kind of thinking pretty typical in societies that are plagued by denial and complacency.

What about the noncomplacent segments of the world? I've already written that immigrants are among the least complacent of Americans. They come to America knowing they are in for big changes of culture, language, and jobs whether they like all of those changes or not; this may even make them slightly neurotic, or perhaps immigration selects for the neurotic in the first place. Yet immigrants start new businesses at much higher rates than native-born Americans and overall they take more chances. By definition, they have no status quo to preserve and they are already walking out on a wire of sorts.

Overall, I see the political equilibrium in the United States as moving against the immigrants. The Trump administration has instituted a variety of measures to make immigration harder. Although Trump will not be in power forever, the pro-immigration forces within the Republican Party have grown progressively weaker. It is hard to see America arriving at a bipartisan consensus on immigration policy anytime soon, and so pro-immigration forces are mostly on the defensive these days and perhaps for some time to come. In the longer run, that will make America a more complacent country.

Another force against complacency in American society has been the entrepreneurs of Silicon Valley. As I discuss in the book, often the *products* of Silicon Valley make us more complacent, but still the *leaders* of the major tech companies have been very dynamic cultural and economic forces. That's great, but right now we seem to be in a moment where the tech world has stultified just a bit. The giants of Facebook, Google, Amazon, and Apple dominate what is right now a fairly static landscape, at least compared to the overall performance of Silicon Valley over the last few decades. I don't begrudge those companies their successes, but the world of tech seems to have hit a temporary lull. It runs the risk of becoming another somewhat bureaucratic force basically pushing for a slightly improved version of the status quo. I still hold out hope here, but we haven't been seeing the radical tech transformations that we did during say the first decade of this century, including for instance the rise of Google, Amazon, and the smartphone.

I also predicted in this book that we were entering a new era of cyberwar, much crime would shift to the internet, and the internet would prove to be an extraordinarily weak link in Western society. All of this has come true far more quickly than I had imagined. When I wrote that part of *The Complacent Class*, I had little inkling of all the cyberhacks that would accelerate, the phenomenon of "fake news" as an ideological weapon, the hacking and publication of Hillary Clinton's and others' emails, and the general realization of just how thin our cybersecurity has been. There even have been recent hacking attempts directed at our nuclear power infrastructure.

On those issues too, we seem to be complacent. The risk of a major cyberattack, even along Pearl Harbor lines, is very real, yet America is not doing nearly enough to protect its core cyber- and physical infrastructure from such a disastrous event. Instead, we simply seem to be assuming "it can't happen here." That too is another form of complacency, and one of the most dangerous manifestations of our lassitude.

In America, segregation by income seems to be worsening, as the fundamental trend of gentrification continues unchecked. We're still paranoid about exposing our kids to any dangers at all, and we are still overly reliant on medication. Most of all, we are complacent about our own complacency.

Yes, I do still have hope for the future. America has more talent than ever before, even if much of that talent is not being mobilized properly. But what will it take for this country to rediscover its properly innovative and dynamic heritage? I am still afraid of just how rough and bumpy that ride is going to be.

Tyler Cowen, July 2017

NOTES

Chapter 1

1. See Burrough (2015, p. 5). On Watts, see Bloom and Martin (2013, p. 29) and Barber (2010).
2. Hsieh and Moretti (2015).
3. For all of these points about car culture, I have drawn on Fisher (2015) and also Samuelson (2016) and Highway Loss Data Institute (2013).
4. Graeber (2015, pp. 109–110).
5. Steuerle (2014).
6. "Bailout Barometer" (2016).
7. See Bossard (1932) and Ansari and Klinenberg (2015).
8. See *Attica* (1972).
9. On the continuing popularity of Austen, see A. McCall Smith (2015).
10. See Sharpe (2015) and Schwarz (2015).
11. See Sax (2015, p. 59). I find the blizzard of conflicting estimates here daunting, but in general the estimates are quite high.
12. See Sax (2015, pp. 41–42), and for primary sources Robinson (1969) and Kaiser Family Foundation (2010).
13. On tag, see Boehm (2015), and on *Star Wars*, see Quinn (2015).
14. See "Student Testing in America's Great City Schools" (2015).
15. See Thompson (2016).
16. See Cowen (2013, p. 53).

Chapter 2

1. See Jasper (2000, p. 75).
2. Tocqueville (1969), bk. 1, pp. 374–77.
3. Ferrie (2005, p. 17).
4. For a skeptical view of African American migration leading to systematically higher average wages, see Eichenlaub, Tolnay, and Alexander (2010). For evidence that the migrants experienced shorter life spans, see D. Black, Sanders, Taylor, and Taylor (2015).
5. Lemann (1991, p. 95).
6. Lemann (1991, p. 201).
7. Sharkey (2015).
8. Molloy, Smith, and Wozniak (2014). For another general look at the decline in the mobility of labor across jobs, see Hyatt and Spletzer (2013).
9. Molloy, Smith, and Wozniak (2014). As for regions, geographic mobility is currently lowest in the American South, and that is a part of the country with a disproportionate share of American poverty. But moving away is no longer clearly the way out of this predicament. For instance, in 2010, 80 percent of the mothers who had been born in Texas also gave birth there. In part that is because Texas is a big state and offers greater opportunities for migration within the state, but in part living in the South seems to be especially "sticky" these days. Seven of the eleven states with the highest rates of "staying moms" are in the South. The other states with high rates of staying—measured across the behavior of the moms—are Wisconsin, Ohio, Indiana, and Michigan, a mix of Midwest and Rust Belt locales (Livingston, 2014).
10. Malamud and Wozniak (2010). There is good evidence that the connection between education and mobility is a causal one, namely that going to school changes how you think about your future place of residence and makes you more willing to move around.
11. On these points, see Livingston (2014) and Sharkey (2015).
12. Davis and Haltiwanger (2014), and more broadly see Molloy, Smith, and Wozniak (2013).
13. See Molloy, Smith, and Wozniak (2014); also "Three-in-Ten U.S. Jobs Are Held by the Self-Employed and the Workers They Hire" (2015) and Hyatt and Spletzer (2016). Molloy, Smith, Trezzi, and Wozniak (2016) also document a decline in American labor market fluidity.
14. Hyatt and Spletzer (2016, p. 2).
15. See Scott (2015).
16. See Ganong and Shoag (2012). By the way, this diminution in cross-state convergence also feeds into the issue of income inequality. Between 1940 and 1980,

cross-state convergence may have accounted for about 30 percent of the decline in hourly wage inequality.

17. See Hyatt and Spletzer (2013).

18. See Kleiner and Krueger (2013), Occupational Licensing (2015), and Rodrigue and Reeves (2016). And on lower levels of cross-state mobility, see Kleiner (2015).

19. See Bergin, Feenstra, and Hanson (2009).

20. The analysis here is from Cadena and Kovak (2013).

21. Molloy, Smith, and Wozniak (2014) consider this hypothesis in depth.

22. On the lower job surplus for less educated workers and how it may hinder mobility, see, for instance, Amior (2015).

23. See Davis and Haltiwanger (2014). Just to refresh your memory, the discussions on income mobility in this chapter use the standard definitions and frameworks. The population is divided up into segments by income, or sometimes by education, such as tenths or fifths. If a parent is in, say, the top tenth, how likely is it that the children of that parent also place high in terms of income? To the extent the intergenerational income correlation is high, income mobility is low; alternatively, this can be expressed in terms of an elasticity, namely how much a higher parental income increases the expected incomes of the children. If you have lots of parents in the bottom deciles or quintiles, with their kids climbing up into higher standing, then income mobility is relatively high. Income mobility is therefore not the same as inequality, which measures gaps between rich and poor at a particular time slice. Income mobility estimates also are not the same as measures of absolute opportunity, such as how many poor people climbed out of poverty. Mainstream measures of income mobility are fundamentally about a churn in relative income standing, as relative rankings of family incomes, and thus also family social standings, change across the generations.

24. A related mechanism is outlined by Costa and Kahn (2000). By the way, these authors are a married couple who found two good jobs together in Los Angeles.

25. On this mobility decline, see Dao, Furceri, and Loungani (2014).

26. See Winship (2015, pp. 9–10).

27. See Graif (2015). On location affecting poor children the most, see Chetty, Hendren, Kline, and Saez (2014, p. 1557).

28. For the study, see Chetty, Hendren, and Katz (2015); Wolfers (2015) provides a useful summary of this and related work. On half of the children being older than twelve, see Sampson (2008). Another interesting discovery was that the children who moved in their teen years were made *worse off* by the move. Arguably they already had absorbed the culture and norms of the old neighborhood and now had to adjust to a better school and a bit more discipline. They just didn't fit in, but they couldn't adapt to the new world either. These children also faced a possible

disruption from the act of moving itself, and on average they were getting less than three years' exposure to the better neighborhoods, given their ages. Their later incomes measure as 13 to 15 percent lower than those who did not move, although the statistical significance for that estimate is weak. In any case, these children were not seeing gains. That said, the measured adverse outcomes were much more likely to apply to the older males who moved than to the older females; perhaps for the girls there was an easier adjustment process to the new neighborhood and also a benefit from simply getting out of the more dangerous neighborhood. The adults who move, by the way, don't seem to be affected at all by their new environs when it comes to their economic outcomes. The girls who grew up in the better neighborhoods saw gains of a different sort. They were more likely to end up married and more likely to maintain an active relationship of some kind with the father of their children. They also ended up living in better neighborhoods as adults. On gender effects and mobility, see Leventhal, Dupéré, and Shuey (2015, pp. 516–517).

29. See Sampson (2008); on the exact take-up rate, see Chetty, Hendren, and Katz (2015, p. 2).

30. See Sampson (2000) and Chetty, Hendren, and Katz (2015, p. 13) on these neighborhoods.

31. See Rubinowitz and Rosenbaum (2000) for one study of Gatreaux. For the very recent study, see Chyn (2015). For general surveys of neighborhood effects, see Leventhal and Brooks-Gunn (2000); Sampson, Morenoff, and Gannon-Rowley (2002); Burdick-Will, Ludwig, Raudenbush, Sampson, Sanbonmatsu, and Sharkey (2010); and Leventhal, Dupéré, and Shuey (2015).

32. On the latter point, see Ganong and Shoag (2012).

33. Streithorst (2015).

34. Streithorst (2015). On the gentrification of the South Bronx, see Kaysen (2015). On the median salary, 83.9 percent of national median salary on rent = (3750*12 / 53657). On the 1980s comparison, see Edlund, Machado, and Sviatchi (2015).

35. Hsieh and Moretti (2015); the quotation is from their abstract.

Chapter 3

1. Reardon and Bischoff (2011a, 2011b). On school lunch segregation, see Owens, Reardon, and Jencks (2014).

2. Reardon and Bischoff (2011a, 2011b).

3. Reardon and Bischoff (2011a, pp. 18–19).

4. Florida and Mellander (2015, pp. 44–45).

5. Florida and Mellander (2015, pp. 44–45). Some of that segregation comes from the presence of the universities themselves, but I do not see why this should not

count in the metrics. A lot of American universities are fairly segregated places and also exert a very real or sometimes even dominant cultural influence on their towns and cities.

6. Florida and Mellander (2015, p. 9). For San Francisco, see *Zumper National Rent Report* (2015).

7. Florida and Mellander (2015, pp. 37–38).

8. Florida and Mellander (2015, p. 28).

9. See Florida and Mellander (2015), "Segregated City." For an overview, see Badger (2015). On the logic of segregation in terms of models, see, for instance, Sethi and Somanathan (2004). On the connection between building restrictions and income segregation, see Lens and Monkkonen (2016).

10. Reardon and Bischoff (2011a, 2011b).

11. Florida and Mellander (2015, pp. 9, 37, passim). Sometimes college students are cited as a kind of "excuse" for high levels of measured segregation, and thus these measurements are sometimes called "mismeasurements." But colleges contribute to the feel of a place as much as other institutions do, maybe more given their influence, their high endowments, and their connections with powerful and influential people across many broader communities.

12. See Campoy (2015).

13. See Bishop (2008, p. 131) and also online data from the U.S. Census Bureau.

14. On these results, see Stroub and Richards (2013).

15. See J. R. Logan (2011, passim, and esp. p. 3).

16. Orfield and Frankenberg (2014, p. 10).

17. Orfield and Frankenberg (2014, p.12).

18. Orfield and Frankenberg (2014, p. 14).

19. Orfield and Frankenberg (2014, pp. 14, 25). On the trend, see J. R. Logan (2011).

20. Orfield and Frankenberg (2014, p. 18).

21. Orfield and Frankenberg (2014, p. 19). On the importance of integrated schooling for life outcomes, see R. C. Johnson (2015).

22. Orfield and Frankenberg (2014, p. 20).

23. Kucsera with Orfield (2014, pp. vi–viii).

24. "New Racial Segregation Measures for Large Metropolitan Areas" (2015). See also D. Hertz (2014) for a discussion of this data.

25. See K. Taylor (2015) and Hannah-Jones (2016).

26. See J. R. Logan (2011), with the quotation from p. 3.

27. That is from Vara (2016).

28. For Latino and Asian data, see J. R. Logan (2011).

29. See Chetty, Hendren, Kline, and Saez (2014).

30. On the halting of convergence, see Mazumder (2014).

31. On this theme of sorting and polarization, see Bishop (2008).
32. See Fiorina (2014).
33. On the rise in imprisonment, see "Public Safety, Public Spending" (2007) and also "One in 31" (2009). On Tocqueville, see Liptak (2008).
34. Neal and Rick (2014).
35. See Murakawa (2014, pp. 121–122).

Chapter 4

1. On Gates, see Friedman (2014).
2. See Hathaway and Litan (2014). For the exact numbers on start-ups, see Haltiwanger, Jarmin, and Miranda (2012); for the numbers on new tech firms, see Haltiwanger, Hathaway, and Miranda (2014). See Casselman (2014) for a popular overview of some of this data. In general, the numbers come from the Census Bureau's Longitudinal Business Database; see Decker, Haltiwanger, Jarmin, and Miranda (2014) for a discussion. See also Decker, Haltiwanger, Jarmin, and Miranda (2015) in particular on the lack of major upside for young firms.
3. Decker, Haltiwanger, Jarmin, and Miranda (2014, pp. 11, passim).
4. See Decker, Haltiwanger, Jarmin, and Miranda (2014, pp. 11, passim) and also Decker (2013). Information on employment at newly opened firms is from JP Morgan economist Michael Feroli, as summarized by Pethoukis (2014).
5. Decker, Haltiwanger, Jarmin, and Miranda (2014, pp. 19, passim).
6. Decker, Haltiwanger, Jarmin, and Miranda (2014, pp. 19, 29). See Decker, Haltiwanger, Jarmin, and Miranda (2015) on the decline in unicorns.
7. Decker, Haltiwanger, Jarmin, and Miranda (2014, p. 16).
8. See Healy (2014).
9. For instance, on the health care sector, see Mathews (2015).
10. See Ip (2015).
11. See Francis and Knutson (2015).
12. The growing import of intangibles is easiest to see in the tech sector. A lot of what tech companies have built, or are building, will be obsolete in less than ten years' time, at least in terms of their tangible products and software. The successful tech companies have high valuations in part because investors understand that they have a phenomenal ability to recruit human talent and apply it to rapidly changing problems in the tech sector. That is an intangible.
13. On net investment, see Mandel (2011); on capital services and the trend of nonresidential investment, see Mandel (2015), drawing on Bureau of Labor Statistics figures, and also Furman (2015). The capital services variable attempts to mea-

sure the productive flow of value from capital for the relevant time period. Since corporations own their capital, however, this measure is not based directly on market prices, and it is necessarily imprecise, requiring, for instance, estimates of deterioration and depreciation.

14. See Fontanella-Khan and Massoudi (2015).

15. See Boroush (2015).

16. On manufacturing research and development, see Lawrence and Edwards (2013).

17. Steinbock (2015).

18. The quotation is from Fernald and Wang (2015). On all of these measures, see also Field (2009) and Fernald (2014a, 2014b). The basic TFP numbers are taken from the Bureau of Labor Statistics; to the extent you may see variation in reported TFP numbers, it may stem for whether and how they are adjusted for business cycles and changes in capacity utilization. Still, those differences do not change the basic story told in text. If you are wondering, TFP estimates for the late nineteenth century run between 1 and 2 percent, see Field (2009), although these numbers are somewhat speculative.

19. That is from the U.S. Department of Labor, Bureau of Labor Statistics.

20. See the work of Berger (2012) on restructuring productivity.

21. See Yglesias (2015) on this point.

22. See, for instance, Andrews, Criscuolo, and Gal (2015), and also Mueller, Ouimet, and Simintzi (2015).

23. See McKenna and Tung (2015) and Schwartz (2015).

24. *Economic Report of the President* (2015, chap. 1).

25. For a variety of pessimistic labor market indicators, see Cowen (2013). On Mexican migration, see Passel, Cohn, and Gonzalez-Barrera (2012). On mortality, see Case and Deaton (2015).

26. See Hilger (2015). For other relevant studies of income mobility, with broadly consistent results, see Long and Ferrie (2013); Chetty, Hendren, Kline, Saez, and Tuner (2014); Hertz (2007); and Lee and Solon (2009).

27. On progress in high school graduation, see, for instance, Goldin (1998), or Census Bureau data. Gordon (2016) provides a detailed look at the differences in the progress of 1870 to 1970 versus more recent times.

28. See U.S. Department of Transportation, Bureau of Transportation Statistics.

29. On Apollo as a percentage of GDP, see Stine (2009).

30. For another detailed study of whether mismeasured information technology can account for the productivity gap, see Byrne, Fernald, and Reinsdorf (2016), who conclude it cannot. See also Syverson (2016).

31. See Nakamura and Soloveichik (2016).

Chapter 5

1. See Heath (2015).
2. See Van Buskirk (2015).
3. For the global comparison, see S. Johnson (2015). For the other numbers, and related analysis, see Boluk (2015).
4. See S. Johnson (2015). The figures are from the Department of Labor, ultimately the Occupational Employment Statistics.
5. See Bossard (1932). Ansari (2015) provides an overview of modern matching in the field of marriage and romance.
6. On Sizzl, see Wehner (2015).
7. On Once, see McAlone (2016).
8. On the latter point, see Eastwick and Finkel (2007).
9. See Swanson (2015).
10. See Greenwood, Guner, Kocharkov, and Santos (2015).
11. On some potential gains and costs, see Eastwick and Finkel (2008) and Eastwick, Luchies, Finkel, and Hunt (2013). The quotation is from Finkel, Eastwick, Karney, Reis, and Sprecher (2012, p. 46), which is more generally a very good overview of its topic.
12. See Tanner (2015) on ads that follow you around.
13. Quote is from Goodin (2015).
14. See Koncius (2015).
15. On how these markets work, see Nosowitz (2015).
16. "Is GDP Wildly Underestimating GDP?" (2015) considers how we may be underestimating the current value of our stock of goods and services, and underestimating the value of cumulated savings, and how such underestimation would help clear up some anomalies in the data.
17. On the decline in pet euthanasia, see "Pets by the Numbers" (N.d.), Nakai (2010), and "The New Shelter Dog" (2015).
18. On this and related services, see Jolly (2015).
19. See Chandra, Finkelstein, Sacarny, and Syverson (2015, including p. 20).
20. See Şahin, Song, Topa, and Violante (2014).
21. See Nunn (2013).
22. Smedley (2014).
23. Ansari (2015, pp. 89–90).

Chapter 6

1. See Burrough (2015, p. 5).
2. See Bloom and Martin (2013, p. 29) and Barber (2010, p. 32).
3. Newton (2009, p. 128).

4. Goldstein (1979, pp. 430–432). On the number of protests, see McPhail, Schweingruber, and McCarthy (1998, p. 55).
5. See Bausum (2015, p. 49).
6. See Cobb (2015, pp. 7, 129, passim).
7. See, for instance, "Dogs, Fire Hoses Used to Disperse Negro Marchers" (1963); on the refusal to use fire hoses against the six-year-olds, see "Dogs and Fire Hoses Turned on Negroes" (1963).
8. See Krotoszynski (2015).
9. For the quotation, see Hudson (2006, p. 115).
10. Franck and Huang (2012, p. 16). On Chase Manhattan being the original plan, see Gillham, Edwards, and Noakes (2013, p. 84).
11. See Smithsimon (2012, p. 42) for a discussion of these tactics.
12. On the legal and practical import of private-sector involvement, see Eisenberg (2012).
13. See Zick (2009, pp. 1–2).
14. On these different kinds of styles, see Gillham (2007); on the different kind of zones, see Gillham (2011).
15. See Mitchell and Staeheli (2005).
16. See Mitchell and Staeheli (2005).
17. On these developments, see Benton-Short (2007).
18. On the problems with the impromptu gatherings in Seattle, see Mitchell (2003).
19. See Mitchell and Staeheli (2005) on surveillance and Benton-Short (2007) on CCTV.
20. On this perspective, see Zick (2009, esp. p. 25).
21. See Zick (2009, pp. 53, passim).
22. The first quotation is from Kalven (1965, p. 139); see Kalven (1965, pp. 139–143) on the Court and p. 179 on Justice Stewart. On the March on Washington, see Gentile (1983, pp. 65–71).

Chapter 7

1. I am not aware of trustworthy data for this period, but it is not unusual to see suggestions of less than $100 per capita per year. I would urge caution, but in any case, standards of living were quite low.
2. See, for instance, Anger and Heineck (2010) and Grönqvist, Vlachos, and Öckert (2010) for some different estimates on transmission mechanisms.
3. See Hertz, Jayasundera, Piraino, Selcuk, Smith, and Verashchagina (2008).
4. Partnership for a New American Economy (2011).
5. For an overview of the fight to legalize same-sex marriage, see Pierceson (2013).
6. See Warner (1999).

Chapter 8

1. Congressional Budget Office (N.d.).
2. Steuerle (2014, pp. 7–8).
3. See Office of Management and Budget; Budget of the United States FY2017, within that source Summary Tables; Table S-4 and Table S-12.
4. See T. Taylor (2015).
5. Based on author calculations from http://ec.europa.eu/eurostat/statistics-explained /index.php/File:Current_healthcare_expenditure,_2012_(%C2%B9)_YB15.png, http://ec.europa.eu/eurostat/statistics-explained/images/9/92/Healthcare _expenditure_YB2015.xlsx, http://ec.europa.eu/eurostat/statistics-explained/index .php/Healthcare_expenditure_statistics, http://data.worldbank.org/indicator/SH .XPD.PCAP.
6. "Social Spending Is Falling in Some Countries (OECD, 2014).
7. On these themes, see Krastev (2014, pp. 39 and passim).
8. On this shift in perspective, see Hacker and Pierson (2014).
9. Tocqueville (1969), vol. 2, bk. 2, chap. 16, p. 536 for the quotation, and see also vol. 2, bk. 2, chap. 16, and p. 613 in particular on the causes of this democratic restlessness.
10. Tocqueville (1969, vol. 1, bk. 1, pp. 374–377).
11. Tocqueville, (1969, vol. 2, bk. 1, p. 548).
12. Tocqueville (1969, vol. 2, bk. 2, part 3, chap. 21, p. 645).
13. On these points, see Tocqueville (1969), passim, and vol. 1, bk. 1, part 1, chap. 7; and also Lawler (1993, pp. 34–36), with the quotation coming on p. 36.
14. Tocqueville (1969), vol. 1, pp. 377–378; see also pp. 376 and 381. Schleifer (2000) discusses this theme in Tocqueville.
15. Tocqueville (1969), vol. 2, bk. 2, Part 4, chap. 6, p. 691.
16. Tocqueville (1969), vol. 2, bk 2, Part 4, chap. 6, p. 693.
17. For one example of a Chinese reaction to American democracy, see "Red Flag Manuscript: 'Chaos' in Western Democracy" (2014).

Chapter 9

1. For one source on all of these developments, see Eligon (2015).
2. For the Nigerian estimate, see "Millions of Victims Lost $12.7B Last Year Falling for Nigerian Scams" (2014), but please note that I don't trust any of the estimates for internet crime, least of all for this area. On the costs of spam, see Rao and Reiley (2012) for this relatively conservative estimate.
3. See Latzer (2016, p. 102) and also Bell (1962 [1960], chapter 8 and in particular p. 151).

4. For those pie charts, see Roeder, Eisen, and Bowling (2015, p. 6). On the parallel with Canada, see Latzer (2016, p. 247).
5. "Beyond Distrust" (2015).
6. On declining trust across the two parties, see, for instance, Haidt and Hetherington (2012).
7. See, for instance, Purtill (2016) and Silver (2016).
8. See Solt (2008, 2015). On the World Values Survey, see Krieckhaus, Son, Bellinger, and Wells (2014).
9. See Ashok, Kuziemko, and Washington (2015). In general these trends are robust long-run trends and they do not require the particular start date of 1970.
10. On female education and the number of children, see Hazan and Zoabi (2015).
11. See Global Peace Index 2016 (2016) and also Freedom in the World (2016).
12. See Cline (2014).

Afterword to the 2018 Edition

1. "America's Placebo President?" https://www.the-american-interest.com/2017/03 /06/americas-placebo-president/.

REFERENCES

Amior, Michael. "Why Are Higher Skilled Workers More Mobile Geographically? The Role of the Job Surplus." CEP Discussion Paper 1338, 2015.

Andrews, Dan, Chiara Criscuolo, and Peter N. Gal. "Frontier Firms, Technology Diffusion and Public Policy: Micro Evidence from OECD Countries." OECD working paper, 2015.

Anger, Silke, and Guido Heineck. "Do Smart Parents Raise Smart Children? The Intergenerational Transmission of Cognitive Abilities." *Journal of Population Economics* 23 (2010): 1255, 1282.

Ansari, Aziz, and Eric Klinenberg. "How to Make On-Line Dating Work." *The New York Times*, June 13, 2015.

Ansari, Aziz, with Eric Klinenberg. *Modern Romance*. New York: Penguin Press, 2015.

Attica: The Official Report of the New York State Special Commission on Attica. New York: Bantam Books, 1972.

Ashok, Vivekinan, Ilyana Kuziemko, and Ebonya Washington. "Support for Redistribution in an Age of Rising Inequality: New Stylized Facts and Some Tentative Explanations." National Bureau of Economic Research Working Paper 21529, September 2015.

Badger, Emily. "The Wealthy Are Walling Themselves Off in Cities Increasingly Segregated by Class." *The Washington Post*, Wonkblog, February 23, 2015.

"Bailout Barometer: How Large Is the Financial Safety Net?" Federal Reserve Bank of Richmond, February 3, 2016.

Barber, David. *A Hard Rain Fell: SDS and Why it Failed*. Jackson: University of Mississippi Press, 2010.

Bausum, Ann. *Stonewall: Breaking Out in the Fight for Gay Rights*. New York: Viking Press, 2015.

Bell, Daniel. *The End of Ideology: On the Exhaustion of Political Ideas in the Fifties*. New York: The Free Press, 1962 [1960].

Benton-Short, Lisa. "Bollards, Bunkers, and Barriers: Securing the National Mall in Washington, DC." *Environment and Planning D: Society and Space* 25 (2007): 424–446.

Berger, David W. "Countercyclical Restructuring and Jobless Recoveries." Yale University working paper, 2012.

Bergin, Paul R., Robert C. Feenstra, and Gordon H. Hanson. "Offshoring and Volatility: Evidence from Mexico's Maquiladora Industry." *American Economic Review* 99, no. 4 (September 2009): 1664–671.

"Beyond Distrust: How Americans View Their Government." Pew Research Center, November 23, 2015.

Bishop, Bill. *The Big Sort: Why the Clustering of Like-Minded America Is Tearing Us Apart*. Boston: Houghton Mifflin, 2008.

Black, Dan A., Seth G. Sanders, Evan J. Taylor, and Lowell J. Taylor, "The Impact of the Great Migration on Mortality of African Americans: Evidence from the Deep South." *American Economic Review* 105, no. 2 (February 2015): 477–503.

Bloom, Joshua, and Waldo E. Martin Jr. *Blacks against Empire: The History and Politics of the Black Panther Party*. Berkeley: University of California Press, 2013.

Boehm, Eric. "You're It: School District Bans Tag during Recess." *The Daily Signal*, October 8, 2015.

Boluk, Liam. "Ride or Die: Less Money, Mo' Music & Lots of Problems: A Look at the Music Biz." Redef.com, August 13, 2015.

Boroush, Mark. "U.S. R&D Increased in 2013, Well Ahead of the Pace of Gross Domestic Product." InfoBrief, National Science Foundation, National Center for Science and Engineering Statistics, September 2015.

Bossard, James H. S. "Residential Propinquity as a Factor in Marriage Selection." *American Journal of Sociology* 38, no. 2 (September 1932): 219–224.

Burdick-Will, Julia, Jens Ludwig, Stephen W. Raudenbush, Robert J. Sampson, Lisa Sanbonmatsu, and Patrick Sharkey. "Converging Evidence for Neighborhood Effects on Children's Test Scores: An Experimental, Quasi-experimental, and Observational Comparison." Working paper, 2010.

Burrough, Bryan. *Days of Rage: America's Radical Underground, the FBI, and the Forgotten Age of Revolutionary Violence*. New York: Penguin Press, 2015.

Byrne, David M., John G. Fernald, and Marshall B. Reinsdorf. "Does the United

States Have a Productivity Slowdown or a Measurement Problem?" Working paper, March 1, 2016.

Cadena, Brian C., and Brian K. Kovak. "Immigrants Equilibrate Local Labor Markets: Evidence from the Great Recession." Unpublished working paper, 2013.

Campoy, Ana. "Boom Times Test Austin's Music Scene." *The Wall Street Journal*, August 26, 2015.

Case, Anne, and Deaton, Angus. "Rising Morbidity and Mortality in Midlife among White Non-Hispanic Americans in the 21st Century." *PNAS* 112, no. 49 (2015): 15078–83.

Casselman, Ben. "Corporate America Hasn't Been Disrupted." *FiveThirtyEight*, August 8, 2014.

Chandra, Amitabh, Amy Finkelstein, Adam Sacarny, and Chad Syverson. "Healthcare Exceptionalism? Performance and Allocation in the U.S. Healthcare Sector." National Bureau of Economic Research Working Paper 21603, October 2015.

Chetty, Raj, Nathaniel Hendren, and Lawrence F. Katz. "The Effects of Exposure to Better Neighborhoods on Children: New Evidence from the Moving to Opportunity Experiment." National Bureau of Economic Research Working Paper 21156, May 2015.

Chetty, Raj, Nathaniel Hendren, Patrick Kline, Emmanuel Saez, and Nicholas Turner. "Is the United States Still a Land of Opportunity? Recent Trends in Intergenerational Mobility." National Bureau of Economic Research Working Paper 19844, January 2014.

Chetty, Raj, Nathaniel Hendren, Patrick Kline, and Emmanuel Saez. "Where Is the Land of Opportunity? The Geography of Intergenerational Mobility in the United States." *Quarterly Journal of Economics* 129, no. 4 (November 2014): 1553–1623.

Chyn, Eric. "Moved to Opportunity: The Long-Run Effect of Public Housing Demolition on Labor Market Outcomes of Children." Working paper, University of Michigan, 2015.

Cline, Eric H. *1177: The Year Civilization Collapsed*. Princeton, NJ: Princeton University Press, 2014.

Cobb, Charles E. Jr. *This Nonviolent Stuff'll Get You Killed: How Guns Made the Civil Rights Movement Possible*. New York: Basic Books, 2015.

Congressional Budget Office. "An Update to the Budget and Economic Outlook: 2015 to 2025." https://www.cbo.gov/sites/default/files/114th-congress-2015-2016/reports/50724-BudEconOutlook-3.pdf.

Costa, Dora L., and Matthew E. Kahn. "Power Couples: Changes in the Locational Choice of the College Educated." *Quarterly Journal of Economics* 115, no. 4 (November 2000): 1287–1315.

Cowen, Tyler. *Average Is Over: Powering America beyond the Age of the Great Stagnation.* New York: Dutton, 2013.

Dao, Mai, Davide Furceri, and Prakash Loungani. "Regional Labor Market Adjustments in the United States and Europe." IMF working paper, February 2014.

Davis, Steven J., and John Haltiwanger. "Labor Market Fluidity and Economic Performance." National Bureau of Economic Research Working Paper 20479, September 2014.

Decker, Ryan. "We're Getting Old and Fat!" *Updated Priors* blog, March 18, 2013, http://updatedpriors.blogspot.com/2013/03/were-getting-old-and-fat.html.

Decker, Ryan, John Haltiwanger, Ron S. Jarmin, and Javier Miranda. "The Secular Business Dynamism in the U.S." Working paper, June 2014.

Decker, Ryan, John Haltiwanger, Ron S. Jarmin, and Javier Miranda. "Where Has all the Skewness Gone? The Decline in High-Growth (Young) Firms in the U.S." National Bureau of Economic Research Working Paper 21776, December 2015.

"Dogs and Fire Hoses Turned on Negroes: Marchers Sent Sprawling." *Chicago Tribune*, May 4, 1963.

"Dogs, Fire Hoses Used to Disperse Negro Marchers." *St. Petersburg Times*, May 4, 1963.

Eastwick, Paul W., and Eli J. Finkel. "Selective vs. Unselective Romantic Desire: Not All Reciprocity Is Created Equal." *Psychological Science* 18 (April 2007): 317–319.

Eastwick, Paul W., and Eli J. Finkel. "Sex Differences in Mate Preferences Revisited: Do People Know What They Initially Desire in a Romantic Partner?" *Journal of Personality and Social Psychology* 94, no. 2 (2008): 245–264.

Eastwick, Paul W., Laura B. Luchies, Eli J. Finkel, and Lucy L. Hunt. "The Predictive Validity of Ideal Partner Preferences: A Review and Meta-Analysis." *Psychological Bulletin* 140, no. 3 (May 2013): 623–665.

Economic Report of the President. Washington, DC: presented to Congress February 2015.

Edlund, Lena, Cecilia Machado, and Michaela Sviatchi. "Bright Minds, Big Rent: Gentrification and the Rising Returns to Skill." National Bureau of Economic Research Working Paper 21729, November 2015.

Eichenlaub, Suzanne C., Stewart E. Tolnay, and J. Trent Alexander. "Moving Out but Not Up: Economic Outcomes in the Great Migration." *American Sociological Review* 75, no. 1 (February 2010): 101–125.

Eisenberg, Arthur. "Some Unresolved Constitutional Questions." In Ron Shiffman, Rick Bell, Lance Jay Brown, and Lynne Elizabeth, eds., *Beyond Zuccotti Park: Freedom of Assembly and the Occupation of Public Space*, 74–86. Oakland, CA: New Village Press, 2012.

Eligon, John. "Black Students See a University Riven by Race." *The New York Times*, November 12, 2015.

Fernald, John. "Productivity and Potential Output Before, During, and After the Great Recession." National Bureau of Economic Research Working Paper 20248, June 2014a.

Fernald, John. "A Quarterly, Utilization-Adjusted Series on Total Factor Productivity." Federal Reserve Board of San Francisco, April 2014b.

Fernald, John, and Bing Wang. "The Recent Rise and Fall of Rapid Productivity Growth." Federal Reserve Bank of San Francisco, February 9, 2015.

Ferrie, Joseph P. "The End of American Exceptionalism? Mobility in the U.S. since 1850." Northwestern University working paper, 2005.

Field, Alexander J. "US Economic Growth in the Gilded Age." *Journal of Macroeconomics* 31 (2009): 173–190.

Finkel, Eli J., Paul W. Eastwick, Benjamin R. Karney, Harry T. Reis, and Susan Sprecher. "Online Dating: A Critical Analysis from the Perspective of Psychological Science." *Psychological Science in the Public Interest* 20, no. 10 (2012): 1–64.

Fiorina, Morris. "Americans Have Not Become More Politically Polarized." *The Washington Post*, June 23, 2014.

Fisher, Marc. "A Love Affair in Reverse: For a Generation Hooked on Smartphones, Social Media and Uber, Car Culture Is Fading." *The Washington Post*, September 6, 2015.

Florida, Richard, and Charlotta Mellander. "Segregated City: The Geography of Economic Segregation in America's Metros." Martin Prosperity Institute, University of Toronto, 2015.

Fontanella-Khan, James, and Arash Massoudi. "Megadeals for 2015 Hit Record High." *The Financial Times*, September 18, 2015.

Francis, Theo, and Ryan Knutson. "Wave of Megadeals Tests Antitrust Limits in U.S." *The Wall Street Journal*, October 18, 2015.

Franck, Karen A., and Te-Sheng Huang. "Occupying Public Space, 2011: From Tahrir Square to Zuccotti Park." In Ron Shiffman, Rick Bell, Lance Jay Brown, and Lynne Elizabeth, eds., *Beyond Zuccotti Park: Freedom of Assembly and the Occupation of Public Space*, 3–20. Oakland, CA: New Village Press, 2012.

Freedom House, "Freedom in the World 2016." https://freedomhouse.org/report/freedom-world/freedom-world-2016.

Friedman, Uri. "Bill Gates: "The Idea That Innovation Is Slowing Down Is . . . Stupid." *The Atlantic*, March 12, 2014.

Furman, Jason. "Business Investment in the United States: Facts, Explanations, Puzzles, and Policy." Remarks delivered at the Progressive Policy Institute, September 30, 2015, online at https://m.whitehouse.gov/sites/default/files/page/files/20150930_business_investment_in_the_united_states.pdf.

Ganong, Peter, and Daniel Shoag. "Why Has Regional Convergence in the U.S. Stopped?" Harvard Kennedy School working paper, June 2012.

Gentile, Thomas. *March on Washington: August 28, 1963*. Washington, DC: New Day Publications, 1983.

Gillham, Patrick. "'More than a March in a Circle': Transgressive Protests and the Limits of Negotiated Management." *Mobilization: An International Quarterly* 12, no. 4 (January 2007): 341–357.

Gillham, Patrick F. "Securitizing America: Strategic Incapacitation and the Policing of Protest since the 11 September 2001 Terrorist Attacks." *Sociology Compass* 5/7 (2011): 636–652.

Gillham, Patrick F., Bob Edwards, and John A. Noakes. "Strategic Incapacitation and the Policing of Occupy Wall Street Protests in New York City, 2011." *Policing and Society* 23, no.2 (2013): 81–102.

Global Peace Index 2016. Institute for Economics and Peace, 2016.

Goldin, Claudia. "America's Graduation from High School: The Evolution and Spread of Secondary Schooling in the Twentieth Century." *Journal of Economic History* 58, no. 2 (1998): 345–74.

Goldstein, Robert Justin. *Political Repression in Modern America: From 1870 to the Present*. Cambridge, MA: Schenkman Publishing, 1979.

Goodin, Dan. "Beware of Ads That Use Inaudible Sound to Link Your Phone, TV, Tablet, and PC." *Ars Technica*, November 13, 2015.

Gordon, Robert J. *The Rise and Fall of American Growth: The U.S. Standard of Living since the Civil War*. Princeton, NJ: Princeton University Press, 2016.

Graeber, David. *The Utopia of Rules: On Technology, Stupidity, and the Secret Joys of Bureaucracy*. Brooklyn: Melville House, 2015.

Graif, Corina. "(Un)natural Disaster; Vulnerability, Long-Distance Displacement, and the Extended Geography of Neighborhood Distress and Attainment after Katrina." *Population and Environment* (August 2015): 1–31.

Greenwood, Jeremy, Nezih Guner, Georgi Kocharkov, and Cezar Santos. "Technology and the Changing Family: A Unified Model of Marriage, Divorce, Educational Attainment and Married Female Labor-Force Participation." *American Economic Journal: Macroeconomics* 8, no. 1 (December 2015): 1–41.

Grönqvist, Erik, Jonas Vlachos, and Björn Öckert. "The Intergenerational Transmission of Cognitive and Non-Cognitive abilities." IFAU—Institute for Labour Market Policy Evaluation working paper, 2010.

Hacker, Jacob S., and Paul Pierson, "After the 'Master Theory': Downs, Schattschneider, and the Rebirth of Policy-Focused Analysis." *Perspectives on Politics* 12, no. 3 (January 2014).

Haidt, Jonathan, and Marc J. Hetherington. "Look How Far We've Come Apart." *The New York Times*, September 17, 2012.

Haltiwanger, John, Ian Hathaway, and Javier Miranda. "Declining Business Dynamism in the U.S. High-Technology Sector." Ewing Marion Kauffman Foundation, February 2014.

Haltiwanger, John, Ron Jarmin, and Javier Miranda. "Where Have All the Young Firms Gone?" Ewing Marion Kauffman Foundation, May 2012.

Hannah-Jones, Nikole. "Choosing a School for My Daughter in a Segregated City." *The New York Times*, June 9, 2016.

Harrington, Jesse R., and Michele J. Gelfand. "Tightness-Looseness across the 50 United States." *PNAS* 111, no. 22 (June 2014): 7990–7995.

Hathaway, Ian, and Robert E. Litan. "Declining Business Dynamism in the United States: A Look at States and Metros." *Economic Studies at Brookings* (May 2014).

Hazan, Moshe, and Hosny Zoabi. "Do Highly Educated Women Choose Smaller Families?" *Economic Journal* (September 2015): 1191-26.

Healy, Kieran. "The Persistence of the Old Regime." *Crooked Timber* blog, August 6, 2014.

Heath, Alex. "Spotify Is Getting Unbelievably Good at Picking Music—Here's an Inside Look at How." *Tech Insider*, September 3, 2015.

Hertz, Daniel. "How Segregated Is New York City?" *NewGeography*, October 15, 2014, http://www.newgeography.com/content/004568-how-segregated-is-new-york-city.

Hertz, Tom. "Trends in the Intergenerational Elasticity of Family Income in the United States." *Industrial Relations* 46, no. 1 (January 2007): 22–50.

Hertz, Tom, Tamara Jayasundera, Patrizio Piraino, Sibel Selcuk, Nicole Smith, and Alina Verashchagina. "The Inheritance of Educational Inequality: International Comparisons and Fifty-Year Trends." *B.E. Journal of Economic Analysis and Policy* 7 (January 2008): 2.

Highway Loss Data Institute. "Evaluation of Changes in Teenage Driver Exposure." *Bulletin Bulletin* 30, no. 17 (September 2013).

Hilger, Nathaniel G. "The Great Escape: Intergenerational Mobility since 1940." National Bureau of Economic Research Working Paper 21217, May 2015.

Hsieh, Chang-Tai, and Enrico Moretti. "Why Do Cities Matter? Local Growth and Aggregate Growth." National Bureau of Economic Research Working Paper 21154, May 2015.

Hudson, David L. Jr. "Freedom of Assembly Was Crucial to the Civil Rights Movement." In Robert Winters, ed., *Freedom of Assembly and Petition*, 114–119. Farmington Hills, MI: 2006.

Hyatt, Henry R., and James R. Spletzer. "The Recent Decline in Employment Dynamics." IZA Working Paper 7231, February 2013.

Hyatt, Henry R., and James R. Spletzer. "The Shifting Job Tenure Distribution." U.S. Census Bureau Working Paper CES 16-12, February 2016.

Ingraham, Christopher. "Teen Marijuana Use Falls as More States Legalize." *The Washington Post*, December 16, 2014.

Ip, Greg. "Why Corporate America Could Use More Competition." *The Wall Street Journal*, July 8, 2015.

"Is GDP Wildly Underestimating GDP?" *Asymptosis* blog, November 27, 2015.

Jaffe, Eric. "The Mystery of Our Declining Mobility." *CityLab*, December 17, 2012.

Jasper, James M. *Restless Nation: Starting Over in America*. Chicago: University of Chicago Press, 2000.

Jencks, Christopher, and Susan E. Mayer. "The Social Consequences of Growing Up in a Poor Neighborhood." In Laurence E. Lynn Jr. and Michael G. H. McGeary, eds., *Inner-City Poverty in the United States*, 111–186. Washington, DC: National Academies Press, 1990.

Johnson, Rucker C. "Long-Run Impacts of School Desegregation & School Quality on Adult Attainments." National Bureau of Economic Research Working Paper 16664, August 2015.

Johnson, Steven. "The Creative Apocalypse That Wasn't." *The New York Times Magazine*, August 23, 2015.

Jolly, Jennifer. "Matchmaking, with Dogs as Dates." *The New York Times*, November 17, 2015.

Kaiser Family Foundation. *"Generation M2: Media in the Lives of 8- to 18-Year-Olds."* January 20, 2010.

Kalven, Harry Jr. *The Negro and the First Amendment*. Chicago: University of Chicago Press, 1965.

Kaysen, Ronda. "The South Bronx Beckons." *The New York Times*, September 21, 2015.

Kim, Sukkoo. "Economic Integration and Convergence: U.S. Regions, 1840–1987." *Journal of Economic History* 58, no. 3 (September 1998): 659–683.

Kleiner, Morris M. "Border Battles: The Influence of Occupational Licensing on Interstate Migration." W. E. Upjohn Institute for Employment Research, *Employment Research Newsletter* 22, no. 4 (2015): 4–6.

Kleiner, Morris M., and Alan B. Krueger. "Analyzing the Extent and Influence of Occupational Licensing on the Labor Market." *Journal of Labor Economics* 31, no. 2 (April 2013): S173–S202.

Koncius, Jura. "Stuff It: Millenials Nix Their Parents' Treasures." *The Washington Post*, September 21, 2015.

Krastev, Ivan. *Democracy Disrupted: The Politics of Global Protest*. Philadelphia: University of Pennsylvania Press, 2014.

Krieckhaus, Jonathan, Byunghwan Son, Nisha Mukherjee Bellinger, and Jason M. Wells. "Economic Inequality and Democratic Support." *Journal of Politics* 76, no. 1 (January 2014): 139–151.

Krotoszynski, Ronald J. "Could a Selma-like Protest Happen Today? Probably Not." *The Los Angeles Times*, March 7, 2015.

Kucsera, John, with Gary Orfield. *New York State's Extreme School Segregation: Inequality, Inaction and a Damaged Future*. N.p.: The Civil Rights Project, March 2014.

Latzer, Barry. *The Rise and Fall of Violent Crime in America*. New York: Encounter Books, 2016.

Lawler, Peter Augustine. *The Restless Mind: Alexis de Tocqueville on the Origin and Perpetuation of Human Liberty*. Lanham, MD: Rowman & Littlefield, 1993.

Lawrence, Robert Z., and Lawrence Edwards. "US Employment Deindustrialization: Insights from History and the International Experience." Peterson Institute for International Economics, Policy Brief PB13-27, October 2013.

Lee, Chul-In, and Gary Solon. "Trends in Intergenerational Income Mobility." *Review of Economics and Statistics* 91, no. 4 (November 2009): 766–772.

Lemann, Nicholas. *The Promised Land: The Great Black Migration and How It Changed America*. New York: Vintage Books, 1991.

Lens, Michael C., and Paavo Monkkonen. "Do Strict Land Use Regulations Make Metropolitan Areas More Segregated by Income?" *Journal of the American Planning Association* 82, no. 1 (Winter 2016): 6–21.

Leventhal, Tama, and Jeanne Brooks-Gunn. "The Neighborhoods They Live In: The Effects of Neighborhood Residence on Child and Adolescent Outcomes." *Psychological Bulletin* 126, no. 2 (2000): 309–337.

Leventhal, Tama, Véronique Dupéré, and Elizabeth A. Shuey. "Children in Neighborhoods." In Marc H. Bornstein and Tama Leventhal, eds., *Handbook of Child Psychology and Development Science*, 493–533. Hoboken, NJ: Wiley, 2015.

Liptak, Adam. "U.S. Prison Population Dwarfs That of Other Nations." *The New York Times*, April 23, 2008.

Livingston, Gretchen. "Texas Moms Are Most Likely to Give Birth in the Same State They Were Born." Pew Research Center, September 25, 2014.

Logan, John R. "Separate and Unequal: The Neighborhood Gap for Blacks, Hispanics and Asians in Metropolitan America." US2010 report, July 2011.

Long, Jason, and Joseph Ferrie. "Intergenerational Occupational Mobility in Great Britain and the United States since 1850." *American Economic Review* 103, no. 4 (2013): 1109–1137.

Ludwig, Jens, Greg J. Duncan, Lisa A. Gennetian, Lawrence F. Katz, Ronald C. Kessler, Jeffrey R. Kling, and Lisa Sanbonmatsu. "Long-Term Neighborhood Effects on Low-Income Families: Evidence from Moving to Opportunity." *American Economic Review* 103, no. 3 (2013): 226–231.

Malamud, Ofer, and Abigail K. Wozniak. "The Impact of College Education of Geographic Mobility: Identifying Education Using Multiple Components of Vietnam Draft Risk." National Bureau of Economic Research Working Paper 16463, October 2010.

Mandel, Michael. "My Chart of the Year: The Investment Drought Continues." *Mandel on Innovation and Growth*, December 30, 2011.

Mandel, Michael. "U.S. Investment Heroes of 2015: Why Innovation Drives Investment." Progressive Policy Institute, September 2015.

Mathews, Anna Wilde. "Health-Care Providers, Insurers Supersize." *The Wall Street Journal*, September 21, 2015.

Mazumder, Bhashkar. "Black–White Differences in Intergenerational Economic Mobility in the United States." Federal Reserve Bank of Chicago, 2014.

McAlone, Nathan. "This Dating App Uses Your Heartbeat to Help You Find a Match." *Business Insider,* January 14, 2016.

McKenna, Claire, and Irene Tung. *Occupational Wage Declines since the Great Recession: Low-Wage Occupations See Largest Real Wage Declines.* Washington, DC: National Law Employment Project, September 2, 2015.

McPhail, Clark, David Schweingruber, and John McCarthy. "Policing Protest in the United States: 1960–1995." In Donatella Della Porta and Herbert Reiter, eds., *Policing Protest: The Control of Mass Demonstrations in Western Democracies*, 49–69. Minneapolis: University of Minnesota Press, 1998.

"Millions of Victims Lost $12.7B Last Year Falling for Nigerian Scams," *Geektime*, July 21, 2014, http://www.geektime.com/2014/07/21/millions-of-victims-lost-12-7b-last-year-falling-for-nigerian-scams/.

Mitchell, Don. "The Liberalization of Free Speech: Or, How Protest in Public Space Is Silenced." Unpublished manuscript, Stanford University, 2003.

Mitchell, Don, and Lynn A. Staeheli. "Permitting Protest: Parsing the Fine Geography of Dissent in America." *International Journal of Urban and Regional Research*, 29, no. 4 (December 2005): 796–813.

Molloy, Raven S., Christopher L. Smith, Riccardo Trezzi, and Abigail Wozniak. "Understanding Declining Fluidity in the U.S. Labor Market." Finance and Economics Discussion Series, Federal Reserve Board, Washington, DC, 2016.

Molloy, Raven, Christopher L. Smith, and Abigail Wozniak. "Declining Migration Within the US: The Role of the Labor Market." National Bureau of Economic Research Working Paper 20065, April 2014.

Mueller, Holger M., Paige Ouimet, and Elena Simintzi. "Wage Inequality and Firm Growth." Centre for Economic Policy Research working paper, 2015.

Murakawa, Naomi. *The First Civil Right: How Liberals Built Prison America*. Oxford: Oxford University Press, 2014.

Nakai, Daisuke. "Percentage of Animals Put to Death in Shelters Reaches Low." *The New York Times*, April 12, 2010.

Nakamura, Leonard, and Rachel Soloveichik. "Capturing the Productivity Impact of the 'Free' Apps and Other Online Media." Working paper, February 18, 2016.

Neal, Derek, and Armin Rick. "The Prison Boom & the Lack of Black Progress after Smith & Welch." National Bureau of Economic Research Working Paper 20283, July 2014.

"New Racial Segregation Measures for Large Metropolitan Areas: Analysis of the 1990–2010 Decennial Censuses." Population Studies Center, University of Michigan, 2015.

"The New Shelter Dog: Smart Pet Adoption Brings Joy Instead of Stigma." *The New York Times*, October 2015 (paid post), http://paidpost.nytimes.com/purina-one/the -new-shelter-dog.html.

Newton, Huey P. *Revolutionary Suicide*. New York: Penguin Classics, 2009 [1973].

Nosowitz, Dan. "A Penny for Your Books." *The New York Times*, October 26, 2015.

Nunn, Ryan. "Match Quality with Unpriced Amenities." University of Michigan job market paper, April 2013.

"Occupational Licensing: A Framework for Policymakers." The White House, July 2015.

Office of Management and Budget, Budget of the United States FY2017.

"One in 31: The Long Reach of American Corrections." Philadelphia: Pew Charitable Trusts, March 2009.

Orfield, Gary, Erica Frankenberg, with Jongyeon Ee and John Kuscera. "Brown at 60: Great Progress, a Long Retreat and an Uncertain Future." The Civil Rights Project, May 15, 2014.

Owens, Ann, Sean F. Reardon, and Christopher Jencks. "Trends in School Economic Segregation, 1970 to 2010." Center for Education Policy Analysis, Stanford University, working paper, 2014.

Partnership for a New American Economy. "The 'New American' Fortune 500." June 2011.

Passel, Jeffrey S., D'Vera Cohn, and Ana Gonzlez-Barrera. "Net Migration from Mexico Falls to Zero—and Perhaps Less." Pew Research Center Hispanc Trends, April 23, 2012.

Pethoukis, James. "America Suffering from 'Economic Calcification'—JP Morgan." American Enterprise Institute, September 2, 2014.

"Pets by the Numbers." U.S. Humane Society, at http://www.humanesociety.org/issues/pet_overpopulation/facts/pet_ownership_statistics.html.

Pierceson, Jason. *Same-Sex Marriage in the United States: The Road to the Supreme Court and Beyond*. Lanham, MD: Rowman & Littlefield, 2013.

"Public Safety, Public Spending: Forecasting America's Prison Population 2007–2011." Philadelphia: Pew Charitable Trusts, February 14, 2007, revised June 2007.

Purtill, Corinne. "Trump Voters Earn More and Are Better Educated than the Typical American." *Quartz*, May 9, 2016.

Quinn, Kevin. "7th Grader Told His Star Wars Shirt Isn't Allowed in School." ABC13, December 11, 2015.

Rao, Justin M., and David H. Reiley, "The Economics of Spam." *Journal of Economic Perspectives* 26, no. 3 (2012): 87–110.

Reardon, Sean F., and Kendra Bischoff. "Growth in the Residential Segregation of Families by Income, 1970–2009." USA 2010 Project, November 2011a.

Reardon, Sean F., and Kendra Bischoff. "Income Inequality and Income Segregation." *American Journal of Sociology* 116, no. 4 (2011b): 1092–1153.

"Red Flag Manuscript: 'Chaos' in Western Democracy." http://chinascope.org/main/content/view/6505/103. Republished in Qiushi, July 23, 2014, http://www.qstheory.cn/dukan/hqwg/2014-07/23/c_1111750512.htm.

Robinson, John P. "Television and Leisure Time: Yesterday, Today, and (Maybe) Tomorrow." *Public Opinion Quarterly* 33, no. 2 (1969): 210–222.

Rodrigue, Edward, and Richard V. Reeves. "Four Ways Occupational Licensing Damages Social Mobility." Brookings, Social Mobility Memos, February 24, 2016.

Roeder, Oliver, Lauren-Brooke Eisen, and Julia Bowling. "What Caused the Crime Decline?" Brennan Center for Justice, New York University School of Law, 2015.

Rubinowitz, Leonard S., and James E. Rosenbaum. *Crossing the Class and Color Lines: From Public Housing to White Suburbia*. Chicago: University of Chicago Press, 2000.

Şahin, Yşegül, Joseph Song, Giorgio Topa, and Giovanni L. Violante. "Mismatch Unemployment." *American Economic Review* 104, no. 11 (2014): 3529–3564.

Sampson, Robert J. *Great American City: Chicago and the Enduring Neighborhood Effect*. Chicago: University of Chicago Press, 2000.

Sampson, Robert J. "Moving to Inequality: Neighborhood Effects and Experiments Meet Structure." *American Journal of Sociology* 114, no. 11 (July 2008): 189–231.

Sampson, Robert J., Jeffrey D. Morenoff, and Thomas Gannon-Rowley. "Assessing 'Neighborhood Effects': Social Processes and New Directions in Research." *Annual Review of Sociology* 28 (2002): 443–478.

Samuelson, Robert J. "Is the Car Culture Dying?" *Washington Post*, July 11, 2016.

Sax, Leonard. *The Collapse of Parenting: How We Hurt Our Kids when We Treat Them Like Grown-Ups*. New York: Basic Books, 2015.

Schleifer, James T. *The Making of Tocqueville's Democracy in America*. 2nd ed. Indianapolis: Liberty Fund, 2000.

Schwartz, Nelson D. "Low-Income Workers See Biggest Drop in Paychecks." *The New York Times*, September 2, 2015.

Schwarz, Alan. "Still in a Crib, Yet Being Given Antipsychotics." *The New York Times*, December 10, 2015.

Scott, Robert E. "The Manufacturing Footprint and the Importance of U.S. Manufacturing Jobs." Economic Policy Institute Briefing Paper 388, January 22, 2015.

Sethi, Rajiv, and Rohini Somanathan. "Inequality and Segregation." *Journal of Political Economy* 112, no. 6 (December 2004): 1296–1321.

Sharkey, Patrick. "Geographic Migration of Black and White Families over Four Generations." *Demography* 52 (February 2015): 209–231.

Sharpe, Katherine. "The Silence of Prozac." *The Lancet* 2 (October 2015): 871–873.

Silver, Nate. "The Mythology of Trump's 'Working Class' Support." *FiveThirtyEight*, May 3, 2016.

Smedley, Tim. "Forget the CV, Data Decide Careers." *Financial Times*, July 9, 2014.

Smith, Alexander McCall. "The Secret of the Jane Austen Industry." *The Wall Street Journal*, March 27, 2015.

Smith, James P., and Finis R. Welch. "Black Economic Progress after Myrdal." *Journal of Economic Literature* 27 (June 1989): 519–564.

Smithsimon, Gregory. " 'A Stiff Clarifying Test Is in Order': Occupy and Negotiating Rights in Public Space." In Ron Shiffman, Rick Bell, Lance Jay Brown, and Lynne Elizabeth, eds., *Beyond Zuccotti Park: Freedom of Assembly and the Occupation of Public Space*, 34–48. Oakland, CA: New Village Press, 2012.

"Social Spending Is Falling in Some Countries, But in Many Others It Remains at Historically High Levels." OECD, *Social Expenditure Update*, November 2014.

Solt, Frederick. "Economic Inequality and Democratic Political Engagement." *American Journal of Political Science* 52, no. 1 (January 2008): 48–60.

Solt, Frederick. "Economic Inequality and Nonviolent Protest." *Social Science Quarterly* 96, no. 5 (2015): 1314–1327.

Steinbock, Dan. "American Innovation under Structural Erosion and Global Pressures." The Information Technology & Innovation Foundation, February 2015.

Steuerle, C. Eugene. *Dead Men Ruling: How to Restore Fiscal Freedom and Rescue Our Future*. New York: Century Foundation Press, 2014.

Stine, Deborah D. "The Manhattan Project, the Apollo Program, and Federal Energy Technology R&D Programs: A Comparative Analysis." Congressional Research Service, June 30, 2009.

Streithorst, Tom. "Why the Rent Is so High and Your Pay Is so Low." *The Los Angeles Review of Books*, August 4, 2015.

Stroub, Kori J., and Meredith P. Richards. "From Resegregation to Reintegration: Trends in the Racial/Ethnic Segregation of Metropolitan Public Schools, 1993–2009." *American Educational Research Journal* 20, no. 10 (2013): 1–35.

"Student Testing in America's Great City Schools: An Inventory and Preliminary Analysis." Council of the Great City Schools, 2015.

Swanson, Ana. "These Are the Jobs Where People Are Most Likely to Marry One Another." *The Washington Post*, September 21, 2015.

Syverson, Chad. "Challenges to Mismeasurement Explanations for the U.S. Productivity Slowdown." National Bureau of Economic Research Working Paper 21974, February 2016.

Taleb, Nassim Nicholas, and Gregory F. Treverton. "The Calm Before the Storm: Why Volatility Signals Stability, and Vice Versa." *Foreign Affairs* (January/February 2015).

Tanner, Adam. "How Ads Follow You from Phone to Desktop to Tablet." *MIT Technology Review*, July 1, 2015.

Taylor, Kate. "Race and Class Collide in a Plan for Two Brooklyn Schools." *The New York Times*, September 22, 2015.

Taylor, Timothy. "The Surprising Stability of the Federal Budget." *Conversable Economist,* January 27, 2015.

Thompson, Derek. "The Myth of the Millennial Entrepreneur." *The Atlantic,* July 6, 2016.

"Three-in-Ten U.S. Jobs Are Held by the Self-Employed and the Workers They Hire." Pew Research Center, Social & Demographic Trends, October 22, 2015.

Tocqueville, Alexis de. *Democracy in America*. Vols. 1 and 2. Translated by George Lawrence. New York: Doubleday, 1969 [1835, 1840].

U.S. Department of Labor, Bureau of Labor Statistics. "Productivity Change in the Nonfarm Business Sector, 1947–2014." http://www.bls.gov/lpc/prodybar.htm.

U.S. Department of Transportation, Bureau of Transportation Statistics. Figure 3-10: Daily Person-miles of Travel (PMT) by Age Group: 1983, 1990, and 1995 NPTS, and 2001 and 2009 NHTS, http://www.rita.dot.gov/bts/sites/rita.dot.gov.bts/files/publications/transportation_statistics_annual_report/2013/figure3_10.html.

Van Buskirk, Eliot. "50 Genres with the Strangest Names on Spotify." *Hypebot.com*, October 2, 2015, http://www.hypebot.com/hypebot/2015/10/spotify-identifies-50-genres-with-the-strangest-names.html.

Vara, Vauhini. "Why Doesn't Silicon Valley Hire Black Coders?" *Bloomberg Businessweek*, January 21, 2016.

Waldmeir, Patti. "Living China's Dream." *The Financial Times*, September 13, 2015.

Warner, Michael. *The Trouble with Normal: Sex, Politics, and the Ethics of Queer Life*. Cambridge, MA: Harvard University Press, 1999.

Wehner, Mike. "Love Bacon? This Dating App Is Made Just for You." *The Daily Dot*, September 16, 2015.

Winship, Scott. "When Moving Matters: Residential and Economic Mobility Trends in America, 1880–2010." Manhattan Institute e21 report, November 2015.

Wolfers, Justin. "Why the New Research on Mobility Matters: An Economist's View." *The New York Times*, May 4, 2015.

Yglesias, Matthew. "All This Digital Technology Isn't Making Us More Productive." *Vox*, July 9, 2015.

Zick, Timothy. *Speech out of Doors: Preserving First Amendment Liberties in Public Places*. Cambridge: Cambridge University Press, 2009.

Zumper National Rent Report. October 2015, www.zumper.com, https://www.zumper.com/blog/2015/10/zumper-national-rent-report-october-2015/?utm_content=bufferf5f6e&utm_medium=social&utm_source=twitter.com&utm_campaign=buffer.

INDEX